Ian POPPLE Otto WAGNER Peter McDOUGALL



SCUBA DIVE SNORKEL SURF

# CURAÇAO

Turner Publishing Company
Nashville, Tennessee
www.turnerpublishing.com



Reef Smart team contributors: Ian Popple, Otto Wagner, Peter McDougall

Front cover photo Turtle & Ray Productions
Back cover photo NaturePicsFilms/Shutterstock

Curaçao: Scuba Dive. Snorkel. Surf.
ISBNs: (pb) 978-1-68481-478-7 (e) 978-1-68481-479-4
BISAC: SPO059000, SPORTS & RECREATION / Water Sports / Scuba & Snorkeling
LCCN: 2023944135

Printed in the United States of America

FSC
www.fsc.org
MIX
Paper | Supporting responsible forestry
FSC® C005010

## Acknowledgments

Reef Smart is indebted to numerous individuals and organizations who contributed their advice, knowledge, artwork and support to the production of this guidebook. We would particularly like to thank Marcel Hissink, Remy Kwak and Paul Coolen at Palm Trading (Curaçao). Their support and valuable insights were crucial to the completion of this book. Rudy Davelaar, dive market representative at the Curaçao Tourism Board, and Bryan Horne of Dive Curaçao also provided feedback on some of the sites featured in this book. In addition, particular thanks go to Daan Drechsel and the team at Dive Center Pietermaai; Jeremiah Peek and the team at Ocean Encounters; Andhiela van Hoof-Buso and Bernardo van Hoof and the team at Goby Divers; Miranda Cannegieter and Louis Rameriz and the team at Go West Diving; Mick Bossman and the team at Dive Division. Each of these individuals and their organizations were always available to provide advice and frequently helped our mapping team reach dive sites during our data collection trip. We are also grateful to numerous recreational divers, too many to name, who happened to be visiting Curaçao during our fieldwork and were happy to share their experiences on all aspects of the island, from the dive sites to the Relax & Recharge options. We are grateful to Turtle & Ray Productions who provided many of the photos in this guidebook, including the cover shot. Last, but not least, we would like to thank Loic Pravaz, John DiGenova and Julie Quenneville, who accompanied us and helped collect 3D mapping data at many of the locations featured in this book.

**About Reef Smart:**

Reef Smart creates detailed guides of the marine environment, particularly coral reefs and shipwrecks, for recreational divers and snorkelers. Our products are available as printed guidebooks, waterproof cards, wall art, dive briefing charts, weatherproof beach signage and 3D interactive maps, which can be used on websites and as apps. Reef Smart also provides additional services to resorts that are dedicated to offering an environmentally aware experience for their guests; these include marine biology training for dive professionals and resort staff, implementation of reef monitoring and restoration programs, and the development of sustainable use practices that reduce the impact of operations on the natural environment.

**www.reefsmartguides.com**

# Table of Contents

# How to use this book

## Objective

The main objective of this guidebook is to provide a resource for people, particularly divers and snorkelers, who are interested in exploring the underwater environment of Curaçao. This guide is designed to be used alongside Reef Smart waterproof cards, which can be taken into the water. This book will be most useful for watersports enthusiasts, but it also includes information that any visitor to the area will find useful.

## Mapping

We have attempted to catalog as many of the region's dive and snorkel sites as we can, from the northwest to the southeast and out to the island of Klein Curaçao. We have presented these sites using Reef Smart's unique 3D-mapping technology. These maps provide useful information such as depths, expected currents and waves, suggested routes, potential hazards and unique attributes.

## Disclaimer

Reef Smart guides are for recreational use only – they are not navigational charts and should not be used as such. We have attempted to provide accurate and up-to-date information for each site, as well as activities to enjoy in the surrounding areas. However, businesses close and new ones open, prices are adjusted, and change is inevitable in the marine environment. The information contained in this guide is accurate only at the time of publication. The size and location of structures may vary. Depths and distances are approximated in both metric and imperial units, and the suggested route is optional. Every diver should dive to their certification and level of experience.

**Reef Smart assumes no responsibility for inaccuracies and omissions and assumes no liability for the use of these maps. If you identify information that should be updated, please contact us at: info@reefsmartguides.com**

### DID YOU KNOW?

Curaçao has some of the most incredible coral reefs in the Caribbean. The island is ringed by fringing reefs that almost completely encircle the island. As such, divers and snorkelers can pretty much explore anywhere they can enter the water. With so much reef to choose from, it is inevitable that differences of opinion about where specific dives sites are found and what they are called will develop over time. This guidebook is an attempt to consolidate all the available information about dive and snorkel site names and locations. We have worked with input from local divers, dive operators and with the government to develop what we consider to be the closest thing to a definitive list of Curaçao dive and snorkel sites.

## Information boxes

Additional information for the featured sites is provided in the form of special information boxes that appear throughout the book:

**DID YOU KNOW?**
Interesting facts about the site or the surrounding area.

**SAFETY TIP**
Advice that aims to improve safety.

**ECO TIP**
Information that will help limit damage to the ecosystem or improve environmental awareness.

**RELAX & RECHARGE**
Information on where refreshments can be purchased, or where to unwind on land. No compensation was received in exchange for featuring these establishments.

**SCIENTIFIC INSIGHT**
Information of a scientific nature that can help you understand what you see and experience.

## Map icons

- Scuba dive
- Snorkel
- Wreck
- Access by boat
- Access by swim
- Access by car
- Access by walk
- Surf
- Kiteboard
- Wind surf

## Species identification

The species listed for each location were chosen to represent the most unique or common organisms found at each site, as determined from personal observations, discussions with divers and snorkelers who have experienced these sites, and from scientific studies conducted in these areas. Many of the species described in this publication are mobile or cryptic (or both), and so may not always be found where indicated. However, we have attempted to place key species on maps in the locations where they are most commonly found.

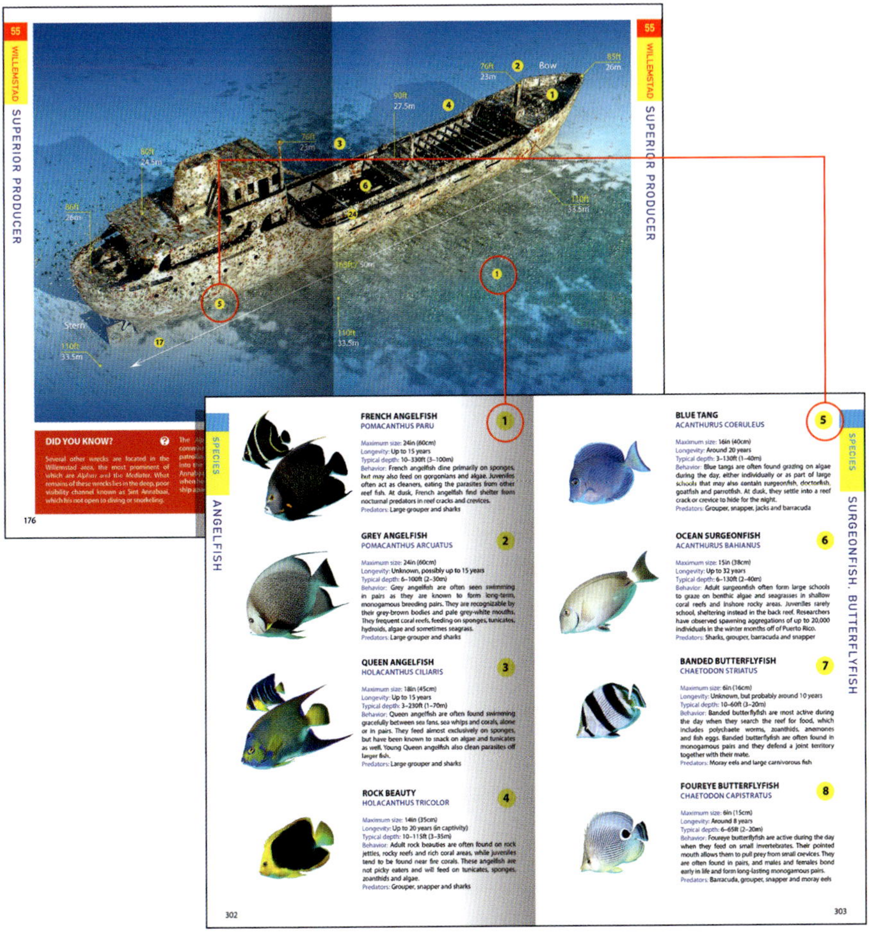


## Species description

The species letters and numbers on various maps link to descriptions located at the back of the book (on pages 272–300). Reef Smart uses the most frequently cited common name for a species. As common names vary from place to place, we have also provided the scientific name for each species, which remains the same worldwide. Scientific names are usually of Latin or Greek origin and consist of two words: a genus name followed by a species name. By definition, a species is typically a group of organisms that can reproduce together such that it results in fertile offspring; a genus is a group of closely related species.

The descriptions of each species are based on the scientific literature as it existed at the time of publication. Scientific knowledge often advances, however, and the authors welcome any information that helps improve or correct future editions of this guidebook. In-depth species profiles, including images and videos, are available for free on our website.
Visit: **Reefsmartguides.com**.

# Our "blue planet"

## Ocean

Water covers nearly three-quarters of our planet's surface and approximately 96 percent of this water is contained in the ocean. The ocean drives our planet's weather, regulates its climate and provides us with breathable air, which ultimately supports every living creature on Earth.

The ocean is also vital to our global economy. It produces the food that billions of people depend on for survival, while being a source of resources, including essential medicines that treat a wide range of ailments and diseases. The ocean also drives local and regional economies through tourism. Every year, millions of travelers are drawn to coastal regions around the world to enjoy activities above and below the water's surface. Considering how important the ocean is to our way of life, it is incredible how relatively little we know about what lies beneath its surface.

## Coral reefs

The ocean includes a wide range of different ecosystems, but perhaps one of the most frequently visited marine ecosystems are coral reefs. Coral reefs are known as the "rainforests of the sea" for good reason – they are one of the most diverse ecosystems on the planet, supporting about a quarter of all known ocean species. This figure is even more astounding when you consider that coral reefs comprise just a fraction of one percent of the ocean floor. They are also particularly vulnerable to degradation, given they are only found in a narrow window of temperature, salinity and depth.

Humans have studied the biology and physiology of corals for decades, but the underwater environment remains largely foreign to many people. Fact is, we have more accurate maps of the surface of Mars than we do of the seafloor. And guides of the marine environment suitable for recreational users are almost non-existent.

Reef Smart aims to change this situation. Our detailed guides seek to educate snorkelers and divers alike. Our goal is to improve safety and enhance the marine experience by allowing users to discover the unique features and species that can be found at each site.

## Preserve and protect

Hopefully our guidebooks, handheld waterproof cards and digital models will help you get to know the underwater environment in general, and reefs in particular. We believe that the more people that can come to appreciate the beauty of the underwater world, the more they will be willing to take steps to protect and preserve it.

The world is connected by a single ocean that is experiencing incredible pressures from all sides. Rising temperatures, increasing acidification and an astonishing volume of plastics that end up both in the water and in marine organisms are negatively impacting this precious system.

There are some big problems to overcome. But a better, more sustainable future is possible. Each and every one of us can make a difference in the choices we make and the actions we take. Together we can help make sure the coral reefs of this world are still around for future generations of snorkelers and divers to enjoy.

Sincerely, the Reef Smart team

### ECO TIP

We hope this guide enhances your in-water experience. Share your passion for exploring the marine environment with others, because our ocean, and particularly coral reefs, need all the "likes" they can get. Coral reefs, as well as mangrove and seagrass ecosystems, are under serious pressure from a multitude of threats that include coastal development, pollution, over-fishing and global climate change. Some estimates put over half the world's remaining coral reefs at significant risk of being lost in the next 25 years; raising awareness can help protect them.

# About Curaçao

## Location and formation

Curaçao is located to the west of the chain of Caribbean islands known as the Lesser Antilles. It sits at the center of the three Netherlands Antilles islands, with the island of Aruba 47 miles (75 kilometers) to the west and the island of Bonaire 25 miles (40 kilometers) to the east. Collectively, these three islands are often referred to as the ABC islands, and they form a line roughly 50 miles (80 kilometers) north of the coast of Venezuela.

Curaçao is known for its fantastic diving and snorkeling, particularly its shore-accessible sites located along the island's south coast. The island is considered by many divers to offer an experience comparable to that of Bonaire, even though the latter island often dominates the headlines. Like its sister island, Curaçao is flat, rocky and dry. Its highest point is Mount Christoffel, or Christoffelberg, located in the north of the island with an elevation of just 1,230 feet (375 meters). Curaçao has a total area of 171 square miles (444 square kilometers) with an approximate length of 40 miles (64 kilometers) and a maximum width of around 10 miles (16 kilometers).

Like the other ABC islands, Curaçao is located within the boundary zone between the South American and Caribbean tectonic plates. The core of the island is composed of ocean floor basalts (pillow lava) that were extruded onto the seafloor during the late Cretaceous Period, about 70 million years ago. Tectonic activity and faulting caused uplift, which moved the entire island into the sunlit photic zone where reefs could start to develop. As sea levels rose and fell during the Pleistocene era, which dates from 2.6 million years ago to just 11,700 years ago, the limestone from these ancient reefs grew and eroded. This repetitive action produced numerous terraces that are still present today, both above and below modern-day sea level. Some of these terraces contain caves, such as the Hato Caves, which are well worth exploring during any trip to the island.

## The history of Curaçao

### Early history

Evidence of early human activity in Curaçao suggests the first settlers of the island were indigenous people, known as Arawaks, who arrived from South America. Shell middens and cave paintings dating from 3000 BC have been

**DID YOU KNOW?**

The Hato Caves, located close to the island's airport, are about 800 feet (250 meters) in length and cover an area of approximately 52,000 square feet (5,000 square meters) – or about half the size of the adjacent airport terminal building. The caves were carved by natural processes over millennia and are filled with stalactites and stalagmites. Both the Caiquetio Indians from northern Venezuela and the Arawak Indians appear to have used the caves for ritual purposes, including burials. The caves also provided shelter to runaway slaves during European colonization. Today, they offer visitors a chance to see unique flora and fauna, such as long-nosed fruit bats.

Gail Johnson/Shutterstock©

The Hato Caves are located just a few minutes drive from the airport and are more than 300,000 years old.

## DID YOU KNOW?

By 1513, Europeans had deported the entire indigenous population of Curaçao to the island of Hispaniola (modern-day Haiti and the Dominican Republic), along with the indigenous populations of Bonaire and Aruba. Once on Hispaniola, they were forced to work as slaves in the island's copper mines.

found in several locations around Curaçao and the earliest human remains were discovered in St. Michielsberg, dating from between 1900 BC and 1730 BC.

The first European explorers to visit Curaçao were Amerigo Vespucci and Alonso de Ojeda in 1499. They claimed the island for Spain, although they did not establish a permanent settlement on the island. The name Curaçao was spelled Qúracao in early maps of the area and is believed to have been derived from the sound of the word that the native inhabitants used to identify themselves.

In the early 17th century, the Dutch West India Company recognized Curaçao's strategic location and established a major trading and shipping hub on the island. This new port trafficked in many goods, but it was focused on the lucrative slave trade that existed between Africa, the Americas and Europe.

The capital city of Willemstad is a UNESCO World Heritage Site known for its colorful colonial architecture.

Izabela23/Shutterstock©

**DID YOU KNOW?**

The names of Curaçao's dive and snorkel sites are an interesting mix of words from English, Dutch and Papiamentu. As such, many of the sites described in this book have a different name depending on the language used. The words: playa, cas, baai, boca, santu/sint appear numerous times throughout this guide and refer to beach, house, bay, mouth (as in river mouth) and saint, respectively.

Curaçao prospered economically over the next century and the island's population diversified, including the addition of Jewish settlers. With Amerindian, Dutch, Spanish and Portuguese languages present on the island, as well as several African-origin languages, Curaçao had the basic linguistic ingredients that led to the development of Papiamentu. This language is first referenced in the early 18th century as 'español bastardeado' (bastardized Spanish).

In 1795, a slave known as Tula led a slave revolt that eventually led to emancipation nearly 70 years later. You can read more about this on pages 89 and 166. Curaçao briefly fell under British control during the Napoleonic Wars, which began around 1800. However, the island returned to Dutch rule by 1816 under the terms of the Treaty of Paris.

## Recent history

In the 20th century, Curaçao went through several political changes. In 1954, it became part of the newly formed autonomous country of the Netherlands Antilles. Then, with the establishment of the Royal Dutch Shell oil refinery on the island, the oil industry brought economic growth to Curaçao. The capital city of Willemstad developed as a vibrant cultural and economic center featuring colorful Dutch colonial architecture that is now recognized as a UNESCO World Heritage Site.

In 2010, the Netherlands Antilles was dissolved, and Curaçao became a separate constituent country within the Kingdom of the Netherlands, along with Sint Maarten. This position provides Curaçao with a high degree of autonomy in its internal affairs while still maintaining ties with the Netherlands.

**DID YOU KNOW?**

In 1817, Governor-General Albert Kikkert decreed that houses in Willemstad could no longer be whitewashed, as was common at the time. It was believed that the glare of the tropical sun, when reflected from these white walls, was harmful to the eyes. From this point on, the buildings in Willemstad would be painted various shades of red, yellow, blue and green. The tradition has continued, which now gives the town its current, distinctive look.

Gail Johnson/Shutterstock©

## Curaçao today

### Population

Curaçao has a population of just over 150,000 people. The island's economy is largely based on tourism. However, the shipping, oil refining and financial services sectors are also well-developed on the island. Curaçao has one of the highest standards of living in the Caribbean.

### The basics

Curaçao is situated in the Atlantic Standard Time -0400 UTC zone and does not observe daylight savings time. The official languages of Curaçao are Dutch, Papiamentu and English. However, Dutch is the sole language for all administration and legal matters on the island. The most widely spoken language is Papiamentu. The local currency in Curaçao is the Netherlands Antillean guilder, also called the Florin, but the US Dollar is also widely accepted. The rate of the local currency is fixed to the US Dollar at approximately 1.80 guilders to $1 USD.

The electricity supply in Curaçao is not quite a match for either North American or European standards: 127 volts / 50 hertz. The outlets are designed for both European and U.S. standard plugs, and most appliances should work well enough. But travelers may want to purchase (or rent) converters and surge protectors while on the island to help protect their more sensitive electronics due to any differences in voltage. The internet is widely available, with many free Wi-Fi zones established around the island. Tap water is safe to drink and is generated through desalination – a process where the salt and minerals in seawater are filtered out, leaving clean fresh water.

### Visitors

The peak tourist season in Curaçao is from December to April, when the weather is dry and sunny. The rainy season is from October to February, but even during this time, the island still receives plenty of sunshine. Most visitors to Curaçao are from the Netherlands, followed by visitors from the United States and Canada.

**SAFETY TIP**

It is generally not a good idea to leave bags unattended on beaches or cliffs. Nor is it advised to leave valuables in the car, whether hidden from view or not. Valuables are most vulnerable to theft at remote sites, such as Blue Room and Directors Bay.

The Queen Emma Bridge by night.

Most visitors stay in the area around the capital Willemstad. Curaçao is generally considered a safe island, but there are certain remote areas that may require visitors to take basic safety precautions, such as avoiding walking alone at night and keeping valuables secure.

## Getting there and getting around

### Getting there

Curaçao is a popular Caribbean destination with more than 800,000 visitors per year, more than half of which represent overnight visitors. It is also a very popular cruise destination. Most people arrive and depart through the Curaçao International Airport at Hato, which is located just a 20-minute drive from the capital city of Willemstad. The airport welcomes regular flights from North America, Europe and Central America, as well as from other Caribbean islands.

### Getting around

Public transport is limited in Curaçao. Large buses (often called Konvois) and minivans (often called buses) operate mainly from terminals in front of the post offices in Willemstad. Their schedule is usually hourly, except during weekends. It can be challenging to go long distances using the public transportation system, however. Taxis operate across the island and are government-regulated with mostly standard fares (although they are not metered). Always inquire about fares for any destination in advance. Ride sharing aps such as Uber and Lyft do not operate in Curaçao.

Rental cars offer visitors the most flexibility and the ability to reach the more remote destinations around the island, like some of the dive and snorkel sites described in this guidebook. North Americans will be comforted to learn that driving is on the right side of the road, although Curaçao relies more heavily on traffic circles or roundabouts to manage traffic flow through intersections than in North America. Scooters, quads (four-wheel all-terrain vehicles) and pedal bicycles of various formats are also available for rent.

It does not often rain on the island outside of the rainy season, but when it does rain, the roads can get very slippery. Be careful and obey the speed limits (which are posted in kilometers per hour). Roads are also narrow and not always in the best shape – particularly some of the dirt roads that service the sites in the northwest.

Finding your way around Curaçao is relatively easy. Free island maps featuring the main roads and popular attractions around the island are available from most car rental companies, hotels, tourism operators and tourism offices. Phone apps can also be useful, with most locals recommending **maps.me** as the most accurate.

**DID YOU KNOW?** ?

Two unique bridges span the Annabaai channel and connect the Willemstad districts of Punda and Otrobanda. The Queen Emma Bridge is a 551-foot-long (168-meter) pedestrian bridge that rests on pontoons so the bridge can be opened and closed to allow the passage of ships. The bridge was originally opened in 1888 and replaced in 1939. The Queen Juliana Bridge, which opened in 1974, was designed for vehicular traffic. At a height of 185 feet (56 meters), it is the tallest bridge in the Caribbean.

# Environment

## Weather

Curaçao is located just north of the Equator, which means the climate is warm and sunny all year round. Average highs range from 90°F (32°C) in August down to 86°F (30°C) in December and January. Average lows show little variation from month to month, ranging from 77°F (25°C) to 81°F (27°C) throughout the year.

Curaçao's rainy season is from December through March, and though a regular daily shower might be expected during this time, the rain does not stick around for long. Curaçao lies outside of the Caribbean hurricane belt.

Water temperatures in Curaçao are also quite stable throughout the year. They average around 79°F (26°C) in February and March and rise to 84°F (29°C) in September and October. Many divers wear only a rash-guard for protection. But if you get cold easily, consider bringing a wetsuit or renting one from a local dive center.

## Waves and visibility

Curaçao experiences steady, easterly trade winds for most of the year, which are strongest in the spring. As a result, the protected west coast rarely experiences large waves or rough seas while the less-developed east coast has very strong surf. The latter is exposed to the full force of the wind except during late August and September, when the trade winds change direction and blow from the west. The corals of Curaçao thrive in the protected lee of the island. Another factor that contributes to the high quality of the reef is the crystal-clear waters. Visibility often exceeds 80 feet (25 meters) and great viz paired with steady sunshine and white coral sand turn the waters between the shore and the fringing reef a gorgeous azure-blue color that people have come to expect from a tropical paradise.

## Currents and tides

The tidal cycle in Curaçao is mild, measuring a mere foot to a foot and a half (less than half a meter). It is enough to make a difference in some of the entry points over shallow reefs, but nothing that will unduly impact a day of diving. Currents along the west coast are typically light, although they can be moderate and even strong at some sites depending on the underwater topography. A few dive sites near the far south of the island and in the extreme north regularly experience strong currents, particularly where the east coast currents wrap around either end of the island and come into contact with the calmer waters of the west coast.

Curaçao is known for its exceptionally beautiful beaches, its stunning diving and snorkeling site and also its flamingos.

Natalia Barsukova /Shutterstock©

**SAFETY TIP**

According to the regulations of the Curaçao Maritime Authority, all divers and snorkelers are required to display a dive flag when in the water. Violating this regulation can technically result in a fine, although this is highly unlikely. More importantly, however, carrying a dive flag helps protect divers and snorkelers from boat traffic that can be quite common around certain dive sites. The use of a surface marker buoy (SMB) is therefore highly recommended when diving or snorkeling in Curaçao at all times, particularly when shore diving.

## Ecosystems

Curaçao is home to one of the most biodiverse coral reef systems in the entire Caribbean. It is estimated that up to 70 per cent of all Caribbean coral species are found around the island. This provides an incredible habitat that in turn attracts as many as 400 different species of fish, mollusc, crustacean and other marine organisms.

### Coral reefs

Curaçao is surrounded by fringing reefs that extend from the shore to approximately 150 to 350 feet (46 to 107 meters) before sloping, sometimes steeply, from a depth of about 25 feet (7.5 meters) into much deeper water. These reefs are incredibly healthy compared to many other islands in the Caribbean, largely because of the island's limited rivers and coastal development. These factors help keep the water clear and unpolluted, particularly in the northwest and southeast of the island and along the relatively unpopulated east coast. Coral cover along these sections can reach more that 70 percent. Curaçao's coral reefs are estimated to have a total surface area of 7.7 square miles (20 square kilometers). Many of these reefs can be accessed from shore, which makes Curaçao a paradise for divers and snorkelers.

### Seagrass and mangroves

Seagrass and mangrove ecosystems are important nursery areas for many species found on coral reefs. Mangroves also provide important nesting habitat for a wide variety of birds. In Curaçao, mangroves and seagrasses are largely found in and along the shoreline of inland bays that are partially connected to the open ocean through narrow channels. Examples of these bays include Santa Martha, Jan Kok, Piscadera and Spanish Water. These relatively shallow areas often have water quality that is not generally suited to diving or snorkeling.

The numerous inland bays around Curaçao support important mangrove and seagrass ecosystems.

Gail Johnson /Shutterstock©

## Marine conservation and management

**Caribbean Research and Management of Biodiversity (CARMABI)** is a non-profit foundation that was originally established in 1955 as a marine research institute. Today, the organization's focus spans both marine and terrestrial research and consultancy work. CARMABI scientists conduct research and monitoring activities to assess the health of Curaçao's marine ecosystems, including monitoring water quality, tracking coral reef health and biodiversity, and studying the behavior and migration patterns of marine species. The data collected helps inform conservation strategies and policies to ensure the long-term preservation of the marine environment. The institute's education department is continuously producing and organizing school programs on nature and the environment, which are given both in the classroom and in the field. Finally, CARMABI is also responsible for managing Curaçao's four national parks: Christoffel National Park, Shete Boka National Park, the Curaçao Rif Mangrove Park and the Curaçao Marine Park, all of which are described in more detail below. Visit: **Carmabi.org**

- **Christoffel National Park** is a terrestrial reserve located around Curaçao's largest peak. It is Curaçao's largest park and offers multiple hiking trails suitable for all levels of hikers. It is known for its biodiversity, including numerous bird species and white-tailed deer. The park also features the Savonet Museum. Visit: **Christoffelpark.org**

- **Shete Boka National Park** lies adjacent to Christoffel National Park, and it covers a large section of Curaçao's rocky, wave-exposed northeast coast, including Boca Tabla and Boca Pistol. The park was established in 1994 to protect important turtle nesting beaches and at least three species of sea turtle are known to nest here. Visit: **Shetebokapark.org**

- **The Curaçao Rif Mangrove Park** is located just a seven-minute walk from the cruise ship terminal in Otrobanda (follow the signs to the Gouverneur van Slobbeweg). The park allows visitors to tour the mangroves via elevated walkways and learn about the different species living there and the importance of this valuable ecosystem. Visit: **Mangrovepark.org**

- **The Curaçao National Marine Park** was opened in 2020 and includes much of southeastern Curaçao. The park stretches from Beacon Point, around Oostpunt (East Point), and up the east coast past Tarpon Bridge. It encompasses 17 different dive and snorkel sites and approximately 536 acres (217 hectares) of coral reef.

**Reef Renewal Curaçao** is an initiative started by dive and snorkel operator Ocean Encounters. The organization seeks to train, engage, and inspire the local and international community through volunteering, educational events, and outreach. They are working to develop new ways to restore reefs with the goal of sharing these methods with restoration projects worldwide. Reef Renewal Curaçao has active nurseries at numerous locations across the island, including: Avila Beach Hotel, Baoase Luxury Resort, Kontiki Beach Resort, Marie Pampoen, LionsDive Beach Resort and Eel Valley. They also offer a Coral Restoration Specialty Course through Ocean Encounters, which helps divers learn about coral restoration and get directly involved in the process. Visit: **Reefrenewalcuracao.org**

**Coral Reef Restoration Curaçao** aims to protect and restore coral reefs in Curaçao and create awareness about the importance of healthy reefs. They train locals and visitors who wish to assist with the maintenance and out-planting of corals. They also collaborate with other marine organizations to increase the knowledge base for the betterment of the coral reef ecosystem. Their ultimate goal is to share their sustainable method

NaturePicsFilms/Shutterstock©

Boca Pistol, part of the Shete Boka National Park.

## DID YOU KNOW?

In 2020, Proteus Ocean Group unveiled plans to build an advanced underwater research station in the Curaçao National Marine Park, called PROTEUS. According to the group's website, PROTEUS will be an ocean observatory and research platform that will enable scientists, innovators, and global customers to search for and reveal solutions to our planet's most critical concerns, including new medicinal discoveries, food sustainability, and the impacts of climate change. The habitat will be sustainably powered from hybrid sources including wind and solar. It will also feature a full-scale video production facility to provide continuous live streaming for educational programming.

to grow more corals and restore Curaçao's reefs. Visit: **Coralreefrestorationcuracao.com**

**BRANCH Coral Foundation**, which stands for Building Reefs And Nurseries for Coral Habitats, was founded in 2022. Their work aims to restore and enhance Curaçao's coral reefs using a range of restoration techniques, such as building coral nurseries filled with endangered staghorn coral and educating the local and international community. They also give volunteers the chance to become part of the team and to contribute to restoration efforts through fun and informative diving experiences. Visit: **Branchcoralfoundation.com**

**Sea Turtle Conservation Curaçao** is a non-profit organization that protects sea turtles and marine wildlife through direct action, such as rescues, rehabilitation, and research activities as well as generating awareness within the community. Several times a week, dedicated volunteers check the beaches for nesting activity, injured individuals, and other notable situations, intervening where necessary. If you see a sea turtle or nest in danger, call or WhatsApp on +599-9-664-7970. Visit: **Seaturtleconservationcuracao.org**

aquapix/Shutterstock©

Corals grow on an artificial frame before out-planting.

# In case of emergency

There are many organisms that can put a damper on a visit to Curaçao, from jellyfish and stingrays to invasive lionfish. Many of these potentially dangerous marine creatures are listed in a special section toward the back of the book (pages 276-279). We have included information in that section on the harm these species can cause, as well as some common treatments that might help. That said, this book is not intended as a substitute for professional medical help.

For visitors unlucky enough to become injured while enjoying their time in the waters around Curaçao, there are many organizations they can visit to receive emergency care, including the standard government emergency services and a few non-profits, such as the sea rescue organization CITRO Curaçao and a first responder organization known as Koninklijke Nederlandse Vereniging EHBO.

The main hospital on the island is the Curaçao Medical Center, which has a 24-hour emergency room, and operates the island's only intensive care unit. The hospital was opened in 2019, so the facilities are modern. There is a second hospital known as The Antillean Adventist Hospital, which offers a wide range of medical services and access to specialists. For less urgent injuries, visitors should consider seeking help from one of Curaçao's many medical clinics or pharmacies, also known as botikas.

Curaçao's medical facilities are generally known to provide high-quality care. Visitors to the island must pay for their treatment. Prices tend to be reasonable, but it is a good idea to arrange appropriate health insurance prior to any visit. Without coverage, a major health incident could be costly.

Should the unthinkable happen, we have listed some important numbers and places for visitors to keep in mind should they need to seek help:

## Emergency contacts

**Police:** 911
**Fire:** 911
**Ambulance:** 912
**Hospital and Recompression Chamber:** 910
**Coast Guard:** 913
**Curaçao Road Service:** 199

## Other emergency services

**CITRO:** +599-9-747-1600
**EHBO:** +599-9-462-4949

## Emergency care hospital

**Curaçao Medical Center**
Open 24 hours
J.H.J. Hamelbergweg z/n,

Madelein Wolfaardt/Shutterstock©

Otrobanda, Willemstad
Tel: +599-9-745-0000
Email: info@cmc.cw
**Cmc.cw**

## Other hospitals and clinics

**The Antillean Adventist Hospital**
5 Groot Davelaarweg, Willemstad
Tel: +599-9-737-0611
Email: contact@aahospital.org
**Adventhospital.com**

**Porto Medico**
Hato International Airport
Tel: +599-9-888-7511
Email: info@portomedico.com
**Portomedico.com**

**Sentro Mediko De Savaan**
De Savaan 108, Willemstad
Tel: +599-9-868-3035
Email: bali@sentropasalu.com
**Sentropasalu.com**

**The Green Clinic Curaçao**
32 Hoogstraat, Willemstad
Tel: +599-9-679-7244
Email: thegreencliniccuracao@gmail.com
**Thegreenclinic-curacao.com**

## Pharmacies

Pharmacies are present in almost every neighborhood in Curaçao. They sell both over-the-counter medicines and those that require prescriptions. Most pharmacies close at 5 or 6 PM. However, there is a "pharmacy on duty" system in Curaçao (referred to locally as "botika na warda") where at least two pharmacies remain open throughout the night on a rotating schedule. Visit: **Botikadiservisio.com** to view the schedule, which shows which pharmacies on the island will be open overnight for the next three months.

# Curaçao Beaches





Curaçao is renowned for its beautiful beaches, considered by many as among the best in the Caribbean. The island boasts a wide array of beach options, each with its own unique charm and features. Whether you're looking for secluded coves with pristine white sands, crystal-clear waters and a relaxing vibe, or a lively beach atmosphere with dining options and other entertainment, Curaçao has it all. All the beaches in Curaçao have associated dive and snorkel sites that are covered more extensively in this book. From north to south – these are Curaçao's most popular beaches:



Cas Abao, with its natural palm-covered palapas, is a stunning beach located in Curaçao's northwest.

# CURAÇAO BEACHES

Gail Johnson/Shutterstock©

It is possible to cliff dive at some of Curaçao's beaches, such as here at Grote Knip.

fokke baarssen/Shutterstock©

# Other aquatic activities

Curaçao has so much more to offer visitors than diving and snorkeling. Visitors who want to mix things up a little might consider trying kiteboarding, wind surfing, stand up paddle boarding (SUP) or surfing. These activities generally take place in areas where diving and snorkeling do not, such as the island's inland waterways, such as Jan Kok and Spanish Water, as well as the rugged north coast, such as Sint Jorisbaai and Playa Kanoa. The best time to surf in Curaçao is between November and March. The best time to kiteboard in Curaçao is between January and August. Here are some additional resources that might be of interest:

**SUP Curaçao**
Caracasbaai
Tel: +599-9-738-0883
Email: bookings@supcuracao.com
**Supcuracao.com**

**Windsurfing Curaçao**
Spanish Water
Tel: +599-9-738-0883
Email: windsurfing@surfspotCuracao.com
**Surfspotcuracao.com**

**NIX Kite School Curaçao**
St. Joris Bay/Ostrich Farm
Tel: +599-9-665-2562
Email: nixkitecuracao@gmail.com
**Nixkitecuracao.com**

**Awa Salu Kiteboarding Curaçao**
St. Joris Bay
Tel: +599-9-562-2022
Email:
Info@awasalu-kiteboarding.com
**Awasalu-kiteboarding.com**

Yana Mavlyutova/Shutterstock©

**Gusty Kiting**
St. Joris Bay
Tel: +599-9-667-4403
Email: info@gustykiting.com
**Gustykiting.com**

**FlowZone Wing Foil**
Willemstad
Tel: +599-9-695-0511
**Flowzone.ws**

**Kitesurf Klein Curaçao**
Willemstad
Tel: +599-9-521-9944
Email: captain@aquaadventurescuracao.com
**Kitesurfkleincuracao.com**

**KitingCuraçao**
Sint Marie
Tel: +599-9-661-3109
Email: info@kitingcuracao.com
**Facebook.com/Kitingcuracao**

**JBay Kiteboarding Curaçao**
Sint Joris Bay
Tel: +599-9-510-8264
Email: info@jbay-kiteboarding-curacao.com
**Jbay-kiteboarding-curacao.com**

**Foil Surf Curaçao**
Spanish Water
Tel: +599-9-522-8317
Email: cfoilsurfcuracao@gmail.com
**FoilsurfCuracao.com**

**Zapata Flyboard Caribbean**
Jan Thiel
Tel: +599-9-512-3359
Email: flyboardcuracao@gmail.com
**Facebook.com/zapataflyboardcaribbean**

# Diving and snorkeling

There are nearly 100 dive and snorkel sites across Curaçao and the neighboring island of Klein Curaçao. Many of these sites are accessible from shore (see page 31), just mere steps down the stunning white sandy beaches that line the island's coasts. The reefs vary from gently sloping sites, such as Mushroom Forest and Pierbaai, to steep walls such as Blue Bay Wall and Bullenbaai. The island also has several notable wrecks, including *Superior Producer* and the *Tugboat*, which are among the most visited sites on the island. Finally, to add an extra touch of diversity, Curaçao also boasts some unique artificial reefs consisting of old automobiles that were sunk decades ago. And although they have mostly become incorporated into the reef, they can still be explored by those able to dive safely at recreational scuba limits or with a tech diving certification.

Some sites in Curaçao are only accessible via boat. These sites tend to be less frequently visited and, as a result, often have slightly healthier reef systems. This includes the tiny undeveloped island of Klein Curaçao that is located just under 7 miles (11.4 kilometers) off the southeast tip of Curaçao. Depending on prevailing conditions, it can take upwards of two hours for most dive operators to make this trip, so visiting this island is usually an all-day affair. The experience is worth the effort, however, provided you have the time. Similarly, the east coast of the island features many dive site that may be worth visiting for more experienced and adventurous divers. The waters on this coast are often turbulent and it is therefore recommended to only visit these sites with a professional guide.

The following pages contain a complete list of dive and snorkel operators that are conducting business in Curaçao at the time of publication. Many of these operators have been featured in greater detail at specific sites within this guide. We have identified these operators with the INFO icon shown here: ⓘ

In addition, a select group of dive operators have been approved by the Curaçao Tourism Board. We have identified these operators with the APPROVED icon shown here: ✓

Finally, a subset of these operators has come together under the Curaçao Hospitality and Tourism Association's (CHATA) Dive Task Force and have established self-regulatory standards that represent a strong commitment to safety, quality, reef care and sustainable tourism. We have identified these operators with the STAR icon shown here: ★

Sven Hansche/Shutterstock©

# Diving and snorkeling services

Businesses are listed based on their location from north to south across the island. This information is up to date as of the publication date of this guidebook.

---

**Go West Diving** *see page 43*
Playa Kalki
Tel: +599-9-560-3319
Email: info@gowestdiving.com
**Gowestdiving.com**

**Westhill Bungalows & Diving**
Playa Forti
Tel: +599-9-510-2837
Email: info@westhillcuracao.com
**Westhillcuracao.com**

**Tec Diving Curaçao**
Westpunt
Tel: +599-9-510-2837
Email: info@tecdivingcuracao.com
**Tecdivingcuracao.com**

**Sublime Diving Curaçao**
Rancho El Sobrino
Resort & Restaurant,
Sabana Westpunt
Tel: +599-9-529-6103
Email: info@sublimediving.com
**Sublimediving.com**

**Bahia Diving** *see page 61*
Playa Lagun
Tel: +599-9-864-1000
Email: info@bahia-apartments.com
**Bahia-apartments.com**

**Let's Go Watersports**
Playa Santa Cruz
Tel: +599-9-864-0438
Email: letsgowatersports@gmail.com
**Therealcaptaingoodlife.com**

**B Diving and Watersports**
Cas Abao Beach
Tel: +599-9-864-0554
Email: information@bdivingcuracao.com
**Bdivingcuracao.com**

**Porto Mari Sports** *see page 105*
Playa Porto Mari
Tel: +599-9-697-8751
Email: info@portomarisports.com
**Portomarisports.com**

**Divers Republic**
Playa Daaibooi
Tel: +599-9-520-3989
Email: info@divers-republic.com
**Divers-republic.com**

**Coral Divers Curaçao**
Coral Estate Centre, Rif Sint Marie
Tel: +599-9-735-2469
Email: Info@coraldiverscuracao.com
**Divecentercuracao.com**

**Dive with Laura**
Grote Berg
Tel: +599-9-684-9187
Email: info@divewithlaura.com
**Facebook.com/DiveWithLauraCuracao**

**Duikstudio Leon**
Grote Berg
Tel: +599 9 665 2303
**Email: duikstudioleon@gmail.com**

**Relaxed Guided Dives**
Grote Berg
Tel: +599-9-868-7710
Email: info@relaxed-guided-dives.com
**Relaxed-guided-dives.com**

**Trunk Divers**
Kokomo beach
Tel: +599-9-868-0663
Email: Trunkdivers@hotmail.com
**Trunkdivers.com**

**Dive Wederfoort**
Boka Samí
Tel: +599-9-888-4414
Email: info@divewederfoort.com
**Divewederfoort.com**

**Boca Beach Oceanclub**
Boka Samí
Tel: +599-9-523-3865
Email: info@boca-oceanclub.com
**Boca-oceanclub.com**

**Curaçao Divers**
Boka Samí
Tel: +599-9-526-1687
Email: info@curacao-divers.com
**Curacao-divers.com**

**At Divers Choice Curaçao**
Sint Michiel
Tel: +599-9-523-9285
Email: info@diverschoicecuracao.com
**Atdiverschoicecuracao.com**

**Red Snapper Diving**
Sint Michiel
Tel: +599-9-682-5216
Email: info@redsnapperdiving.com
**Redsnapperdiving.com**

**Sami Scuba Senter**
Snake Bay
Tel: +599-9-889-0052
Email: info@wederfoort-apartments.com
**Wederfoort-apartments.com**

**Dushi Diving** *see page 163*
Julianadorp
Tel: +599-9-515-6170
Email: dushidiving@gmail.com
**Dushidiving.com**

**Central Dive Curaçao**
Julianadorp
Tel: +599-9-671-4868
Email: info@central-dive-curacao.com
**Central-dive-curacao.com**

**Blue Bay Dive and Watersports**
Blue Bay Beach
Tel: +599-9-888-5450
Email: dive@bluebay-curacao.com
**Diveshopcuracao.com**

**The Dive Shop Curaçao**
Piscadera Bay
Tel: +599-9-684-0434
Email: info@thediveshop-curacao.com
**Thediveshop-curacao.com**

**Caribbean Sea Sports Curaçao**
Dreams Curaçao Resort Spa & Casino
Tel: +599-9-677-8151
Email: divecaribseasports@gmail.com
**Caribseasport.com**

**Goby Divers Curaçao** *see page 159*
Curaçao Marriott Beach Resort
Tel: +599-9-662-2853
Email: info@goby-divers.com
**Goby-divers.com**

**Soul Divers** *see page 167*
Willemstad
Tel: +599-9-664-8000
Email: info@soul-divers.com
**Soul-divers.com**

**Groove Diving**
Corendon Mangrove Resort
Tel: +599-9-522-4205
Email: info@groovediving.com
**Groovediving.com**

**Epsilon Dive Center**
Acoya Hotel and Renaissance Curaçao
Tel: +599-9-682-8238
Email: sales@epsiloncuracao.com
**Epsiloncuracao.com**

**Divers of the Caribbean**
Punda, Willemstad
Tel: +599-9-461-0661
Email: info@diverofthecaribbean.net
**Diversofthecaribbean.net**

**Dive Center Pietermaai** *see page 18*
Pietermaai, Willemstad
Tel: +599-9-684-0434
Email: diving@scubalodge.com
**Divecenterpietermaai.com**

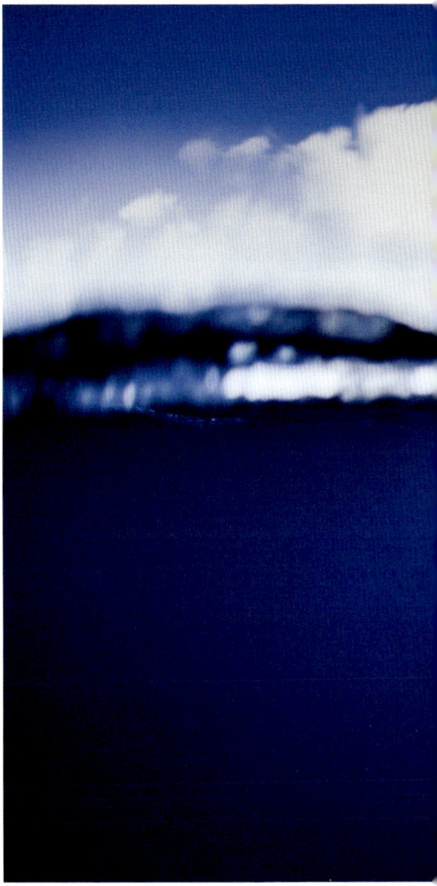

**Scuba Store and More**
Willemstad
Tel: +599-9-738-6640
Email: info@scubastoreandmore.net
**Scubastoreandmore.net**

**Rebel Diving**
Willemstad
Tel: +599-9-519-0152
Email: info@rebeldivingcuracao.com
**Rebeldivingcuracao.com**

**Scubaçao Diving Adventures**
Willemstad
Tel: +599-9-523-8581
Email: info@scubacao.com
**Scubacao.com**

**Twin Divers**
Marie Pampoen
Tel: +599-9-679-2193
Email: info@Twin-Divers.com
**Twin-divers.com**

**The Dive Bus** *see page 187*
Marie Pampoen
Tel: +599-9-693-8305
Email: reservations@the-dive-bus.com
**Thedivebus.com**

**Carrero Diving Curaçao**
Marie Pampoen
Tel: +599-9-666-5195
Email: carrerodiving@gmail.com
**Facebook.com/Carrerospots**

**BLVD Divers Curaçao**
Mambo Beach
Tel: +599-9-461-0122
Email: retail@divedivision.com
**Facebook.com/BLVDDivers**

**Obsession Watersports Curaçao**
Mambo Beach
Tel: +599-9-736-5659
Email: galmeyer@hotmail.com
**Facebook.com/ObsessionWatersportsCuracao**

Warren Metcalf/Shutterstock©

**Ocean Encounters** *see page 201*
Sunscape Curaçao Resort, Spa & Casino and LionsDive Beach Resort
Tel: +599-9-694-0025
Email: info@oceanencounters.com
**Oceanencounters.com**

**SubStation Curaçao**
Bapor Kibra
Tel: +599-9-465-2051
Email: info@substation-curacao.com
**Substation-curacao.com**

**Atlantis Watersports**
Santa Rosa
Tel: +5999 843 8288
Email: scubapro@atlantisdiving.com
**Atlantiscuracao.com**

**Duiken Op Curaçao**
Santa Rosa
Tel: +599-9-513-4224
Email: fredbroer.broer@gmail.com
**Duikenopcuracao.nl**

NaturePicsFilms/Shutterstock©

**Duiken in Curaçao**
Katoen Tuin
Tel: +599-9-665-7276
Email: info@duikenincuracao.nl
**Duikenincuracao.nl**

**Scuba Holics By Locals**
Montaña
Tel: +599-9-79593673
**Email: georvan.mensche@outlook.com**

**Sublub Curaçao**
Montaña
Tel: +599-9-868-8507
**Email: sublubcuracao@gmail.com**

**Duikcentrum van de Ven**
Jan Thiel
Tel: +599-9-514-1267
Email: info@duikcentrumvandeven.com
**Duikcentrumvandeven.com**

**Dive Center Scuba Do** *see page 211*
Jan Thiel Beach
Tel: +599-9-767-9300
Email: info@divecenterscubado.com
**Divecenterscubado.com**

**Jan Thiel Diving**
Livingstone Jan Thiel Beach Resort
Tel: +599-9-567-5511
Email: info@janthieldiving.com
**Janthieldiving.com**

**Fun Diving Curaçao**
Papagayo Beach Hotel
Tel: +599-9-523-9220
Email: hello@fundivingcuracao.com
**Fundivingcuracao.com**

**CURious2Dive**
Caracasbaai
Tel: +599-9-513-2265
Email: info@curious2dive.com
**Curious2dive.com**

**Dive Charter Curaçao**
Caracasbaai
Tel: +599-9-525-3483
Email: divechartercuracao@gmail.com
**Divechartercuracao.com**

**About Jackie Fine Diving**
Caracasbaai
Tel: +599-9-666-5669
Email: info@aboutjackiefinediving.com
**Aboutjackiefinediving.com**

**Cura Divers**
Caracasbaai
Tel: +599-9-693-6657
Email: mario@curadivers.com
**Curadivers.com**

# Dive and snorkel sites

# Dive and snorkel sites

1 Watamula Hole
2 Playa Gipy
3 Watamula Reef
4 Elvin's Plane Wreck
5 Playa Kalki (Alice in Wonderland)
6 Playa Piskado (Playa Grandi)
7 Playa Forti (Sweet Alice)
8 Korta Pe
9 Grote Knip
10 Kleine Knip
11 Playa Jeremi
12 Playa Lagun
13 Playa Santa Cruz
14 Boca Santu Pretu (Black Sand Wreck)
15 Mushroom Forest
16 Sponge Forest
17 Blue Room
18 Playa Hulu
19 Duane's Release
20 Rediho
21 Black Coral Garden
22 Hell's Corner
23 Mako's Mountain
24 Santa Martha (Sunset Waters)
25 Playa Hundu
26 Playa San Juan
27 Playa Chiki
28 Playa Manzaliña
29 Playa Shon Mosa
30 Playa Largu
31 Cas Abao
32 Playa Hunku
33 Playa Porto Mari
34 Daaibooi
35 Witches Kitchen
36 Rif Sint Marie
37 Habitat
38 Light Tower
39 Seldom Reef
40 Spanish Anchor
41 Bullenbaai
42 Pestbaai
43 Kokomo Beach (Vaersenbaai & Car Wrecks)
44 Boka Sami
45 Snake Bay
46 Hole Number 6
47 Blue Bay Wall
48 Blue Bay Garden
49 Rolling Stones
50 Long Beach
51 Piscadera
52 Marriott Beach
53 Fisherman's Wharf
54 Double Reef
55 Superior Producer
56 Tarpon City
57 Dive City
58 Boca Simon
59 Atlantis
60 Pierbaai & Car Pile (Playa Marie Pampoen)
61 Oswaldo's Drop-Off
62 Stella Maris Reef
63 Shipwreck Point
64 Tugboat Saba
65 Sandy's Plateau
66 Jan Thiel (Sweet Bottom)
67 Diver's Leap
68 Beacon Point
69 Lost Anchor
70 La Palapa
71 Caracasbaai
72 Tugboat Curaçao
73 Director's Bay
74 Small Wall
75 Barracuda Point
76 Eel Valley
77 Newport / Booby Trap
78 Kathy's Paradise
79 Smokey's
80 Guliaw
81 Best Reef
82 Piedra Pretu (Black Rock)
83 Punt Kanon
84 Tarpon Bridge
85 Jorisbaai
86 Tunnel of Doom
87 Playa Kanoa
88 Boca San Pedro/Houtjesbaai
89 Boca Ascension
90 Boca Patrick
91 The Cave (North Point)
92 The Edge (Northwest Klein Curaçao)
93 Easy Going (Southwest Klein Curaçao)
94 South Point (Cannon Pile)
95 Klein Curaçao East

# WATAMULA HOLE

| | |
|---|---|
| Difficulty | ●●● |
| Current | ●●● |
| Depth | ●●○ |
| Reef | ★★★ |
| Fauna | ★★★ |

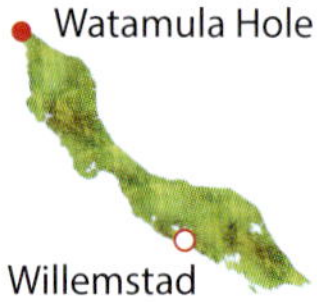


Access about 8 mins from Playa Kalki



**Level** Advanced

## Location

Westpunt, Curaçao
GPS 12°23.471'N, 69° 9.448'W

## Getting there

Watamula Hole dive site is located immediately off shore from the famous Watamula Hole landmark adjacent to Curaçao's northwest point. The best way to explore this site is through one of the local dive operators located nearby, ideally in Westpunt.

## Access

Although Watamula Hole is technically accessible from the cliff edge and the beach at Playa Gipy, it is highly dangerous to access this site from shore. Watamula Hole is just a short boat ride north from Playa Kalki. Rough conditions here often make it easier to drop divers off and then pick them up without tying up to the buoy that is typically present at this site.

## Description

Watamula Hole is the most northerly dive site in Curaçao. The two currents that run along either side of Curaçao collide at this point, creating conditions that make this site better suited for advanced divers. The word watamula comes from the Dutch word "watermolen", which means watermill. The term is a reference to the turbulent conditions often experienced at this site. Watamula Hole is considered one of the island's best sites, with healthy coral formations and large barrel sponges dominating the site. There is also an abundance of reef creatures at this site, including ocean triggerfish, nurse sharks, sea turtles and large populations of grunts, parrotfish and butterflyfish. Divers can often drift dive this site when currents are favorable. A tunnel exists in the direction of Playa Gipy.

# PLAYA GIPY

Difficulty ●●●
Current ●●●
Depth ●●○
Reef ★★☆
Fauna ★★☆

Access about 7 mins from Playa Kalki

**Level** Advanced

## Location

Westpunt, Curaçao
GPS 12°23.269'N, 69°09.540'W

## Getting there

Playa Gipy is located just south of Watamula Hole. The best way to explore this site is through one of the local dive operators located nearby, ideally in Westpunt.

## Access

The Playa Gipy dive site is accessible from the beach at Playa Gipy, although it can be challenging to descend the cliff and enter the water here. The safest way to access the site is via a short boat ride north from Playa Kalki. The dive site's typical rough conditions often make it easier to drop divers off and pick them back up without tying up to the buoy that is usually found here.

## Description

Playa Gipy, sometimes spelled Gepi, Gepy or Guepi, hosts an abundance of healthy corals and sponges, which are scattered among relatively large sand patches. Unlike the sites on either side of Playa Gipy, the reef here is more reminiscent of a rolling meadow than a slope or wall. The reef also has a greater number of soft corals than its neighboring sites. The reef at Playa Gipy supports a wide range of species and provides divers with a diverse habitat to explore. This site is more protected than nearby Watamula Hole, but currents can still be unpredictable here, especially when swimming far from the beach. Divers may find lobsters and moray eels at this site. Yellowtail snapper, bar jacks and horse-eye jacks often feed in the water column above the reef.

NaturePicsFilms/Shutterstock©

# WATAMULA REEF

Difficulty ●●●
Current ●●●
Depth ●●○
Reef ★★★
Fauna ★★☆

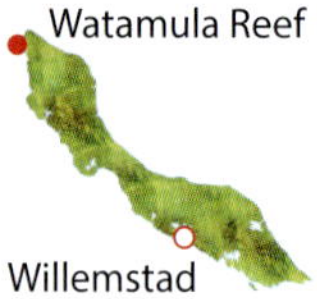


Access about 5 mins from Playa Kalki

**Level** Advanced

## Location

Westpunt, Curaçao
GPS 12°23.126′N, 69° 9.625′W

## Getting there

The best way to visit this boat-accessible site is through one of the local dive operators located along the northwest coast, ideally in Westpunt, as that makes for the shortest boat ride.

## Access

Watamula Reef is located just around the northwest tip of Curaçao from Playa Kalki. Waves and currents often increase significantly as boats round the headland, which can unsettle some divers. But those with the stomach for rough seas will be rewarded by one of the most pristine reefs on the island. Most divers start gearing up and running through their pre-dive checks while the boat is still in motion. At the site, most dive boats usually attach to the mooring buoy that is typically anchored north of the houses along the cliff edge. Once in the water, divers will want to descend straight to the bottom as rapidly as possible, as the currents can pull divers away from the reef.

## Description

Watamula Reef, also sometimes known as Watamula South, requires relatively calm conditions to safely access. Conditions are usually best in the summer months, but divers can still dive these sites throughout the year. The strong currents along this stretch of the coast often mean that drift dives are the best way to explore these sites.

The Watamula sites located along the northwest coast of the island are considered some of the most pristine in Curaçao, with a high density and diversity of hard corals, soft corals and sponges. These reefs also support a wide range of reef creatures, from parrotfish and butterflyfish to boxfish and puffers. The reef itself slopes to a maximum angle of around 45 degrees and is highly rugose with large schools of creole wrasses, boga and chromis often present. Large coral mounds, some of which extend up to 20 feet (6 meters) from the bottom, can be found all along the reef slope. These mounds provide plenty of habitat and overhangs for snapper, goatfish and soldierfish to hide.

The reef slope becomes less steep, and the corals more sparse, as depth increases beyond 80 feet (24.5 meters). There is a ledge ranging in height from 15 to 20 feet (4.5 to 6 meters) along the seaward edge of the reef here. It is undercut in many places along its length, which provides shelter to green morays, black grouper and dog snapper. The remote nature of this site means that lionfish are often more common here than elsewhere.

The deep ledge at Watamula Reef bends around to the northeast and eventually disappears as the reef transitions to the more

### SAFETY TIP

Most dive groups stick together as much as possible when diving the northwest coast of Curaçao. However, differences in air consumption can influence that plan toward the end of a dive, and some buddy pairs will likely need to ascend before others. It is good practice to bring an inflatable surface marker buoy (SMB) whenever diving, but this is particularly the case when diving the north end of Curaçao. Divers can be hard to see in the large swells that are common along this stretch of the Curaçao coastline, and an SMB is an essential piece of safety equipment for divers to mark their position while completing their safety stop and once at the surface.

## SCIENTIFIC INSIGHT

Lionfish are indigenous to the Indo-West Pacific. They were first spotted in the Western Atlantic near Dania Beach in southeastern Florida in 1985. It is suspected that the first individuals were aquarium fish that were intentionally released into local waterways. Since then, the lionfish population has expanded north up the coast of the United States, then south throughout the Caribbean. They were first observed in Curaçao in October 2009 on Watamula Reef. Initial genetic testing suggests that the current Caribbean-wide population originated from just 10 individuals, but more recent studies place the original number of colonists at closer to 120, likely released over multiple instances.

As an invasive species, lionfish pose a serious threat to marine ecosystems in the Western Atlantic. According to a 2018 study, published in the Journal of Applied Ecology, an adult lionfish's diet includes 167 species, many of which are ecologically or economically important. They also reproduce incredibly rapidly, producing thousands of eggs in just a few days. And without any natural predators outside of the Indo-Pacific region, they keep expanding their range and increasing their numbers. As a result, they are causing serious damage to local coral reef ecosystems. Fortunately, lionfish are tasty to eat, and regional efforts are underway to help catch lionfish through popular fishing derbies and other initiatives. What's more, lionfish are now finding their way onto the menus of many Caribbean restaurants.

Dive Division Media/Shutterstock©

Watamula Reef features large mounds of healthy boulder star coral.

undulating meadow-like slope dominated by soft corals that characterizes the Playa Gipy dive site located to the northeast. Porcupinefish, trumpetfish and slender filefish are often found hiding in the branches of these soft corals and both hawksbill and loggerhead sea turtles are commonly spotted here.

### Route

Divers and snorkelers typically enter the water at

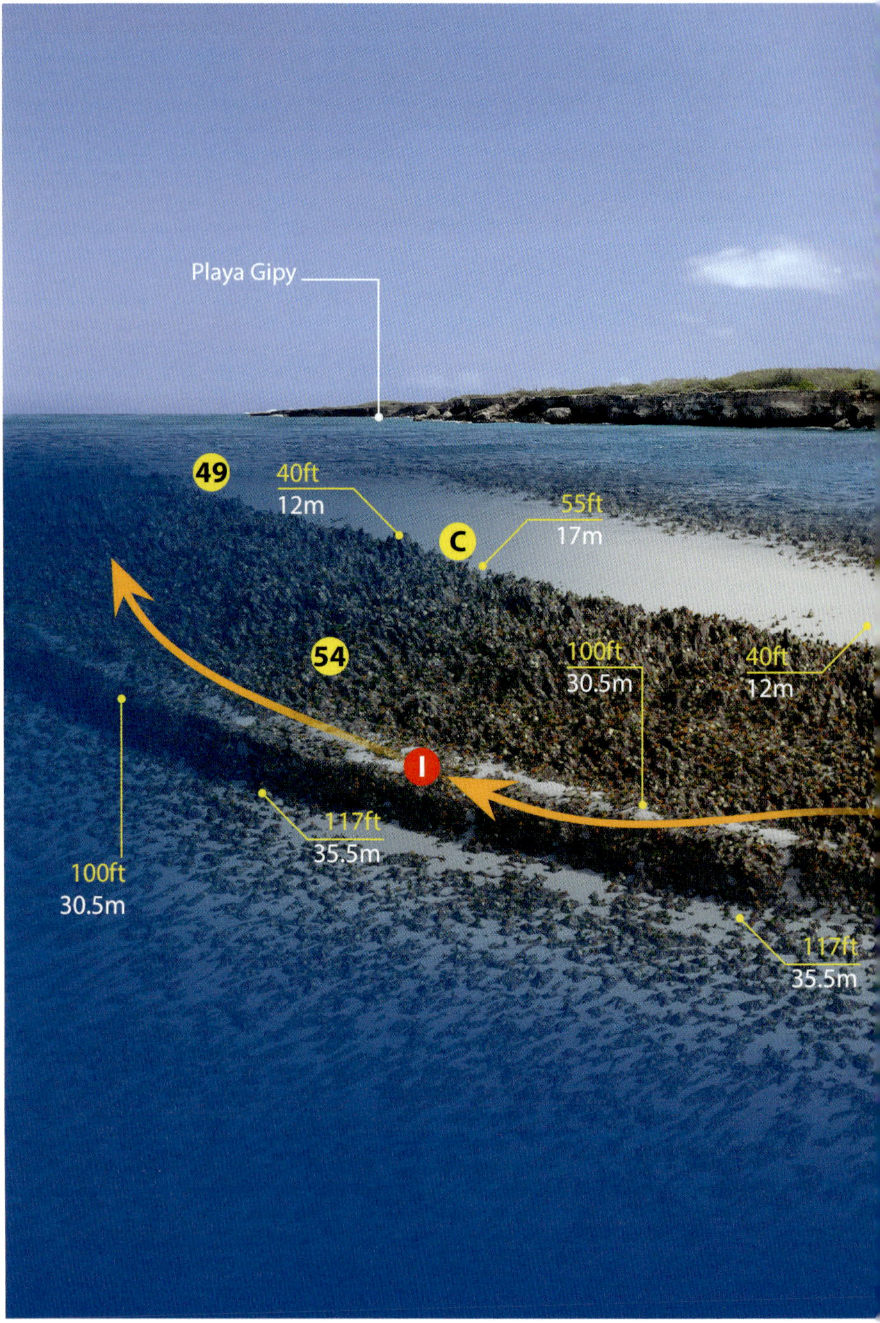


the mooring buoy and usually head in a northerly direction toward Playa Gipy. The ledge that runs along the deeper edge of the reef is an interesting feature to explore but should only be visited by experienced divers due to its depth. The dive usually ends at Playa Gipy provided there is a steady, northerly current present. The shallower reef here, which has a greater abundance of sand patches, allows divers to regain some of the bottom time that they may have lost while exploring the deep ledge.

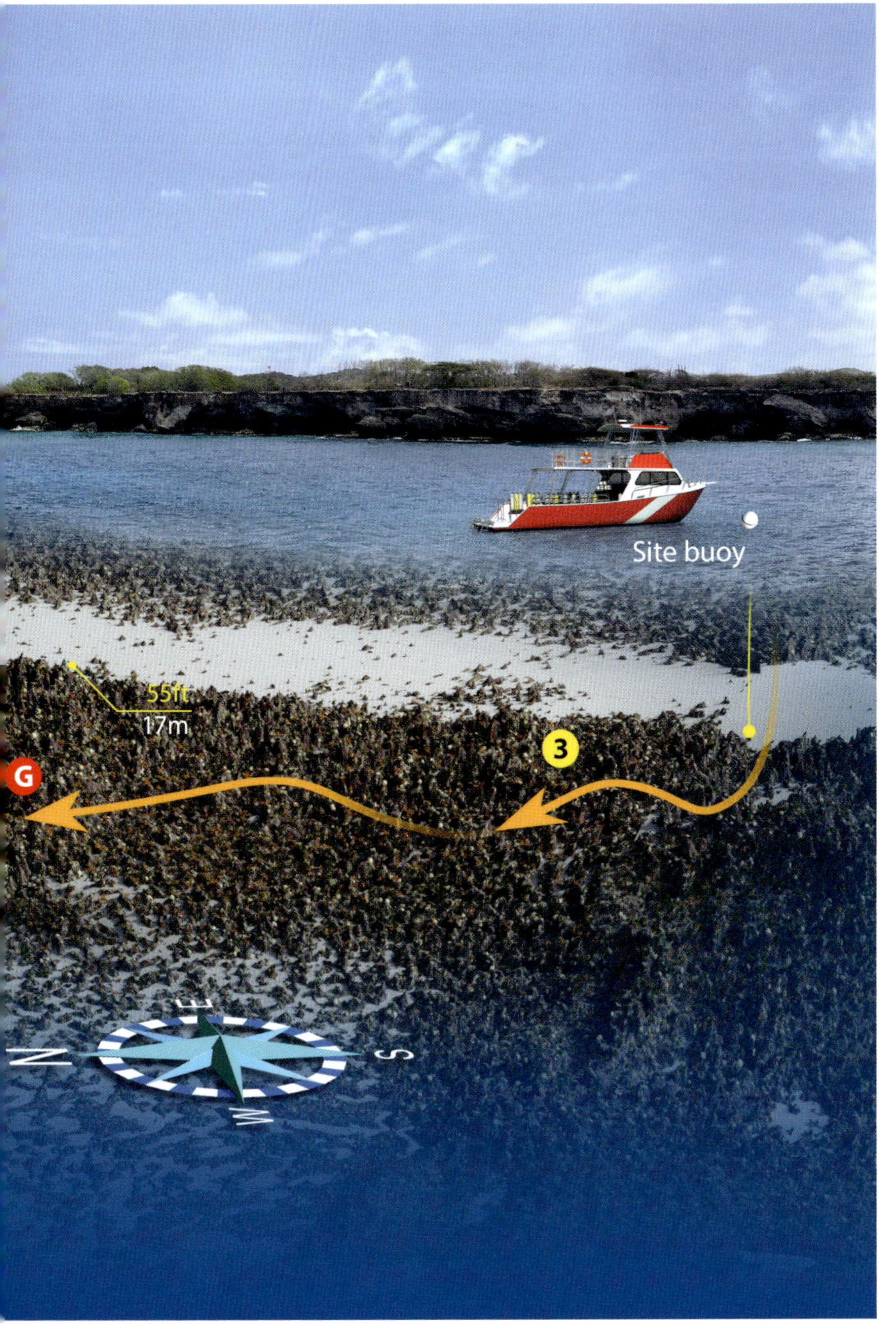
Site buoy
55ft
17m
3
G
N
E
S
W

# ELVIN'S PLANE WRECK

Difficulty ●○○
Current ●○○
Depth ●●○
Reef ★★☆
Fauna ★★☆

Access about 2 mins from Playa Kalki

**Level** Open Water

## Location

Westpunt, Curaçao
GPS 12°22.690'N, 69°09.753'W

## Getting there

The best way to visit Elvin's Plane Wreck is by boat, through one of the local dive operators located along the northwest coast – ideally a shop based in Westpunt, which makes for the shortest boat ride.

## Access

Elvin's Plane Wreck lies only 450 feet (135 meters) off the rocky shoreline, which makes it technically accessible from shore, but only for those with access to the private estate, formerly known as the Kura Hulanda Lodge & Beach Club. The site is about 0.4 miles (0.65 kilometers) from Playa Kalki, which means it is a little too far to reach by shore diving from the nearest public access. A mooring buoy typically marks the site of the wreckage at this site. Elvin's Plane Wreck is suitable for divers of all experience levels – the site might be accessible to more advanced snorkelers capable of free-diving to depths of around 45 feet (14 meters). There is often a mild current along this stretch of the coast, and visibility is usually excellent.

## Description

The aircraft that forms the central feature of the Elvin's Plane Wreck site, is a Fokker Fairchild F-27, which once flew regularly for Antillean Airlines between Aruba, Bonaire and Curaçao. The plane was sunk as an artificial reef in 2006 by All West Apartments & Diving and Go West Diving, after being donated by the Curaçao Fire Department.

Soon after the plane was sunk, swells generated by hurricane Felix, which passed to the north of the ABC islands in 2007, helped break the structure into pieces. Today, only small sections of the aircraft at the Elvin's Plane Wreck site remain recognizable. The cockpit, which is still connected to what remains of the fuselage by wires and cables, sits on a plateau dominated by sand and patch reefs at the top of the reef slope at a depth of approximately 46 feet (14 meters). Another large section of the fuselage, complete with windows, and other assorted wreckage, sits just a few feet to the west. The entire wreck is surrounded by towers of hard coral, brain coral and pencil coral as well as sponges.

While the aircraft at Elvin's Plane Wreck is interesting enough to explore to be worth the trip to the site, most divers also spend time drifting across the surrounding reef. The gentle reef slope on which the wreckage sits is dominated by incredibly rugose habitat that supports a wide range of coral species including brain, lettuce, pencil, massive starlet and pillar corals. Large coral mounds punctuate the gentle sloping reef, which is similar in structure to many of the reefs farther along the headland toward Watamula.

The complex habitat supports large moray eels, lobsters, ocean triggerfish, barracuda and

### DID YOU KNOW?

The Fokker Fairchild F-27 was a popular aircraft that was operated by numerous airlines in the United States, Canada and Central and South America from 1958 to the mid 1980s. These relatively small 40- to 50-seater planes were powered by twin turbo props and were perfect for short hops between islands. In 1972, a Uruguayan Air Force F-27 carrying 45 people crashed in the Andes mountains. The story of the 16 survivors, who survived on the frozen glacier adjacent to the crash site for 72 days by resorting to anthropophagy, became known as the "Miracle in the Andes", and was the subject of the 1974 book "Alive" as well as a 1993 film of the same name.

NaturePicsFilms/Shutterstock©

A diver explores the main fuselage of Elvin's Plane Wreck.

porcupinefish. Smaller species, such as sergeant majors and blue chromis have colonized the wreckage while the occasional eagle ray and schools of bogas can be seen out on the surrounding reef.

## Route

The presence of a steady, gentle current along the coastline at Elvin's Plane Wreck, generally leads most divers to explore the site as part of a drift dive. Depending on the strength of the current, divers may opt to enter the water up current from the buoy that marks the wreck – usually somewhere along the reef between Playa Kalki and the wreckage. Once at the plane wreck, divers can drop down out of the current, as the site is largely sheltered by the surrounding coral mounds. The wreckage is complex but covers a relatively small area, so most divers continue their dive by drifting beyond the wreckage, around the headland and along the reef toward Watamula.

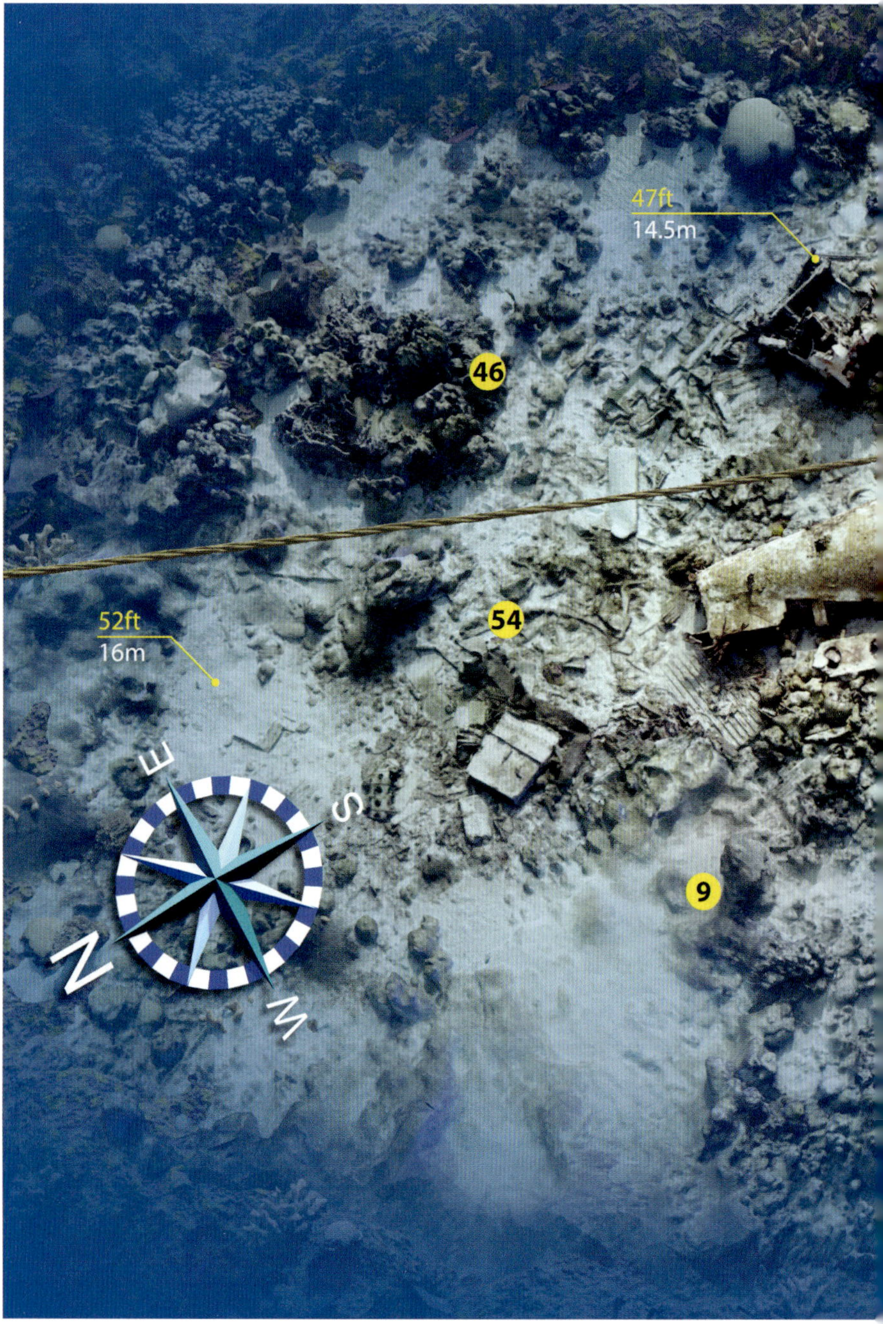
47ft
14.5m
46
54
52ft
16m
9
E
S
N
W

69
50ft
15m
15ft / 4.5m
G
52ft
16m
76

# PLAYA KALKI (ALICE IN WONDERLAND)

Difficulty ●○○
Current ●○○
Depth ●●○
Reef ★★★
Fauna ★★☆

Access about 1 min from Playa Kalki
Access about 45 mins from Willemstad
Access about 3 mins from shore

**Level** Open Water

**Location**
Westpunt, Curaçao
GPS 12°22.533'N, 69°09.465'W

## Getting there

Head north from Willemstad on Weg Naar Westpunt, which bends due west at the northern end of the island. Turn right onto Westpunt D, followed by the first left after about 0.2 miles (0.3 kilometers). Continue along this road until it bends to the left and right before finally reaching a parking lot where a sign indicates Go West Diving. The total distance from Willemstad is approximately 27 miles (43.5 kilometers).

## Access

This shore-accessible dive and snorkel site can be reached by descending the stones steps from the parking lot and entering the water directly from the beach. The beach consists mostly of sand, but there are many large rocks in the shallows, so it is best to wear boots. Those divers using the services of Go West Diving can access this dive and snorkel site by descending the steps at the end of the dive center's jetty or using a giant stride entry. A rope on the bottom leads the way to the reef and runs down the seaward slope, which begins about 150 feet (46 meters) from the end of the jetty.

## Description

Playa Kalki is one of the most northerly beaches in Curaçao. The dive and snorkel site located just off the beach, known as Alice in Wonderland, is a real locals' favorite. The name refers to the fact that this site is a 'wonder' to explore. The word 'kalki' means lime in Papiamentu, probably in reference to the limestone cliffs that surround the site.

The back reef at Playa Kalki consists of sand and coral rubble, about 12 feet (3.5 meters) deep, which is home to a wide range of juvenile reef fish, including wrasses, surgeonfish and grunts, as well as a multitude of bicolor damselfish. At a depth of around 20 feet (6 meters), the reef starts to slope more noticeably and becomes increasingly rugose, with patches of sand between the increasingly large coral heads.

At a depth of about 50 feet (15 meters) the reef slopes more steeply and features extremely large mounds of star coral and lettuce coral, some of which rise nearly 20 feet (6 meters) from the seabed. These coral mounds are often undercut and may shelter spotted moray eels, schoolmaster snapper, mahogany snapper and blackbar soldierfish.

The complex reef habitat, which also includes patches of brain coral, finger coral, large tube sponges and some soft corals, supports a wide diversity of reef fish, including schools of brown chromis, creole wrasses, blue tangs, porcupinefish, bar jacks, and various species of parrotfish. Large schools of bait fish are sometimes present at this site, and delicate black corals can be found in the deeper parts of the reef.

There are two small sculptures that have been placed on the reef here, both located in the upper part of the reef slope. A saxophone statue is located in the middle of the reef at a depth of about 30 feet (9 meters). It was created to honor the memory of a musician and diver whose favorite site was Alice in Wonderland. The second statue, known as Chichi, represents the sensual, rounded figure of a woman – Chichi means 'big sister' in Papiamentu. The statue was created by Serena's Art Factory in Curaçao and placed on the reef in December 2020 at a depth of approximately 26 feet (8 meters).

## Route

From the jetty, the reef extends roughly south to the left and northwest to the right. Divers and snorkelers can head in either direction, but the most common area to explore is to the northwest, which includes the two sculptures. Divers often follow the rope to reach the sand-reef transition and the start of the reef slope. From there they typically descend the slope to explore the deeper parts of the site first. The most common

## FEATURED OPERATOR

**Go West Diving** is Curaçao's most northerly dive center. They service many of the dive and snorkel sites around West Punt, from the incredible Watamula sites to the north to Mushroom Forest in the south. Playa Kalki is the house reef of Go West Diving. It is accessible from the adjacent beach or directly from the end of the dive center's jetty, where their daily boat excursions depart. The dive center is a well-organized operation, with helpful and friendly staff, a wide selection of rental equipment and dive courses. Go West is open seven days a week from 8am to 5pm.

Tel: + 599-9-864-0102
Email: info@gowestdiving.com
Visit: **Gowestdiving.com**

GO WEST Diving Curaçao

The artwork known as Chichi, is one of two sculptures placed on the reef at Playa Kalki.

route has divers rising slowly up the slope as they explore to the northwest before turning around at the halfway point of their dive plan. They can then explore the two sculptures up close and in detail located as they are along the upper part of the reef slope. From there, divers often head back along the sand-reef transition to the rope, using the rope to easily navigate back to the jetty. With any remaining air, divers can search the shallow sand and rubble area for cryptic species and juveniles near the end of the jetty.

PLAYA KALKI (ALICE IN WONDERLAND)

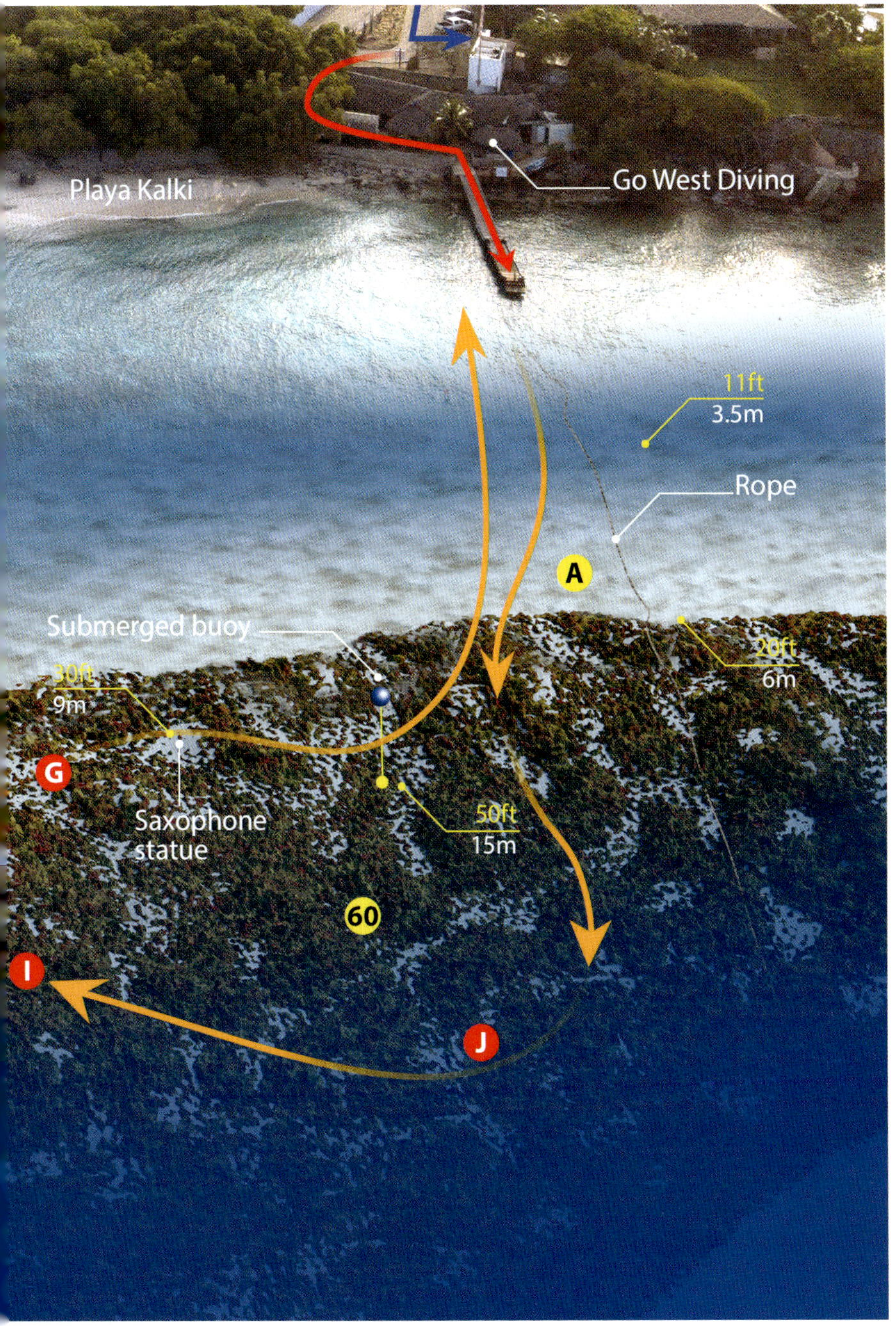

# PLAYA PISKADÓ (PLAYA GRANDI)

Difficulty ●○○
Current ●○○
Depth ●●○
Reef ★★☆
Fauna ★★☆

Access about 2 mins from Playa Kalki
Access about 45 mins from Willemstad
Access about 4 mins from shore

**Level** Open Water

## Location

Westpunt, Curaçao
GPS 12°22.167′N, 69°09.233′W

## Getting there

Head north from Willemstad on Weg Naar Westpunt. The road bends due west at the northern end of the island and returns to the west coast at Playa Grandi, which is the official name of the beach where the dive and snorkel site Playa Piskadó is located, along with Playa Westpunt. There is a car park on the cliff that overlooks the beach. The total distance from Willemstad is approximately 27 miles (44 kilometers).

## Access

This shore-accessible dive and snorkel site can be reached by descending the stone steps from the free parking lot on the cliff above the beach. This location is particularly popular with visitors because of the numerous sea turtles that are found around the jetty. As such, you can expect the beach and parking lot to be relatively crowded at peak times of the day, especially mid-morning. The beach is a mixture of sand and pebbles and there are many large rocks in the shallows, so it is best to wear boots if possible.

Divers and snorkelers often enter the water adjacent to the jetty and surface swim to the reef, which begins about 150 feet (46 meters) due west from the end of the jetty. This site is suitable for divers and snorkelers of all experience levels. Currents are usually mild, and visibility is usually good, but can decline sharply in the waters closer to shore and around the jetty.

## Description

Playa Piskadó is also known as Boca Piskadó, Playa Grandi and sometimes Neptune's Reef. The latter name is due to the statue of Neptune located on the reef slope. The reef is somewhat patchy in the shallows around the center of the site where numerous concrete blocks, chains, ropes and scraps of metal litter the seabed, most likely the anchors for past boat moorings. But the reef becomes significantly more rugose to the south, and even more so to the north. In these areas, the reef consists of large mounds of star, brain and lettuce coral, interspersed with sand patches, similar to many other sites along this stretch of the coast. Coral mounds rise up from the seabed, ranging in height from about 10 to 15 feet (3 to 4.5 meters). Large purple tube sponges and the occasional soft coral are scattered along the reef slope as well, along with patches of mustard hill coral and pencil coral, which round out the reef assemblage.

The statue of Neptune sits on the seabed at a depth of 35 feet (10.5 meters). At a height of 8 feet (2.5 meters), the statue overlooks the reef slope beneath its beautiful crown of tube sponges, which have grown naturally since the statue was placed on the reef in 1997. These tube sponges are full of life, hosting banded coral shrimp, gobies, trumpetfish and slender filefish. In the past, divers used to place coins on the statue to bring good luck. To the south of the pier, and at a depth of 75 feet (23 meters), is a small artificial reef constructed of scrap metal, including car engine blocks.

Divers and snorkelers may encounter large schools of creole wrasses and scad on this reef,

**SAFETY TIP**

Playa Grandi is a busy fishing village with small fishing vessels coming and going throughout the course of the day. As such, a surface marker buoy (SMB) is an important piece of equipment to use when visiting this site. An SMB can help ensure boat operators are aware of divers in the water. Be sure to also look in all directions and listen carefully for approaching boats before surfacing.

**ECO TIP**

Playa Grandi has been home to generations of local fishing families. Over the decades, as fishers cleaned their catch from their anchored boats or along the shoreline, sea turtles have been attracted to the scraps. The sea turtles at Playa Grandi are not shy, so visitors may find themselves being bumped and jostled as the turtles cruise around the shallows, weaving between the swimmers. It is important to remember, however, that these are wild animals, and it is always best to give them space. Never feed the sea turtles, hold them down, attempt to ride them or remove them from the water.

Gail Johnson/Shutterstock©

Divers and snorkelers can often find sea turtles at Playa Piskadó, particularly in the water near the beach.

as well as in the shallow sandy region that sits between the reef and the beach. The reef at Playa Piskado has a particularly high number of rare species, including seahorses, soapfish, goldentail morays, spotted drums, frogfish, flying gurnards and glasseye snapper. The large number of sea turtles found in the bay closer to the beach, means that it is also very common to spot them out on the reef slope, particularly green sea turtles and hawksbills.

## Route

Playa Piskadó is not the best site for snorkeling, but for those who love sea turtles, there is little reason to move beyond the jetty. As many as a dozen turtles are often seen foraging for fish scraps left by the local fishers. There are also plenty of other species to see around the jetty, including snapper, bar jacks, and large schools of scad.

Divers tend to follow the line of the jetty out toward the deeper reef, sometimes heading slightly south down the reef slope, before turning north toward the most rugose part of the reef. The reef slope ends in sand at about 90 feet (27.5 meters) and has a long, wide spur that extends outward at depth. Divers have no need to drop this deep on the slope, however, as the best coral reef life can be found halfway up the slope at a depth of around 45 feet (13.5 meters). Most divers choose to return toward the jetty along the upper reef slope, passing the statue of Neptune along the way.

Playa Grandi
P
A
B
40ft
12m

# PLAYA FORTI (SWEET ALICE)

Difficulty ●○○
Current ●○○
Depth ●●○
Reef ★★☆
Fauna ★★☆

Access about 3 mins from Playa Kalki
Access about 45 mins from Willemstad
Access about 5 mins from shore



**Level** Open Water

## Location

Westpunt, Curaçao
GPS 12°21.985'N, 69°09.225'W

## Getting there

Head north from Willemstad on Weg Naar Westpunt. The road bends due west at the northern end of the island and returns to the west coast at Playa Grandi. Playa Forti is located just over 0.2 miles (0.32 kilometers) to the south. The total distance from Willemstad is approximately 27 miles (44 kilometers).

## Access

There are plenty of parking spaces close to the beach access and adjacent to the restaurant at Playa Forti. A steep staircase runs down the cliff face to a small, sheltered beach that provides access to the water. This site is suitable for divers and snorkelers of all experience levels. There are usually no currents here and visibility is often excellent.

## Description

Playa Forti, also known as Sweet Alice, is an enjoyable, easy-to-access reef with plenty to see, especially in the deeper parts of the site. Divers can explore either to the north or south of the beach, but they must swim beyond the sand plateau that extends about 500 feet (152 meters) from shore in order to encounter decent reef. Angelfish, grunts and snapper are common here, as are sea turtles and moray eels, including the relatively rare chain moray. Snorkelers usually explore along the base of the cliff to the south of the beach but should be aware of people jumping from the cliff above.

### RELAX & RECHARGE

There are decent restaurants on either side of the beach at Playa Forti, both with stunning views overlooking the surrounding shoreline. **Blue View Sunset Terrace** is located north of the beach and offers a range of seafood options, steak, chicken and ribs, along with some vegetarian dishes and a kids' menu. The restaurant has a glass-floored balcony, which adds an interesting flair for those with a head for heights.
Email: **info@blueviewcuracao.com**

To the south of the beach, lies **Restaurant Playa Forti**, whose menu also contains a nice mix of seafood and meat dishes, along with local options, vegetarian meals and a kids' menu. Here, you'll have a ringside seat as people launch themselves from the cliff, literally adjacent to the restaurant's terrace, into the ocean 30 feet (9 meters) below.
Visit: **Playafortirestaurant.com**

# KORTA PE

Difficulty ● ○ ○
Current ● ○ ○
Depth ● ● ○
Reef ★★★
Fauna ★★☆

Access about 3 mins from Playa Kalki

**Level** Open Water

## Location

Westpunt, Curaçao
GPS 12°21.855'N, 69°09.357'W

## Getting there

The best way to visit this boat-accessible site is through one of the local dive operators located along the northwest coast, ideally in Westpunt, which makes for the shortest boat ride.

## Access

There is a staircase on the shore that technically provides access to this dive and snorkel site, but it is on private property. As such, this site is not accessible from shore to anyone other than those staying at the private residence. It is accessible, by boat, however. This site is suitable for divers and snorkelers of all experience levels. Currents are usually mild here and visibility is usually excellent.

## Description

Korta Pe, also sometimes spelled Kortape, is a healthy fringing reef located off shore from the Marazul Dive Resort. The sand plateau in the back reef is nearly half the width of nearby Playa Forti, which means divers have less distance to swim to reach the reef. The reef at Korta Pe hosts a wide range of butterflyfish species, including banded, foureye, long-snout and spotfin. Divers often swim southwest toward the point where a sponge-dominated plateau sits at a depth of around 50 feet (15 meters). Snorkelers usually swim along the cliff edge in either direction to explore the many cracks and crevices.

9

WESTPUNT

# GROTE KNIP

Difficulty ●●○
Current ●○○
Depth ●●○
Reef ★★☆
Fauna ★★☆

Access about 7 mins from Playa Kalki
Access about 47 mins from Willemstad
Access about 9 mins from shore

**Level** Open Water

**Location**
Westpunt, Curaçao
GPS 12°21.103'N, 69°09.093'W

## Getting there

Head north from Willemstad on Weg Naar Westpunt and turn left on Kaminda Monica Kapel Matheeuw about 1.5 miles (2.4 kilometers) past the town of Tera Corá. Continue for another 11 miles (17.7 kilometers), passing Playa Lagun and Playa Jeremi. Just before Landhuis Knip, take the left turn toward Playa Kenepa Grandi and Playa Kenepa Chiki, which are the official names of Grote Knip and Kleine Knip respectively. Playa Kenepa Chiki appears first on the left-hand side of the road. Playa Kenepa Grandi is located about 0.7 miles (1.1 kilometers) farther north on the same road. The total distance from Willemstad is approximately 25.5 miles (41 kilometers).

## Access

There is plenty of free parking at Grote Knip and a trail provides easy access to the beach, which is free to enter. This site is suitable for divers and snorkelers of all experience levels. Currents are usually mild here, but the vast expanse of fine sand in the back reef area can affect visibility close to shore when seas are choppy.

## DID YOU KNOW?

On the cliffs between Grote Knip and Kleine Knip is a large cave known as the "Cave of Love." Local folklore tells of two young lovers who used to meet regularly on the cliff top. One day, upon learning the young man had been lost at sea, his lover threw herself from the cliff in despair. The cave is only accessible from the water, which makes this a popular spot for day boats to bring snorkelers. Some dive centers also visit this site, using it as a starting point for dives that run to the south, in the direction of Kleine Knip. The reef here has numerous sand chutes and divers often see eagle rays cruising by.



### Description

Grote Knip gets its name from the nearby Landhuis Kenepa (often shortened to Knip), which is itself named after the fruit-bearing kenepa tree. This historic plantation was the origin of the Curaçao slave revolt of 1795.

The beach is popular with visitors and locals alike. There is shade in places, and there are beach chairs and sun loungers for rent, as well as public toilets and showers, a snack bar and the occasional food truck. You are welcome to bring your own food and drink to the beach as well. Cliff jumping is a popular pastime at this beach. Jumpers can follow the stairs at the southern end of the beach to access the cliff, but must be aware that this activity is at one's own risk.

Grote Knip is also a popular diving and snorkeling site. The deep reef gradually slopes downward to a depth of over 100 feet (30 meters) seaward of the sandy back reef. Getting to the deep reef requires a significant surface swim, however, typically around 10 minutes depending on conditions. Snorkelers usually stick to the cliff edge to the north or south of the beach, where a range of species can be found, including squid, morays, angelfish and schooling grunts.

# KLEINE KNIP

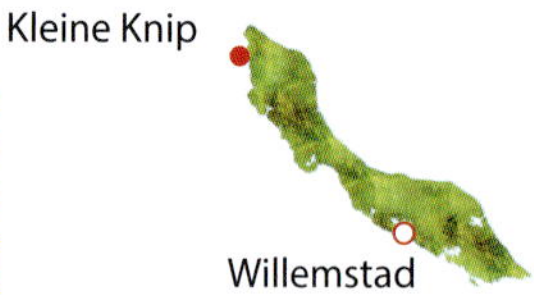


Difficulty ●○○
Current ●○○
Depth ●●○
Reef ★★★
Fauna ★★☆

Access about 10 mins from Playa Kalki
Access about 45 mins from Willemstad
Access about 7 mins from shore

**Level** Open Water

**Location**
Westpunt, Curaçao
GPS 12°20.477'N, 69°09.147'W

### Getting there

Head north from Willemstad on Weg Naar Westpunt and turn left on Kaminda Monica Kapel Matheeuw about 1.5 miles (2.4 kilometers) past the town of Tera Corá. Continue for another 11 miles (17.7 kilometers), passing Playa Lagun and Playa Jeremi. Just before Landhuis Knip, take the left turn toward Playa Kenepa Grandi and Playa Kenepa Chiki, which are the official names of Grote Knip and Kleine Knip respectively. Playa Kenepa Chiki appears first on the left-hand side of the road. The total distance from Willemstad is approximately 25 miles (40 kilometers).

### Access

Kleine Knip is the smaller of the two Kenepa beaches. The advantages of this beach over its neighbor to the north are that divers and snorkelers do not have as far to walk from the car to the water's edge. The reef here is also slightly closer to shore than it is to the north. Currents are usually mild here, but the vast expanse of fine sand in the back reef can affect

Kleine Knip is famous for its clear and calm waters and healthy coral reef.

NaturePicsFilms/Shutterstock©

## RELAX & RECHARGE

Just a short, 2.5 miles (4-kilometer) drive north of Kleine Knip is a local restaurant that gets rave reviews. **Cactus Café** is located on the road, adjacent to Marazul Dive Resort. It has a wonderful menu, packed full of tasty local dishes, such as traditional stews and fresh fish, as well as North American staples, like burgers and fries. Cactus Café also has some rather unique selections, like their African peanut soup, which is a must try, and their coconut curry shrimp. The incredible food, value for money and great service will have you coming back several times during your stay.
Visit: **Facebook.com/CactusCafeCuracao**

visibility close to shore when seas are choppy. Entry to the beach is free of charge.

## Description

Kleine Knip is a gently sloping reef site dominated by numerous large coral mounds in the upper reef area. The reef becomes increasingly patchy at depth, eventually transitioning to sand at a depth of around 100 feet (30 meters). Most of the marine life at this site is focused around the large coral mounds that rise from the bottom at around 45 feet (14 meters) in depth. These coral mounds consist largely of star coral and lettuce coral, some of which are over 10 feet (3 meters) in height. Many are undercut, offering shelter to moray eels, lobsters, snapper, schooling grunts and soldierfish. The coral mounds are interspersed with large barrel and tube sponges as well as sand patches and channels in which divers can sometimes see stingrays.

The back reef at Kleine Knip consists of a mix of sand and coral rubble at an average depth of around 20 feet (6 meters). Divers can often find razorfish and sand tilefish darting in and out of the sand. Patch reefs start to appear at a depth of around 30 feet (9 meters). These patches gradually increase in density and rugosity as divers approach the main reef slope at a depth of around 45 feet (14 meters). Moray eels, angelfish and parrotfish are common at this site – even the relatively rare blue parrotfish is frequently seen here. Large schools of creole wrasses and chromis are present above the reef.

Snorkelers generally explore the base of the cliffs on either side of the beach where small caves and reef recesses can be found, sometimes containing octopuses. There are plenty of healthy patches of elkhorn coral here, along with delicate blade fire coral and small sea fans. It is also possible to encounter sea turtles along the base of the cliff.

## Route

From the beach, divers should enter the water and surface swim out to the reef to better conserve their air. Once they have reached the sand-reef transition, divers should consider taking a compass reading back toward the beach before they descend. That will enable easier navigation on the return portion of the dive if enough air remains for a return along the bottom – a slow return along the bottom can also double as a prolonged safety interval. Divers can choose to head either north or south along the reef at Kleine Knip, as the reef is decent in both directions. The topography of the reef is largely featureless in either direction, but a sharp notch exists at a depth of around 75 feet (23 meters) in the center of the site, which can assist in navigation.

P
2
22
50ft
15m
75ft
23m

Playa Kenepa Chiki
F
L
77
30ft
9m
17
100ft
30.5m
E
S
N
W

# PLAYA JEREMI

Difficulty ●●○
Current ●○○
Depth ●●○
Reef ★★★
Fauna ★★☆

Access about 17 mins from Playa Kalki
Access about 40 mins from Willemstad
Access about 7 mins from shore

**Level** Open Water

**Location**
Westpunt, Curaçao
GPS 12°19.728'N, 69°09.017'W

## Getting there

Head north from Willemstad on Weg Naar Westpunt and turn left on Kaminda Monica Kapel Matheeuw about 1.5 miles (2.4 kilometers) past the town of Tera Corá. Continue for another 10 miles (16 kilometers), passing Playa Lagun. The turn for Playa Jeremi appears on the left-hand side, approximately 0.7 miles 1.1 kilometers after Playa Lagun. The beach is just under 500 feet (150 meters) down the track. The total distance from Willemstad is approximately 23.5 miles (38 kilometers).

## Access

There is plenty of space in the parking lot adjacent to the beach, including some shaded spots beneath the trees. The beach is just a short walk to the west of the lot. Divers and snorkelers can enter the site by simply walking across the sand and into the water. This site is suitable for divers and snorkelers of all experience levels. Currents are usually mild here and visibility is often good.

## DID YOU KNOW?

Approximately half a mile (0.8 kilometers) to the north of Playa Jeremi is an unofficial dive site known as Paradise. This boat-accessible site, which is suitable for divers and snorkelers of all experience levels, is known for its wide diversity of sponges and large coral formations. Large schools of creole wrasses are often present on this reef, which attracts predators such as barracuda. Moray eels and lobsters are often found in the reefs numerous cracks and crevices. A small cave is located close to the cliff edge that contains a resident school of glassy sweepers.

### Description

Playa Jeremi is typically a quieter beach than many of the others in this part of Curaçao. There are multiple palapas that provide shade on the beach. Picnic tables are also present, but there are no other amenities. As with other beaches along this coast, it is common to see people cliff jumping here. The cliffs that drop into the water on either side of the beach are the most interesting areas for snorkelers to explore, but they can also be interesting for divers. The coral cover is dense and healthy, hosting a range of reef species, including parrotfish, surgeonfish, squid and yellowhead jawfish.

The deep reef at Playa Jeremi begins beyond the wide sandy plateau, which extends about 500 feet (152 meters) from the beach. The reef begins as a gradual slope starting at a depth of around 30 feet (9 meters). The slope features numerous large coral mounds for divers to explore. Grunts, snapper and yellow goatfish are common here. There is also a high density of butterflyfish, particularly banded and foureye butterflyfish.

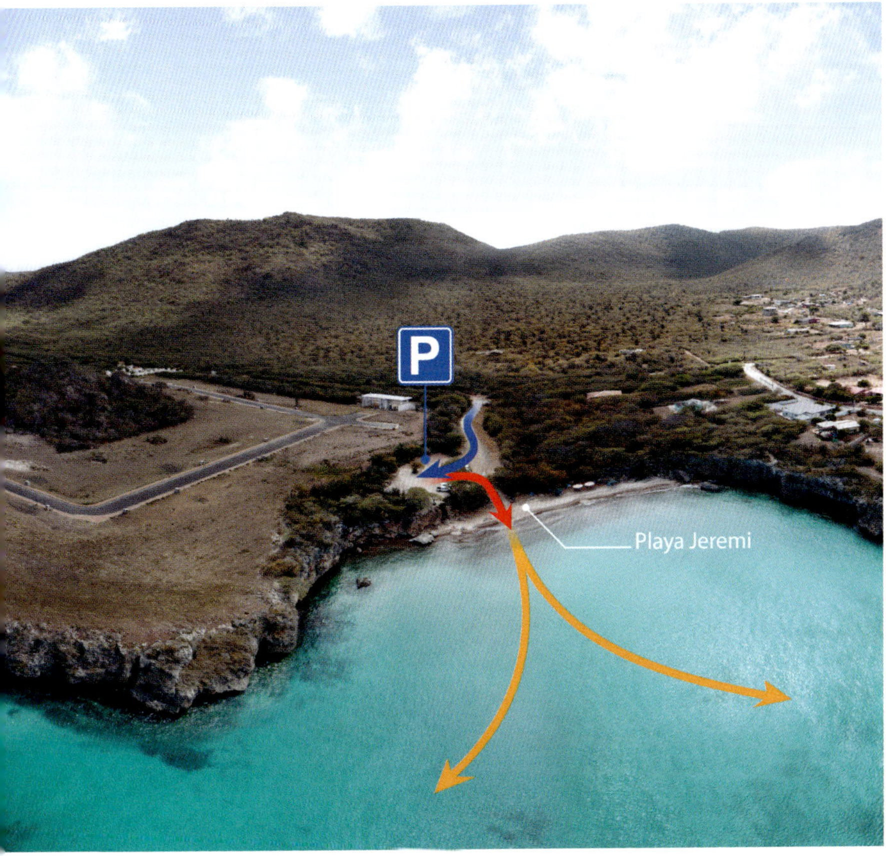

# PLAYA LAGUN

Difficulty ●○○
Current ●○○
Depth ●●○
Reef ★★★
Fauna ★★☆

Access (boat) about 20 mins from Playa Kalki
Access (car) about 40 mins from Willemstad
Access (swim) about 12 mins from shore

**Level** Open Water

## Location

Bandabou, Curaçao
GPS 12°19.093'N, 69°09.032'W

## Getting there

Head north from Willemstad on Weg Naar Westpunt. Approximately 1.5 miles (2.4 kilometers) past Tera Kora, turn left onto Kaminda Monica Kapel Matheeuw. Continue down this road for approximately 9.5 mile (15.3 kilometers) until reaching the well-marked turning for Playa Lagun. The total distance from Willemstad is about 22.5 miles (36.2 kilometers).

## Access

Playa Lagun is one of the most picturesque shore-accessible dive and snorkel sites in Curaçao. Tall cliffs enclose this small, west-facing, beach on either side. A large, free parking lot is located immediately adjacent to the beach. Divers and snorkelers access the water by simply walking across the beach. Like many of the northwest sites in Curaçao, the drop-off is a significant distance from the beach. The advantage of Playa Lagun, however, is that there is plenty to explore in the shallows, as well as to both the north and south along the cliff edge. Divers wishing to explore the outer reef should surface swim to the seaward edge of the channel before dropping to the bottom and continuing west across flat sand until the reef appears. The total distance from the beach to the drop-off is approximately 700 feet (213 meters).

## Description

Playa Lagun is a great place to explore for both divers and snorkelers. Most divers venture across the wide sandy plateau to the outer reef, which is about a 12-minute swim from shore, but well worth the effort. The outer reef begins as a wide space of rubble and scattered patch reefs at a depth of around 40 feet (12 meters). Divers can find all manner of cryptic creatures near the sand-reef transition, including peacock flounders, frogfish and scorpionfish, as well as slender filefish in the branches of the many soft corals.

The reef gradually slopes into deeper water, becoming increasingly rugose, with large mounds of boulder star coral dominating the habitat. Some of these coral mounds rise to a height of 15 feet (4.5 meters) from the seabed. The reef also contains plenty of large soft corals and sponges. At a depth of around 60 feet (18 meters) the reef starts to slope a little more steeply. Large schools of fish move throughout the reef, including grunts, goatfish, surgeonfish and snapper. There are large schoolmaster snapper here as well as a particularly dense population of stoplight parrotfish. Above the reef, divers will commonly see bar jacks, blue runners and chromis.

### RELAX & RECHARGE

You won't go hungry or thirsty at Playa Lagun – the beach is blessed with a couple of great relax and recharge options. **Bahia Beach Bar** is accessible via stairs, directly from the beach and has wonderful, elevated views over the entire bay. The restaurant serves a range of meals and drinks and is a great place for a sundowner when your day of diving and snorkeling is done.
Visit: **Bahia-apartments.com**

**Discover Lagun** is located on the left-hand side of the road when entering Playa Lagun. They serve a range of burgers, including the Sweet & Sour Burger and Blue Cheese Burger, as well as delicious pizzas, including a Futti Di Mare for seafood lovers. For those with a hearty appetite, there is an all-you-can-eat Grill Night on Wednesday evening starting at 5pm for meat and fish.
Visit: **Facebook.com/DiscoverLagun**

## FEATURED OPERATOR

**Bahia Apartments & Diving Curaçao** is ideally situated adjacent to the beach at Playa Lagun. This professional operation is a PADI Dive Resort & SSI Dive Training Center that forms part of the Bahia Apartments & Diving complex located on the cliff top above the bay. Bahia Diving Curaçao offers a range of PADI and SSI courses, equipment rental, guided shore dives, night dives and, for the artists among us, they can organize an underwater painting course. Bahia Diving is open seven days a week.

Tel: + 599-9-864-1000
Email: info@bahia-apartments.com
Visit: **Bahia-apartments.com**

The shallow areas of this site are excellent for both diving and snorkeling. There is a coral restoration project and transplant area located within the channel, adjacent to the beach. Toward the seaward edge of the channel there is also a small artificial reef consisting of boulders.

The cliffs that stretch to the north and south of the channel opening are also worth exploring. There are plenty of large boulders at the base of these cliffs that are interesting to explore, along with large stands of branching elkhorn coral that often support butterflyfish, blennies and spotted drums.

A series of caves and undercuts are located along the base of the cliffs to the south of the channel, which can be fun to explore for those who are comfortable and when conditions allow. One cave is large enough for two divers to enter and explore at the same time. The cave is located approximately 500 feet (150 meters) along the base of the southern cliff. The cave was formed by wave action that eroded the base of the cliff and created a hollow in the limestone that extends back 50 feet (15 meters) from the cliff face. There are two access points along the short slope found at the base of the cliff: one very tight, and one large enough to allow easy access for one diver at a time. The interior space of the cave is close to 30 feet (9 meters) wide, and it reaches just under 20 feet (6 meters) in height. The back of the cave is cut in half by a

The sheltered beach at Playa Lagun provides simple access to the dive and snorkel site.

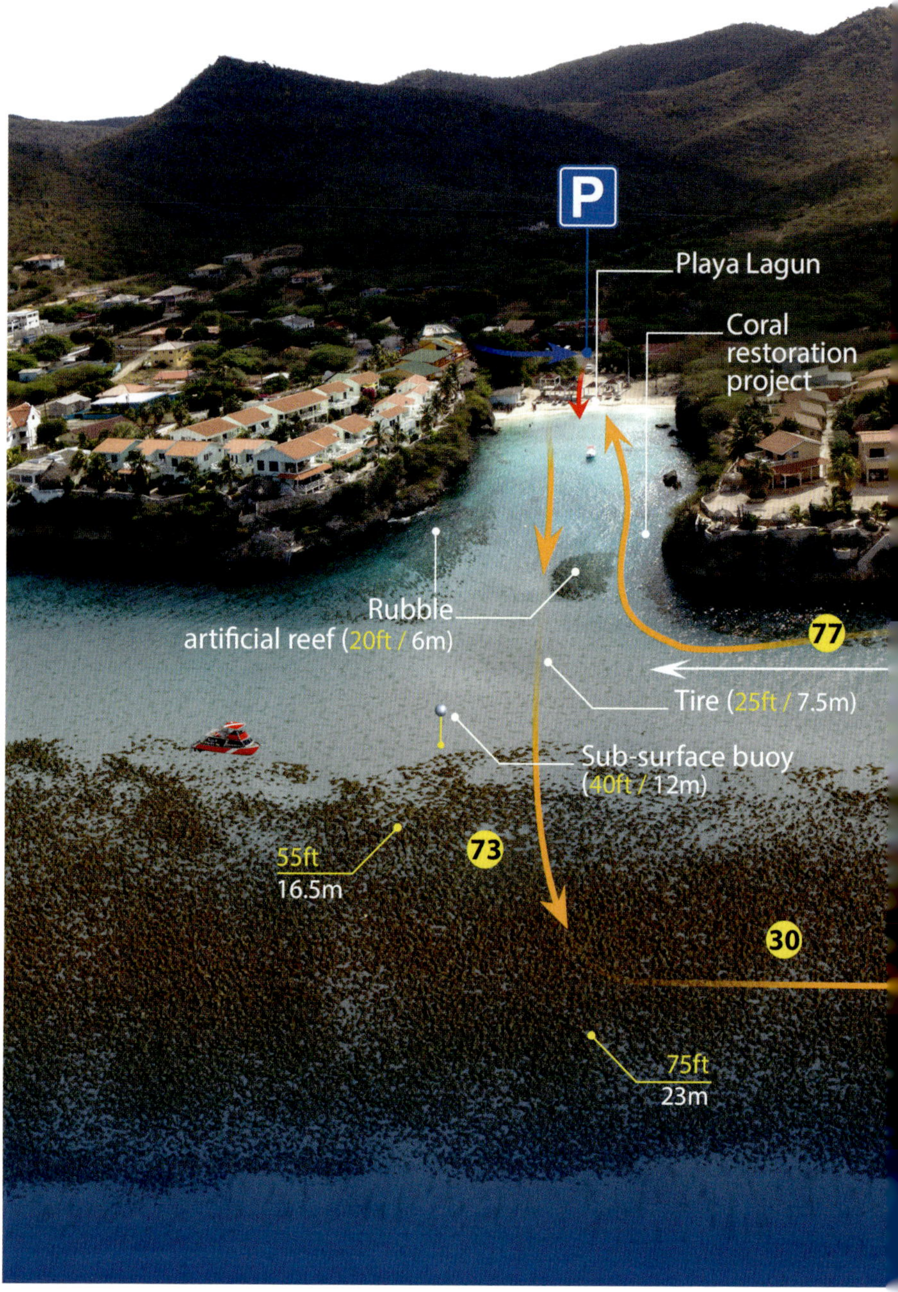


wide flat shelf. Schools of glassy sweepers are often found sheltering in the cave, along with squirrelfish and the occasional lionfish.

## Route

Divers and snorkelers enter the water from the beach. Snorkelers often start exploring the cliff walls along the channel, whereas divers typically surface swim out toward the artificial reef located near the seaward end of the channel. This marks a good point to descend to the bottom. Divers should follow a bearing

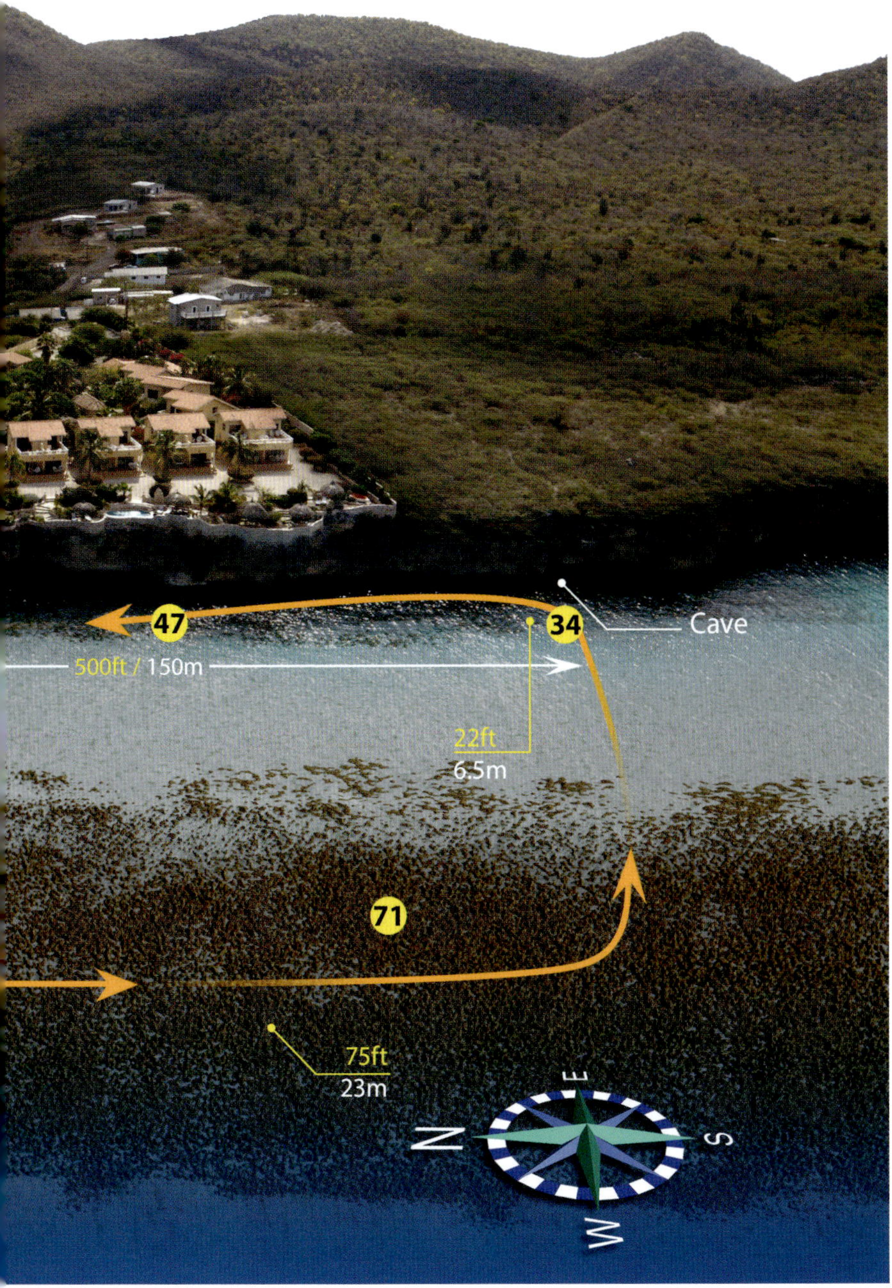


of due west to reach the reef – they usually encounter a car tire about halfway between the channel and the start of the reef slope. A small subsurface buoy marks the edge of the outer reef. Divers usually swim against the current (if one exists) at the outer reef, before heading back to shore and returning to the channel along the cliff edge. At around 22 feet (6.5 meters) depth, the shallow nature of the cliff edge is ideal for extending bottom time and taking a prolonged safety interval.

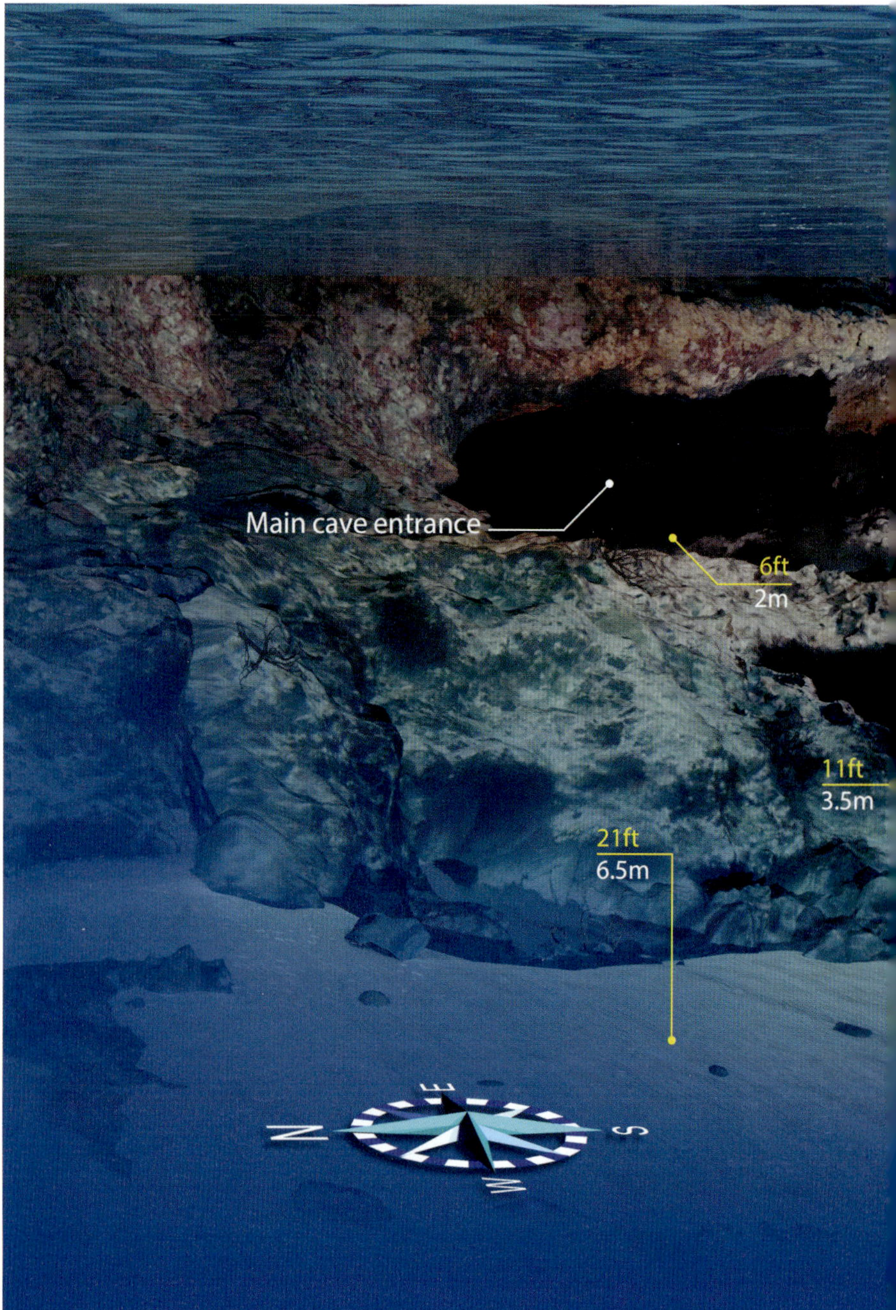
Main cave entrance
6ft
2m
11ft
3.5m
21ft
6.5m
N
E
S
W

Cave entrance
Main cave entrance
Cave entrance
Cave cross section

# PLAYA SANTA CRUZ

Difficulty ● ○ ○
Current ● ○ ○
Depth ● ○ ○
Reef ★★☆
Fauna ★☆☆

Access about 21 mins from Playa Kalki
Access about 40 mins from Willemstad
Access about 2 mins from shore

**Level** Open Water

**Location**
Westpunt, Curaçao
GPS 12°18.348′N, 69°08.728′W

## Getting there

Head north from Willemstad on Weg Naar Westpunt and turn left on Kaminda Monica Kapel Matheeuw about 1.5 miles (2.4 kilometers) past the town of Tera Corá. Continue for another 8.3 miles (13.3 kilometers) and look for a sign on the left-hand side of the road indicating Playa Santa Cruz. The road skirts the edge of Balneario di Santa Cruz for about 0.5 miles (0.85 kilometers) before ending at the beach. The total distance from Willemstad is approximately 22 miles (35.5 kilometers).

## Access

Playa Santa Cruz is free to access and there are plenty of parking spaces available. Divers and snorkelers can gear up at the car and simply walk across the beach to enter the water. This site is suitable for all experience levels. Currents are usually mild here, but visibility can be poor,

so it is recommended to use one of the local boat operators to visit the reef areas located slightly outside of the bay.

## Description

Playa Santa Cruz, also known as Boca Santa Cruz, is a wide beach with plenty of sand for visitors to play ball games, should the mood suit. There are a few palm trees and palapas for shade, and the beach amenities include toilets and a snack bar that opens periodically during busy periods. Kayaks, stand up paddle boards and jet skis can all be rented at the beach.

Divers and snorkelers typically explore the cliff edges along either side of the beach, but the visibility is often poor here, particularly around the outflow from the Balneario di Santa Cruz mangrove area at the northern end of the beach. The best reefs are located approximately 0.5 miles (0.75 kilometers) to the north of the bay, which requires a lift from one of the local boat operators. These reefs support decent coral cover that attracts a range of coral species, including grunts, goatfish, parrotfish, lobsters and moray eels. The cliffs that border the bay feature a series of small caves and undercuts that are popular for divers to explore. Boat rides can also be booked to visit the nearby Black Sand Wreck (page 68) and Blue Room cave (page 75) to the southwest.

There is also a decent reef to explore at the drop-off, due west of the beach, but the distance from shore is just over 0.2 miles (420 meters), making it all but impossible to reach safely, even for divers with incredible air consumption. As such, this reef should also only be visited by boat.

To the south of the beach, just before Let's Go Watersports, there is a small track that leads from the road to the cliff top, allowing visitors to explore the San Nicolas Abou hiking area. It is possible to walk to both Boca Santa Pretu and the Blue Room from Playa Santa Cruz.

# BOCA SANTU PRETU (BLACK SAND WRECK)

Difficulty ●●○
Current ●●○
Depth ●●○
Reef ★☆☆
Fauna ★★☆

Access — about 22 mins from Playa Kalki
Access — about 40 mins from Willemstad
Access — about 7 mins from shore
Access — about 17 mins from Playa Santa Cruz

**Level** Open Water

## Location

Westpunt, Curaçao
GPS 12°18.250'N, 69°08.998'W (wreck)

## Getting there

Head north from Willemstad on Weg Naar Westpunt and turn left on Kaminda Monica Kapel Matheeuw about 1.5 miles (2.4 kilometers) past the town of Tera Corá. Continue for another 8.3 miles (13.3 kilometers) and look for a sign on the left-hand side of the road indicating Playa Santa Cruz. The road skirts the edge of Balneario di Santa Cruz for about 0.5 miles (0.85 kilometers) before ending at the beach. To the south of the beach, just before Let's Go Watersports, there is a small track that leads from the road to the cliff top. The hike to Boca Santa Pretu is approximately 15 minutes. For most divers and snorkelers, the easiest and safest way to visit Boca Santa Pretu and the Black Sand Wreck is through a local dive operator. The total distance from Willemstad is approximately 22.5 miles (36 kilometers).

## Access

The black beach at Boca Santa Pretu is unique, picturesque and often deserted because of its remote location. The *Black Sand Wreck*, which lies approximately 620 feet (190 meters) from the beach, can be reached by a relatively brief, 7-minute surface swim on a heading of approximately 315 degrees taken from the eastern end of the beach. While it is possible to reach this site from shore, most divers and snorkelers prefer to visit the site by boat, rather than hike through the bush with their gear and surface swim to the wreck. Multiple dive operators visit this location, as well as water taxis and snorkel operators from Playa Santa Cruz. Currents are usually mild here, but they can be moderate at times and the sand around the wreck can affect visibility when seas are choppy.

## Description

Boca Santa Pretu is also occasionally referred to as Playa Chikitu and Black Sand Beach, after the black sand that typifies the site. The *Black Sand Wreck* was originally a fishing boat called *Catherine*. This 120-foot (36-meter) wreck lies in two main pieces: a stern section that points toward the shore and a bow section that points out to the deeper reef slope. The wreck is easy to identify from the surface of the water given the shallowness of the sandy seafloor and the dark contrast of the wreck itself. Both main sections of the wreck rest upside down on a sandy seabed that ranges in depth from approximately 29 feet (9 meters) at the bow to 26 feet (8 meters) at the stern.

The hull is covered in numerous small dome-shaped brain and star corals, as well as the

occasional soft coral, making it interesting for divers and snorkelers to closely peruse the hull of the wreck. Smaller pieces of debris are scattered around the site, which add to the complexity of the habitat and help support additional marine life.

The relative shallowness of the *Black Sand Wreck* means that both divers and snorkelers can enjoy exploring the site. Schools of grunts and goatfish can be found around the wreck, as well as trumpetfish, rock beauties, graysbies and various snapper species, as well as several anemones. In the sand around the wreck, divers and snorkelers may find extensive colonies of garden eels.

On the seaward side of the wreck, the sand slopes gradually into deeper water, where a reef develops at a depth of about 35 feet (10.5 meters). The reef, which represents the eastern edge of nearby Mushroom Forest (page 72) sits at a distance of about 200 feet (60 meters) from the bow at a roughly northwestern bearing. Many divers explore this nearby reef as part of their dive after they have fully explored the wreck. Those shore-diving this site may also wish to explore the cliff edges on the way back to the beach, where there is a surprisingly high diversity of marine life.

## Route

Divers and snorkelers who plan on swimming out to the wreck should take a compass heading from the eastern end of the beach and navigate from there. Given the sandy seabed and relative shallowness, visibility can be reduced during choppy conditions, but generally the wreck should be easy to identify. For those exploring the site from a boat, the wreck is easily accessible as it is generally visible from the surface.

Most divers spend at least a quarter of their air exploring the wreck by circling it a few times before spiraling outward to investigate the surrounding debris. Eventually, most divers opt to head toward the reef line on a northwestern heading. From here, divers typically swim into the current to begin their dive along the reef slope,

The relative shallowness of the Black Sand Wreck makes it suitable for both divers and snorkelers.

paying attention to their remaining bottom time so they know when to turn around. A return up the reef slope and back to the wreck can help regain some bottom time.

Alternatively, divers with boat support may opt to conduct the exploration of the nearby reef as part of a drift dive. Depending on the direction and strength of the prevailing current, divers can head southwest toward Mushroom Forest (page 72) or northward up toward Playa Santa Cruz (page 66). They can then surface and signal the boat to come pick them up without having to return to the wreck.

**Name:** *Catherine*
**Type:** Fishing boat
**Previous names:** n/a
**Length:** 120 ft (36.5m)
**Tonnage:** n/a
**Construction:** n/a
**Last owner:** n/a
**Sunk:** n/a

15/16

# SPONGE FOREST & MUSHROOM FOREST

WESTPUNT

Difficulty ● ○ ○
Current ● ○ ○
Depth ● ○ ○
Reef ★★☆
Fauna ★☆☆

Access about 23 mins from Playa Kalki

**Level** Open Water

## Location

Westpunt, Curaçao
GPS 12°17.850'N, 69°09.413'W (Sponge Forest)
GPS 12°17.998'N, 69°09.313'W (Mushroom Forest)

## Getting there

The best way to visit Sponge Forest and Mushroom Forest is through one of the local dive operators located along Curaçao's northwest coast.

## Access

Sponge Forest and Mushroom Forest are located off the northwest shore of the San Nicolas Plantation grounds. There are typically mooring buoys located at these sites, which are suitable for divers and snorkelers of all experience levels. Currents are often moderate here, typically heading in a northeastern direction toward Playa Santa Cruz, which means divers and snorkelers can often enter the water at Sponge Forest and drift though this site and into Mushroom Forest. Visibility is usually excellent at both sites courtesy of the steady currents.

## Description

Sponge Forest and Mushroom Forest are two contiguous reef systems that run for approximately half a mile (0.8 kilometers). Favorable currents can help push divers and snorkelers from one site into

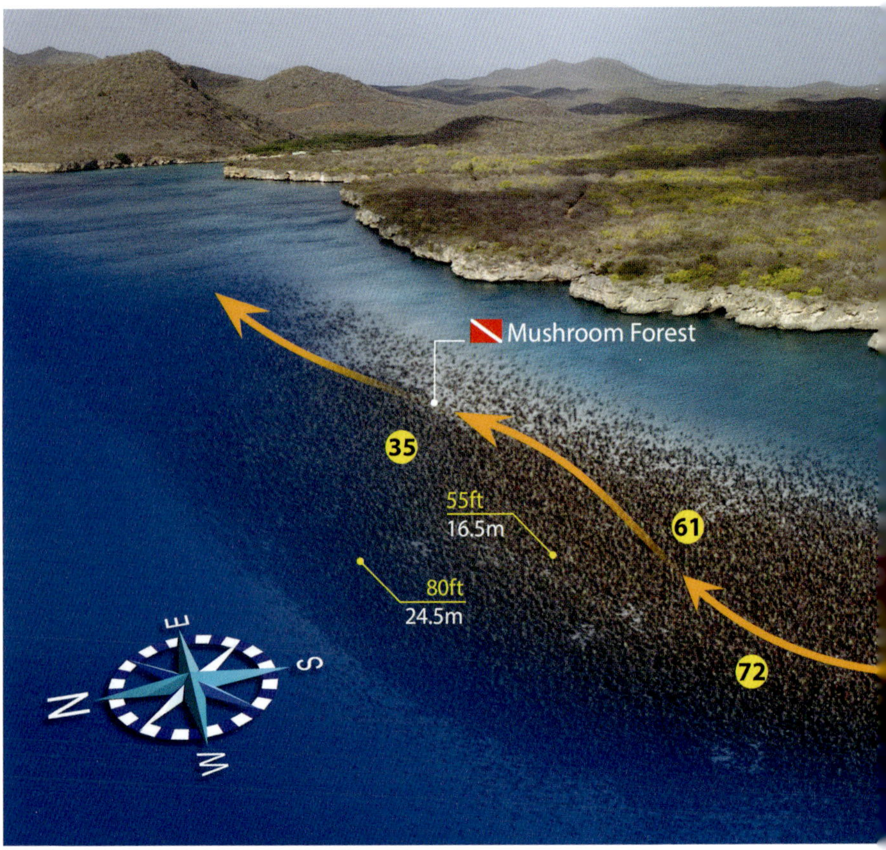

the next, resulting in a wonderfully long experience diving some incredible habitat. The sites essentially consist of a wide, gently sloping plateau that is packed densely with complex reef habitat. While it is possible to snorkel at these two sites, the depth of the plateau, at approximately 50 feet (15 meters), is a little too deep for most and the surface conditions at Sponge Forest can get choppy at times. As a result, these sites are better suited for divers.

The habitat at Sponge Forest is a decent mix of soft and hard corals, interspersed with sand patches at an average depth of 50 feet (15 meters). Divers can often find stingrays or nurse sharks resting in the sand patches, as well as schooling grunts and goatfish. Yellowmouth grouper are often found hiding in the reef itself, while chromis and bar jacks fill the water column above. As the name suggests, the habitat here tends to lean more heavily toward sponges. Divers can see large elephant ear sponges, tube sponges and barrel sponges, particularly in the deeper parts of the site.

As divers transition from Sponge Forest into Mushroom Forest, the number of sand patches begins to diminish and the rugosity of the reef increases. Large mushroom-shaped coral structures, which mainly consist of star coral, but also contain a mix of other species, including lettuce and brain coral, rise from the bottom, sometimes as much as 10 feet (3 meters) in height. The complex habitat creates a labyrinth of crevices that shelter a remarkable array of reef creatures.

In the waters around the mushroom formations, divers can often find angelfish, butterflyfish and nudibranchs. The structures are undercut in many places, and divers may find spotted morays, soapfish, soldierfish, lobsters and the occasional nurse shark hiding underneath the overhangs. Large schools of boga cruise over the reef as well.

## Route

The most used route at these sites is to follow the prevailing current, which usually runs toward the northeast. Navigating to specific coral heads is difficult if not impossible given the relatively featureless nature of the seabed aside from the coral mounds themselves. Fortunately, the entire

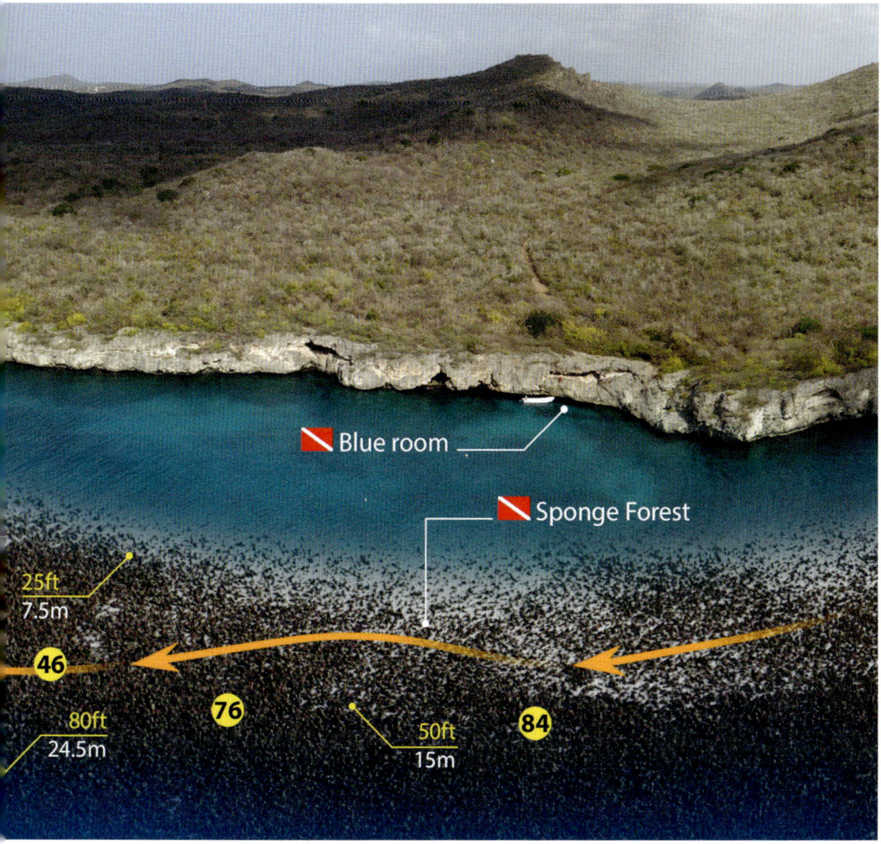

plateau offers divers an incredible experience no matter what path through the coral mounds they take, so visitors need only drift dive anywhere along the reef plateau from Sponge Forest to Mushroom Forest to get the full experience available from these two sites.

Mushroom Forest was named after the towering coral formations present at this site.

Turtle & Ray ©

## SCIENTIFIC INSIGHT

Sponges are incredible filter feeders and provide an invaluable service to the reef by filtering the water column. They collect bacteria from the water and also process carbon, nitrogen and phosphorus. Water passes in through the sponge's pores and is expelled through the osculum, typically located at the top of the sponge. This water movement is driven by specialized cells, called collar cells, which have steadily beating flagella. These collar cells must be replaced constantly by the sponge and, once discarded, become an important food source for other reef organisms. Incredibly, a coral reef sponge is capable of filtering between 10,000 and 30,000 times its volume of seawater each day, which means they are capable of filtering the entire water column above the reef.

# BLUE ROOM

| | |
|---|---|
| Difficulty | ●●○ |
| Current | ●○○ |
| Depth | ●○○ |
| Reef | ★☆☆ |
| Fauna | ★☆☆ |

| | |
|---|---|
| Access (boat) | about 23 mins from Playa Kalki |
| Access (car) | about 40 mins from Willemstad + hike |
| Access (swim) | about 0 mins from shore |
| Access (walk) | about 45 mins from Playa Santa Cruz |

**Level** Open Water

## Location

Westpunt, Curaçao
GPS 12°17.837′N, 69°09.322′W

## Getting there

Head north from Willemstad on Weg Naar Westpunt and turn left on Kaminda Monica Kapel Matheeuw about 1.5 miles (2.4 kilometers) past the town of Tera Corá. Continue for another 5 miles (8 kilometers) and look for the sign on the left-hand side of the road that indicates Playa Santa Cruz. The road skirts the edge of Balneario di Santa Cruz before ending at Playa Santa Cruz. To the south of the beach, just before Let's Go Watersports, there is a small track that leads from the road to the cliff top. The hike to Boca Santa Pretu is approximately 15 minutes. A hike of a further 30 minutes is required to reach Blue Room. Adventurous hikers can follow the edge of the cliff, which is challenging in places and has a 50-foot (15-meter) sheer drop down to the water with no railings – it is not for the faint-hearted. The total distance from Willemstad is approximately 22.5 miles (36 kilometers). For most divers and snorkelers, the easiest and safest way to visit Blue Room is by boat.

## Access

Blue Room typically has a mooring buoy anchored just off the cliff edge at a depth of about 33 feet (10 meters). Divers and snorkelers can easily reach

A diver explores the seabed beneath Blue Room.

NaturePicsFilms/Shutterstock©

the room from this mooring. Those wishing to access the site from shore must drop in from the cliff edge. Currents and wave action are usually mild here, but when surge does exist, it can make entering and exiting Blue Room challenging.

## Description

Blue Room, or Blauwe Kamer in Dutch, is a large cave that cuts back beneath the cliff. As the late afternoon sunlight shines into the cave, it tends to turn the water a vivid blue color, which is how the site came to be named. Over the years, Blue Room has become one of the island's most talked-about aquatic attractions, second perhaps only to *Tugboat* (page 228).

Most people visit Blue Room by swimming or snorkeling. While the entrance to the cave is wide enough for several people to pass at the same time, the roof drops down to the water line at the entrance and is often submerged at high tide or when conditions are rough. As such, a duck-dive is usually required to pass in and out of the cave and a face mask is highly recommended. This is the most dangerous part of the experience. Once inside the cave, the ceiling rises to as much as 12 feet (3.5 meters) above the surface of the water in many places, so the air pocket in the cave is large enough for entire groups of swimmers to breathe at the surface. In addition, the light that passes through the entrance is enough to illuminate the inside of the cave, so there is no need for a flashlight.

There is very little benthic life inside Blue Room, as corals require light to survive. Orange cup corals, which often inhabit shaded locations, are present here however, and it is also common to see large schools of glassy

**SAFETY TIP**

It is important to be aware that thieves are known to operate around Blue Room, specifically targeting bags and other personal possessions that have been left unattended along the shore by those exploring the cave beneath. In addition, while it is possible to clamber down the cliff face and drop into the water at Blue Room, exiting the water at this site can be challenging for many people. Those who cannot climb out and who do not have boat support will be forced to swim along the coast back in the direction of Boca Santa Pretu, which is just over 0.6 miles (1 kilometer) to the north. As such, it is highly recommended to visit this site only by boat.

sweepers, small crabs and shrimp, soldierfish, goatfish and even the occasional nurse shark resting on the bottom.

Blue Room offers a completely unique experience that is rarely found elsewhere. For divers however, the shallow depth and lack of marine life is unlikely to hold their interest for long, which is why a visit to Blue Room is often combined with a dive on nearby Sponge Forest and/or Mushroom Forest.

## Route

No specific route is necessary to explore this site.

## 18 PLAYA HULU

**Level** Open Water
GPS 12°17.260′N, 69°09.162′W

Difficulty ●○○
Current ●○○
Depth ●●○
Reef ★★☆
Fauna ★★☆

Playa Hulu, sometimes known as Boca Hulu, is a relatively sheltered dive and snorkel site located just south of Sponge Forest. The site is believed to be named after an escaped slave, known as Hulu, who lived in this area. The site is technically accessible from shore via the nearby beach of the same name, but the land is part of the San Nicolas plantation, which is currently closed to the public. As such, this site currently can only be reached by boat. The reef at Playa Hulu is a steep slope with lots of healthy corals and sponges. Moray eels are common here, and divers often report finding frogfish at this site. Currents are usually mild and there is limited wave action.

## 19 DUANE'S RELEASE

**Level** Advanced
GPS 12°16.963′N, 69°09.042′W

Difficulty ●●●
Current ●●○
Depth ●●○
Reef ★★★
Fauna ★★☆

Duane's Release is a boat-accessible dive site that sometimes goes by the name Scooter and sometimes by the name Boca Pos Spaño. The site was named after a diver called Duane Hendrix who passed away at a young age and whose ashes were released here. A memorial plaque can also be found underwater, adjacent to the mooring line. Duane's Release lies between Playa Hulu and Rediho on a section of coastline that is more exposed to currents and wave action than its neighbors. These stronger currents often mean this site is best explored as a drift dive, and though it can be explored by divers of all levels on calm days, those with experience will likely feel more at ease when conditions are rough. Snorkelers should consider waiting for calm conditions to visit the site. There are plenty of hard corals, sponges and large soft corals where trumpetfish, seahorses and slender files often hide. Balloonfish, boxfish and angelfish are common here, and divers may also encounter sea turtles and eagle rays.

## 20 REDIHO

**Level** Advanced
GPS 12°16.803′N, 69°08.745′W

Difficulty ●●●
Current ●●●
Depth ●●○
Reef ★★★
Fauna ★★★

Rediho is another dive site that is currently accessible only by boat. The site is adjacent to a small beach located within the San Nicolas plantation, which is currently closed to the public. The relatively exposed position of this site often results in strong currents and choppy surface conditions, which make Rediho less suitable for snorkelers and novice divers, except on calm days. The reef has numerous sandy channels that drop down the steep slope into the depths. Much like Duane's Release located to the north, divers often report seahorses, frogfish, sea turtles and eagle rays at this site. Predatory barracuda, tiger grouper and Nassau grouper are also fairly common here. Visibility is usually excellent at Rediho thanks to strong currents. And when drift diving, the current is often strong enough for divers to reach Duane's Release, which is why these two sites are sometimes collectively called Boca Pos Spaño by some sources.

## 21 BLACK CORAL GARDEN

**Level** Advanced
GPS 12°16.550′N, 69°08.572′W

Difficulty ●●●
Current ●●●
Depth ●●●
Reef ★★★
Fauna ★★☆

Black Coral Garden lies just south of Playa Franki, which is a small beach located within the currently closed-to-the-public San Nicolas plantation. As such, this dive site is currently accessible only by boat. The site is named after the rare black corals that divers can find in the deeper sections of this steeply sloped site, along with large elephant ear sponges, wire corals and plate-form corals. As in the nearby sites to the north, seahorses and frogfish are often found here, as well as sea turtles and barracuda. Currents can be strong at Black Coral Garden, which makes this site ideal for drift diving and helps maintain particularly good visibility. However, it also means that the site is less suited to snorkelers and novice divers except on calm days.

## 22 HELL'S CORNER

**Level** Advanced
GPS 12°16.198'N, 69°08.407'W

Difficulty ●●●
Current ●●●
Depth ●●●
Reef ★★★
Fauna ★★☆

Located on a particularly exposed, south-facing headland, Hell's Corner is named after the strong currents that typify this boat-accessible site. The site is also sometimes referred to as Fallen Rock. Hell's Corner is often completed as a drift dive that can run all the way into Black Coral Garden for those with good air consumption. The typically choppy sea conditions here make this site less ideal for snorkelers except on calm days. The entire reef is healthy, with a decent mix of hard and soft corals as well as sponges. Black coral and plate-form corals typify the deeper areas of the reef. Cubera snapper are also occasionally spotted in the deeper parts of the reef.

## 23 MAKO'S MOUNTAIN

**Level** Advanced
GPS 12°16.042'N, 69°08.153'W

Difficulty ●●●
Current ●●●
Depth ●●●
Reef ★★★
Fauna ★★☆

It is not known how Mako's Mountain (sometimes just Mako Mountain) got its name. There is certainly very little chance of seeing a mako shark here. This exposed site, which is located on a south-facing headland, often has strong currents that can take drift divers all the way into the reef at nearby Hell's Corner. There are tales of shark sightings at Mako's Mountain, but official REEF surveys have yet to record any. Divers are likely to see large horse-eye jacks, bar jacks and mutton snapper, however, as well as large numbers of chromis. These species attract many predatory grouper species, including black, yellowmouth and tiger. The east side of Mako's Mountain, which is sometimes referred to as San Nicolas or Mike's Reef, can make for an interesting snorkel site and is accessible from shore by swimming across the channel adjacent to the beach at Santa Martha, also known as Sunset Waters.

Seahorses are present at many of the sites between Playa Hulu and Mako's Mountain.

Drew McArthur/Shutterstock©

# SANTA MARTHA (SUNSET WATERS)

Difficulty ●○○
Current ●○○
Depth ●●○
Reef ★☆☆
Fauna ★★☆

Access about 25 mins from Rif Sint Marie
Access about 39 mins from Willemstad
Access about 2 mins from shore

**Level** Open Water

## Location

Soto, Curaçao
GPS 12°16.068'N, 69°07.683'W

## Getting there

Head north from Willemstad on Weg Naar Westpunt and turn left on Kaminda Monica Kapel Matheeuw about 1.5 miles (2.4 kilometers) past the town of Tera Corá. Continue for another 5.2 miles (8.4 kilometers) through the town of Soto and take the left turn after the graveyard. This road runs along the southern side of Balneario di Santa Martha, before descending the cliff to the beach at Santa Martha. The total distance from Willemstad is approximately 21 miles (33.5 kilometers).

## Access

Santa Martha is free to access and there are plenty of parking spaces. Divers and snorkelers can gear up at the car and simply walk down the beach and into the water. A small lagoon is enclosed by a semi-circular beach and breakwater, which makes entering and exiting the water relatively simple. The shallow floor is littered with large rocks and rubble, however, so divers and snorkelers should make sure they have protective footwear when they enter the water. This dive site is suitable for all experience levels. Currents are usually mild here, but visibility can be very poor at times.

## Description

Santa Martha dive and snorkel site is known by a whole host of alternate names. Perhaps the best known of these is Sunset Waters, after the resort that used to exist nearby. The site is also known as Airplane Wreck, because of the light aircraft that was positioned just outside the breakwater at the top of the drop-off as an artificial reef and point of attraction for divers. The site is also occasionally referred to as Sunset Beach, Harry's Hole and Wet Suit City, the latter because of the amount of fire coral located here.

Santa Martha beach is a popular bathing spot for locals because the waters inside the breakwater are shallow and calm. The beach here offers little else to attract visitors, however, and its proximity to the channel that connects to the nearby saliña means that visibility at this dive and snorkel site is frequently poor, especially as you swim closer to the channel that borders the northern edge of the site. The poor visibility not only limits divers' ability to explore safely, it also has a negative effect on the health of corals at this site.

Heading out through the breakwater in a roughly southwestern direction, divers and snorkelers will likely first encounter an old anchor, which lies upright on a sandy plateau at a depth of approximately 20 feet (6 meters). What remains of the light aircraft lies to the northwest of the anchor and closer to the drop-off, at a depth of around 22 feet (6.5 meters). The structure is barely recognizable as a plane because it consists of just the cockpit frame and the interior elements. A large barrel sponge sits on top of the plane at a depth of around 16 feet (5 meters). Slightly farther down the reef slope, divers and snorkelers may notice a few other pieces of debris, including what remains of one of the plane's wings.

The reef slope is more of a wall, with cascades of sand that descend the steep slope, broken

### DID YOU KNOW?

Light aircraft are often constructed from light, thin metals, such as aluminum alloys and plastics. These materials are ideal for flight because they have a high strength-to-weight ratio and are corrosion resistant. Aircraft rarely last long in the marine environment, however, as their light weight makes them easy to break apart during times of rough weather, especially when placed in shallow water.

## RELAX & RECHARGE

A few minutes to the north of Santa Marta, on a hill overlooking the town of Jan Donker, is a local gem of a restaurant called **Shelter Rock Paradise**. They focus on local cuisine, prepared in traditional ways. Friday night is Coconut Night, which means your meal of stewed goat, beef, seafood, chicken or vegetables will be slow cooked inside a coconut, directly over the hot coals. This is a relaxed establishment with exceptional food and exceptional views (especially at sunset) – it's a place to unwind, so don't come here if you're in a rush. If you come early enough in the day, and feel the need to build up an appetite, there are one-hour and three-hour hiking trails to explore. There are even salsa/bachata dance classes and camping spots here. Happy hour is every Wednesday from 6-8pm.
Visit: **Shelterrock-paradise.com**

up by large coral patches. The coral and sponge cover is surprisingly dense in places and large star corals rise up from the wall below the plane and transition to plate-form corals in the depths. The wall extends roughly parallel to shore in both directions, featuring a series of slightly scalloped indentations. Visibility is often better down on the wall, and the reef here is interesting to explore.

Along the wall, divers may find moray eels, lobsters and fairy basslets hiding among the coral heads, as well as schoolmaster snapper and grey snapper. Rainbow parrotfish and blue parrotfish can be found in the shallower areas of the reef, as well as butterflyfish, surgeonfish, trunkfish and scorpionfish.

### Route

Most divers typically walk or surface swim out through the breakwater as the lagoon is too shallow to effectively submerge. Once past the rocks, divers can descend to the sand and swim

Green moray eels can be found on the reef wall at Santa Martha.

Jonathan Boggs/Shutterstock©

out to the drop-off along a roughly 220 degree heading. Once at the drop-off, divers typically turn northwest and swim along the sand-reef transition of the drop-off to encounter the anchor and then the wreckage of the airplane. After exploring the wreckage, divers typically descend the reef wall and explore to the southeast, away from the channel. The reef wall descends past 100 feet (30.5 meters) but the highest diversity of coral life can be observed at a depth of around 50 feet (15 meters). Most divers plan on turning around once they reach

a half tank of air, and then return along the top of the drop-off toward the wreckage for a prolonged safety interval.

# SANTA MARTHA (SUNSET WATERS)

16ft
5m
29ft
9m
Plane wreck
25ft
7.5m

# PLAYA HUNDU

Difficulty ●○○
Current ●○○
Depth ●●○
Reef ★★★
Fauna ★★☆

Access about 22 mins from Rif Sint Marie
Access about 42 mins from Willemstad
Access about 3 mins from shore

**Level** Open Water

**Location**
Soto, Curaçao
GPS 12°15.592'N, 69°07.203'W

**Getting there**
Head north from Willemstad on Weg Naar Westpunt and turn left on Kaminda Monica Kapel Matheeuw about 1.5 miles (2.4 kilometers) past the town of Tera Corá. Continue for another 5.2 miles (8.4 kilometers) through the town of Soto and take the left turn after the graveyard. This road is a dirt track that can be challenging to drive along at times. The road bends to the right and then runs relatively straight for about 0.75 miles (1.2 kilometers) until the parking lot adjacent to

the beach. The total distance from Willemstad is approximately 21 miles (33.5 kilometers).

## Access

Playa Hundu is a remote beach that can be challenging to get to, but once there, visitors are often captivated by feelings of peace and tranquility here. The beach is a mix of sand and coral rubble, so footwear is recommended. This dive site is suitable for divers and snorkelers of all levels. Currents are usually mild, and visibility is excellent.

## Description

The shallow back reef at Playa Hundu is a wonderful sunlit plateau that extends approximately 230 feet (69 meters) from shore out to the drop-off. East of the beach, the plateau is dominated by sand, but to the west, the plateau slopes a little deeper and features a wonderful mix of soft and hard corals, with large, healthy stands of blade fire coral as well as stands of staghorn, elkhorn and pillar corals, in some places. The high rugosity habitat of the reef supports a wide diversity of reef creatures, including anemones, filefish, boxfish, frogfish and various snapper and grouper species. At a maximum depth of just 50 feet (15 meters), the plateau is shallow enough to be visible to snorkelers at the surface, as well as deep enough to allow comfortable buoyancy for divers. The site also features a drop-off with a steep, 45-degree slope with numerous ridges and channels cutting through it. Divers can explore the drop-off and the dense coral cover and associated reef species. Divers may also notice the presence of many different hamlet species at this site, including yellowtail, butter, barred and black hamlets.

26

BANDABOU

# PLAYA SAN JUAN

Difficulty ●○○
Current ●○○
Depth ●●○
Reef ★★☆
Fauna ★★☆

Access about 18 mins from Rif Sint Marie
Access about 41 mins from Willemstad
Access about 3 mins from shore

**Level** Open Water

## Location

San Juan, Curaçao
GPS 12°14.952'N, 69°06.410'W

## Getting there

Head north from Willemstad on Weg Naar Westpunt and turn left on Kaminda Monica Kapel Matheeuw, which is about 1.5 miles (2.4 kilometers) past the town of Tera Corá. After approximately 3.3 miles (5.3 kilometers) there is a left turn off the main road that leads to Landhuis San Juan. It takes approximately another mile (1.5 kilometers) to reach the plantation complex from the main road. Visitors must pay a small entrance fee to access the grounds. The road to Playa San Juan is off toward the right immediately after passing the plantation. The road quickly reaches the San Juanbaai and runs along the southern edge of the bay before ending at a small car park. The total distance from Willemstad is approximately 20 miles (32.5 kilometers).

## Access

To access the Playa San Juan dive and snorkel site, visitors must enter the water from the car park and swim across the narrow channel that

## DID YOU KNOW?

Landhuis San Juan was built in 1662, and it is considered one of the oldest plantation houses in Curaçao. The estate was managed by the island's vice-director Matthias Beck and his family, and was involved in growing maize, sugarcane, cotton and indigo, as well as livestock breeding. The house was used as a set for the 2013 movie Tula: The Revolt, which tells the story of Curaçao's slave revolt of 1795. Today, the plantation is known for its stunning beaches, collectively known as the San Juan beaches. From west to east, they are Playas Chiki, Manzalina, Shon Mosa and Largu, each of which has its own associated dive and snorkel site. These beaches are remote and there are no facilities, so it is important to bring whatever food, drinks, sunscreen and other items you need to get through your visit.

connects San Juanbaai to the open ocean. From the mouth of the channel, divers must head west toward the reef slope – a distance of around 440 feet (134 meters). This dive site is suitable for all experience levels. Currents are usually mild here, but visibility can be poor close to the mouth of the channel.

### Description

Playa San Juan is sometimes referred to as Boca Grandi – not to be confused with the site farther north, which is known as Playa Grandi. The sand-bottomed bay transitions to reef away from the mouth of the channel. Blue and brown chromis school in the water column above the reef here, along with bar jacks and squid. On the reef itself, it is possible to find soapfish, flying gurnards and sand tilefish. Snorkelers can cross the channel and explore the shallow reef areas to the west, or they can stay east of the channel and explore the rocky area toward the headland in the direction of Playa Chiki.

27 BANDABOU

# PLAYA CHIKI

Difficulty ●○○
Current ●○○
Depth ●●○
Reef ★★☆
Fauna ★★☆

Access (boat) about 17 mins from Rif Sint Marie
Access (car) about 42 mins from Willemstad
Access (swim) about 1 mins from shore

**Level** Open Water

## Location

San Juan, Curaçao
GPS 12°14.818′N, 69°06.410′W

## Getting there

Follow the directions provided for Playa San Juan, but upon reaching the plantation house, stay on the main track instead of taking the immediate right turn. Continue about 0.2 miles (0.3 kilometers) down the road until the road forks. Take the fork on the right. Over the remaining 0.6 miles (1 kilometer) to the coast, the road forks two more times – take the right fork in both cases. The road ends at a parking lot adjacent to the small and relatively sheltered Playa Chiki, which is confusingly signposted as Playa Hundu. The total distance from Willemstad is approximately 20.5 miles (33 kilometers).

## Access

To access the Playa Chiki dive and snorkel site, walk down the sandy beach and enter the water. The back reef begins just 100 feet

**ECO TIP**

Sea turtles have been documented nesting on many of Curaçao's beaches between the months of May and December, including Klein Curaçao. The island's northwest area, with its quieter beaches, is an important area for sea turtle nesting. This region was declared a national park in 1993, and the coastline was legally designated a conservation area by means of the land-use zoning ordinance. Sea turtles gained legal protection in Curaçao in 1996. Three species of turtle are known to nest regularly in Curaçao – loggerhead, hawksbill and green sea turtles. Leatherback nesting was first documented for the first time in Curaçao in 2005 at Grote Knip. Sea Turtle Conservation Curaçao does important work to protect these endangered creatures around the islands, including monitoring, rescue and beach clean-up efforts. Learn more about this organization on page 17.

(30.5 meters) from the beach. This dive site is suitable for all experience levels. Currents are usually mild here and visibility is usually good.

## Description

Playa Chiki, which translates into "little beach," consists primarily of sand. The beach is also occasionally known as turtle beach, probably because of its potential as a turtle nesting beach. The back reef at Playa Chiki features small patch reefs for the first 150 feet (45 meters) and then transitions to highly complex reef with sand and coral rubble channels. There is a good mix of sponges along with hard and soft corals at this reef, which hosts plenty of reef life. The reef starts to slope more steeply around 360 feet (110 meters) from the beach, which is the closest to shore of any of the three San Juan-associated reefs.

28

BANDABOU

# PLAYA MANZALIÑA

Difficulty ● ○ ○
Current ● ○ ○
Depth ● ● ○
Reef ★★☆
Fauna ★★☆

Access about 16 mins from Rif Sint Marie
Access about 42 mins from Willemstad
Access about 2 mins from shore

**Level** Open Water

**Location**
San Juan, Curaçao
GPS 12°14.723'N, 69°06.322'W

### Getting there

Follow the directions provided for Playa San Juan, but upon reaching the plantation house, stay on the main track instead of taking the immediate right turn. Continue about 0.2 miles (0.3 kilometers) down the road until the road forks and then take the fork on the right. Over the remaining 0.5 miles (0.9 kilometers) to the coast, the road forks two more times: take the right fork followed by the left fork. The road ends at a parking lot adjacent to Playa Manzaliña. The total distance from Willemstad is approximately 20.5 miles (33 kilometers).

### Access

To access the Playa Manzaliña dive and snorkel site, visitors simply need to walk down the sandy beach and enter the water. This dive site is suitable for all experience levels. Currents are mild and visibility is usually good.

## DID YOU KNOW?

The Manzaliña tree that gives this beach its name is more commonly known throughout the Caribbean as manchineel or beach apple *(Hippomane mancinella)*. The full name in Spanish is actually *manzaliña de la muerte*, which means "little apple of death" and references the small toxic apples that grow on the tree. In fact, it is not just the manchineel apples that are toxic, but the entire tree, including the bark, leaves, and even its milky-white sap. The Caribs were known to poison the water supply of their enemies with the leaves of the manchineel tree and the famous Spanish explorer, Juan Ponce de León, died in 1521 in Florida, shortly after being struck by an arrow that had been poisoned with manchineel sap. Even standing beneath the tree during a rain shower can cause skin blistering from the rainwater that drips from the tree.

### Description

Playa Manzaliña is named after the Manzaliña trees found on the beach at this site. This beach is the most popular of the San Juan beaches. Even so, it is uncommon to find more than a handful of people here. Divers and snorkelers can explore the reef in either direction. If the current is favorable, divers can explore the site along with part of the reef off Playa Chiki to the northwest. The distance to the reef slope from the beach is around 400 feet (122 meters), so a slightly longer swim than at Playa Chiki. While creole wrasses and chromis fill the water column here, the site is known for hosting a range of cryptic species, including scorpionfish, flounders and nudibranchs. Swimmers should also look out for anemones with their associated Pederson cleaner shrimp at this site.

# PLAYA SHON MOSA

| | |
|---|---|
| Difficulty | ●○○ |
| Current | ●○○ |
| Depth | ●●○ |
| Reef | ★★☆ |
| Fauna | ★★☆ |

Access (boat) about 16 mins from Rif Sint Marie
Access (car) about 42 mins from Willemstad
Access (swim) about 3 mins from shore

**Level** Open Water

## Location

San Juan, Curaçao
GPS 12°14.633'N, 69°06.257'W

## Getting there

Follow the directions provided for Playa San Juan, but upon reaching the plantation house, stay on the main track instead of taking the immediate right turn. Continue about 0.2 miles (0.3 kilometers) down the road until the road forks and then take the fork on the right. Over the remaining 0.5 miles (0.9 kilometers) to the coast, the road forks two more times: take the left fork followed by the right fork. The road ends at a parking lot adjacent to Playa Shon Mosa. The total distance from Willemstad is approximately 20.5 miles (33 kilometers).

## Access

To access the Playa Shon Mosa dive and snorkel

## DID YOU KNOW?

To the south of Playa Shon Mosa (and to the west of Playa Largu), is an area of coastline that can only be safely accessed by boat. Multiple local operators refer to a dive site in this area as Big Sponge, because of a large individual sponge that existed there in the past. While Big Sponge is not an official Curaçao dive and snorkel site, it is possible to find local operators that will visit this remote location.

site, visitors simply need to walk down the sandy beach and enter the water. This dive site is suitable for all experience levels. Currents are mild and visibility is usually good.

### Description

Playa Shon Mosa is the smallest of the San Juan beaches. It is also the most protected because the coastline juts out to form a headland starting at the southern end of the beach, which provides some shelter from winds and currents. The swim out from the beach is slightly longer than at neighboring sites. The predominantly sandy back reef supports an interesting mix of species, with a slightly higher probability of seeing stingrays, sand tilefish, sand divers, flying gurnards and peacock flounders than at other San Juan sites. Patch reefs appear at about 300 feet (80 meters) from shore and the reef becomes progressively more rugose and starts to slope gradually into the depths at 600 feet (183 meters) from the beach. Divers and snorkelers can explore in either direction. It is a very brief swim north to reach Playa Manzaliña.

# PLAYA LARGU

Difficulty ● ○ ○
Current ● ○ ○
Depth ● ● ○
Reef ★★★
Fauna ★★★

Access — about 12 mins from Rif Sint Marie
Access — about 45 mins from Willemstad
Access — about 3 mins from shore

**Level** Open Water

**Location**
San Juan, Curaçao
GPS 12°14.127'N, 69°05.913'W

## Getting there

Follow the directions provided for Playa San Juan, but upon reaching the plantation house, stay on the main track instead of taking the immediate right turn. Continue about 0.2 miles (0.3 kilometers) down the road until the road forks and then take the fork on the right. The road forks two more times over the next 0.4 miles (0.6 kilometers): take the left fork in both cases. After that, the road is a rough dirt track that twists and turns for another 0.9 miles (1.5 kilometers) before running alongside the southern edge of a small saliña and ending close to the beach. The total distance from Willemstad is approximately 21.5 miles (33.5 kilometers).

## Access

There is plenty of space to park near Playa Largu. To access the dive and snorkel site, visitors simply need to walk across the beach and enter the water. The beach here consists

## DID YOU KNOW?

To the southeast of Playa Largu, in front of the Cas Abou residences, is a dive and snorkel site often referred to as Playa Chikitu (sometimes also called Playa Boto). Like the nearby Big Sponge site on the other side of Playa Largu, this is not an official Curaçao dive and snorkel site. It is, however, regularly visited by local dive operators. It can only be reached by boat because there is no shore access other than through the private residences located adjacent to the site onshore, which is restricted to the general public.

more of sharp coral rubble than sand, so booties or other foot protection are necessary. This dive site is suitable for all experience levels. Currents are mild and visibility is usually good.

### Description

Playa Largu is a long, south-facing beach regarded by many as the best of the San Juan dive and snorkel sites. The site is sometimes referred to as Playa Dushi, which means beautiful, and Long Beach, which is the English transition of largu. The back reef consists mostly of sand and coral rubble, and divers can often find stingrays here. The reef slope begins about 350 feet (105 meters) from the beach and is steeper here than at most of the other San Juan sites. Playa Largu hosts multiple sponge species on its reef slope, including barrel, vase, rope and elephant ear sponges located in the deeper parts of the site. Moray eels are also common at depth, and many divers report large green morays here, as well as grouper and lobsters. Divers can explore in either direction at Playa Largu. For snorkelers, the back reef and along the top of the reef slope support an abundance of soft corals that often shelter trumpetfish and slender filefish.

31

BANDABOU

# CAS ABAO

Difficulty ●●○
Current ●○○
Depth ●●○
Reef ★★☆
Fauna ★★★

Access (boat) about 10 mins from Rif Sint Marie
Access (car) about 33 mins from Willemstad
Access (swim) about 5 mins from shore

**Level** Open Water

## Location

Banda Abou, Curaçao
GPS 12°13.660'N, 69°05.537'W

## Getting there

Head north from Willemstad on Weg Naar Westpunt and turn left on Kaminda Monica Kapel-Matheeuw about 1.5 miles (2.4 kilometers) past the town of Tera Corá. Continue for just over 2 miles (3.3 kilometers) until 1 mile (1.7 kilometers) passed Villapark Fontein. Turn left at the orange entranceway marked by a sign indicating Cas Abao. This paved road stretches 2.3 miles (3.8 kilometers) and leads directly to the beach. Along the way, drivers will pass the Cas Abao Resort on the left-hand side and eventually reach a small booth, where an entrance fee must be paid to access the beach. The fee is paid per car, based on a maximum of four people. There is a surcharge per additional person. The beach is open from 8am to 6pm and the price for entry is slightly higher on Sundays and public holidays. From this point onward, the road is no longer paved. There is a large parking area, with plenty of space located next to the beach. The total distance from Willemstad is approximately 18 miles (29 kilometers).

## Access

Cas Abao is a popular beach among both locals and visitors. Access to diving and snorkeling simply involves walking down the sandy beach and into the water. This dive site is suitable for all experience levels. Currents are usually mild here and visibility is usually excellent.

## Description

Cas Abao is sometimes referred to as Lower House, which is the English translation of its Papiamentu name, and sometimes also Bon Bini Beach. It is widely regarded as one of the best beaches in Curaçao and offers plenty of activities and amenities for the entire family. There are many large palapas as well as a few trees spread out along the beach that provide natural shade. Beach chairs are available to rent, as are kayaks and stand-up paddle boards. There are also toilets and coin-operated showers available. A beach bar serves food and refreshments and even offer free Wi-Fi. And for those visitors who are really looking to relax, there is a spa that offers a range of massages and other treatments.

The dive center at Cas Abao is well set up and the helpful staff are keen to give advice. They are also available for guided dives and snorkel tours, as desired. For those visitors who wish to do their own thing, the best place to enter the water is at the center of the wide beach. The reef begins about 330 feet (100 meters) from shore and slopes rapidly to a depth of approximately 100 feet (30 meters). At this depth, the seabed returns to sand.

## RELAX & RECHARGE

**Cas Abao Beach Bar** has you covered for all your beach refreshment needs. The menu has burgers, sandwiches, wraps and salads, as well as plenty of "beach bites", including nuggets, bitter balls, croquettes, frikandel and chicken satè skewers, among other delicious snacks. There are also several flavors of ice cream. The beverage menu is just as extensive, with plenty of alcoholic and non-alcoholic drinks, including refreshing frozen cocktails, coffee and tea and various fruit smoothies. You can sit on the terrace, at the bar, or simply take your food and drink to the beach – this establishment is plastic-free. Cas Abao Beach Bar is open from 10am to 6pm.
Visit: **Casabaobeach.com/food-drinks**

Divers can head in either direction along the reef slope. To the north, the reef is highly rugose and has a good mix of hard and soft corals as well as sponges, which host a wide variety of reef creatures, including anemones, frogfish, seahorses, sea turtles and even eagle rays. The reef to the south is similar in form, but at depth it features three large spurs that extend out from the reef into deep water, each one increasingly larger in size as you move south. The largest of these spurs features a small wall along which divers can often find schools of mahogany snapper, as well as green moray eels and lobsters tucked into crevices in the reef.

## Route

It is generally a good idea to conduct more than one dive at Cas Abao to allow a full exploration of both directions along the reef slope. Divers usually descend the reef slope and explore the deeper areas of the reef first. To the south, divers usually have enough time to pass each of the three spurs before turning back. A dive tank, remodeled as an underwater sign and located at the top of the reef slope, helps point divers back to the beach. There is also a wooden sign at a depth of 40 feet (12 meters) located directly in line with the dive shop. Divers can often find razorfish, sand divers and peacock flounders in the sand on their way back to the beach.

Snorkelers usually stick to the shallows on the two extremes of the beach, where the cliff drops directly into the water. These regions provide snorkelers with plenty of reef habitat



Large tube sponges can be found along the outer reef slope at Cas Abao.

NaturePicsFilms/Shutterstock©

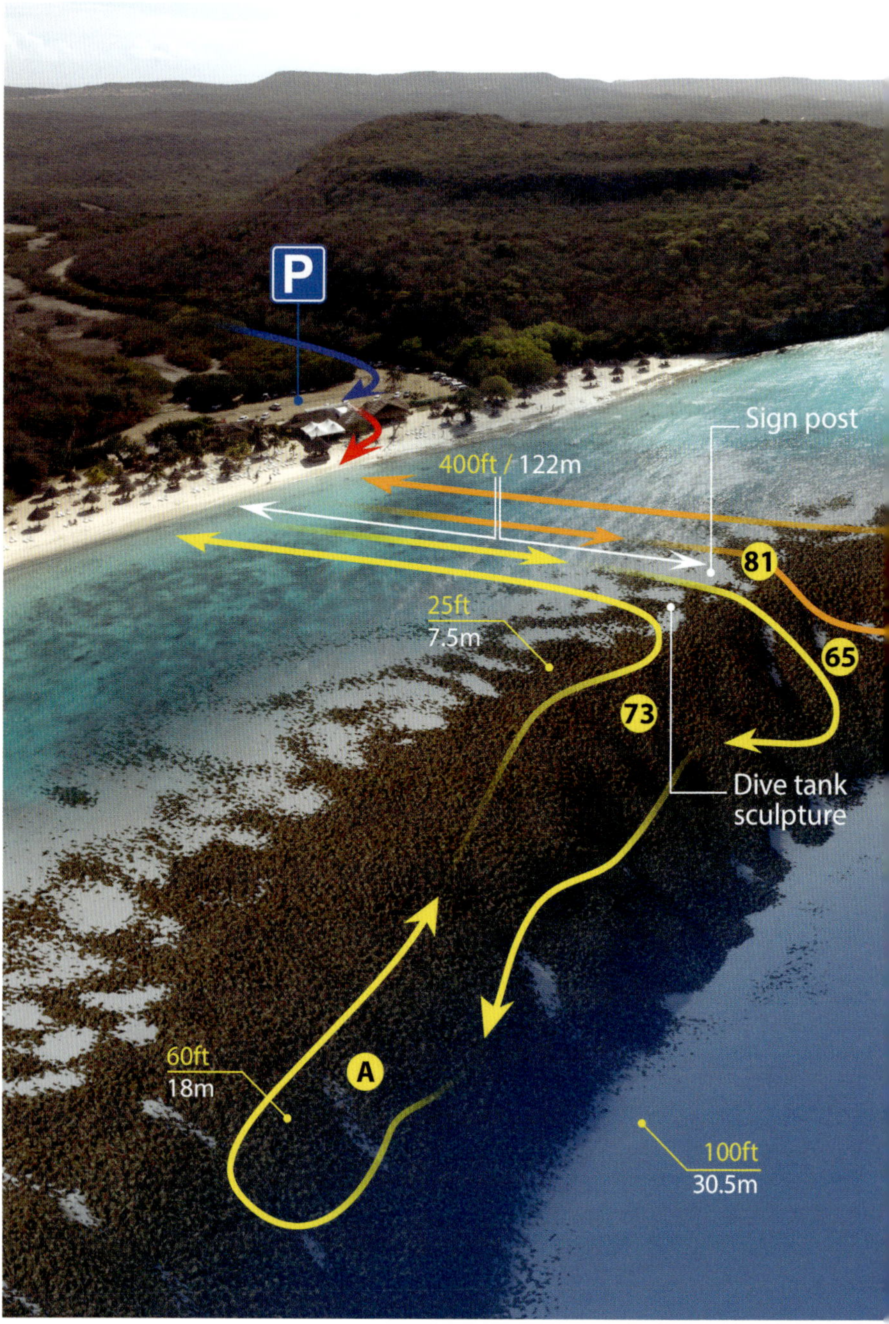


to explore, which supports a variety of reef fish and even the occasional octopus.

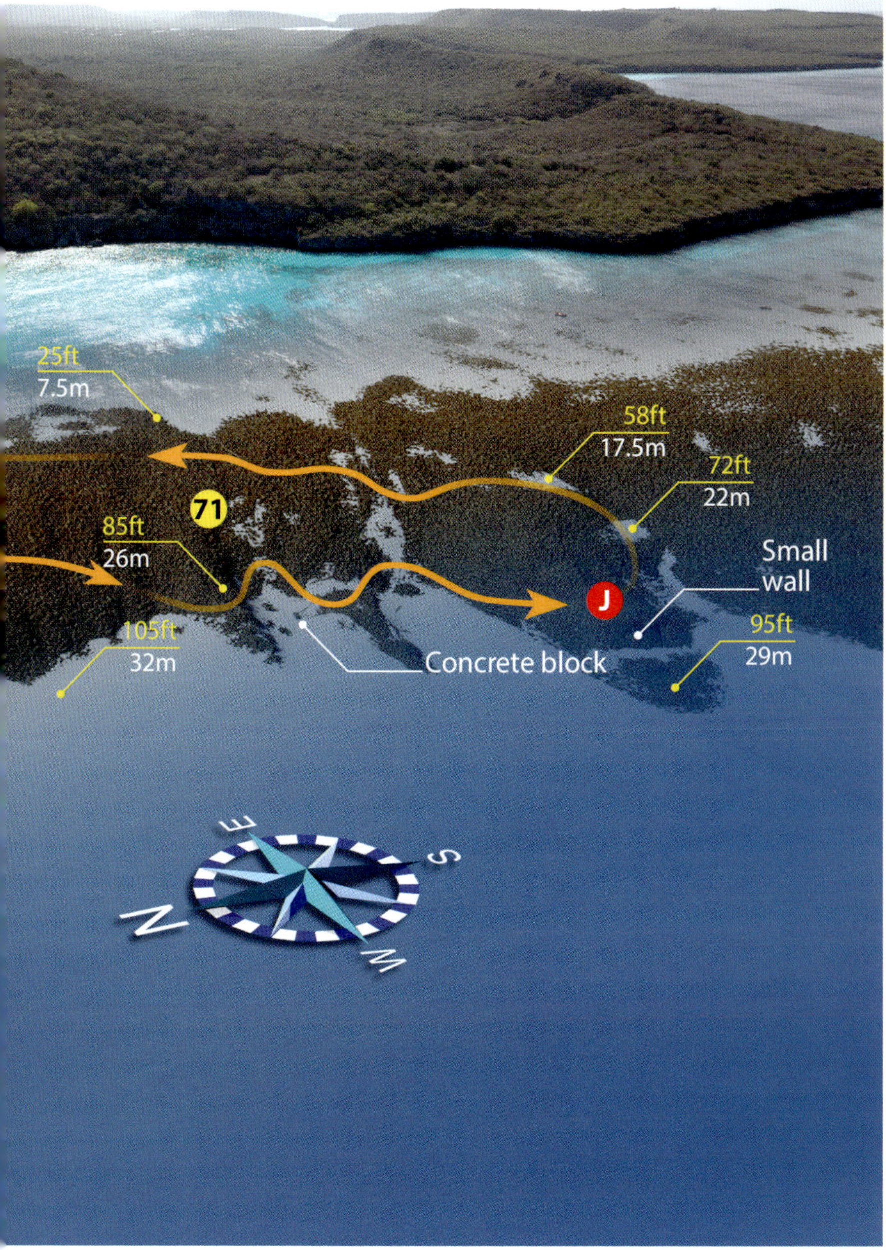
25ft
7.5m
58ft
17.5m
72ft
22m
71
85ft
26m
Small
wall
J
95ft
29m
105ft
32m
Concrete block
E
S
N
W

# PLAYA HUNKU

Difficulty ●●●
Current ●○○
Depth ●●○
Reef ★★★
Fauna ★★☆

Access: about 8 mins from Rif Sint Marie
Access: about 30 mins from Willemstad
Access: about 12 mins from shore

**Level** Open Water

**Location**
Banda Abou, Curaçao
GPS 12°13.213'N, 69°05.417'W

## Getting there

The easiest way to reach Playa Hunku is through one of the island's local dive operators. The site can be reached from shore, but only by way of driving to Playa Porto Mari and swimming 0.3 miles (0.5 kilometers) along the coast. (See driving directions as described for Playa Porto Mari on page 104). However, this long of a surface swim can be challenging for most divers and snorkelers, especially if there is current, and so it is rarely attempted.

## Access

Playa Hunku is a private beach with restricted access. The only way to explore the adjacent dive and snorkel site is either by boat, or by shore from nearby Playa Porto Mari, which is located to the southeast. Accessing the water from Playa Porto Mari involves walking down the sandy beach, usually from the northwestern end

**SAFETY TIP**

It is important for divers and snorkelers to gauge the strength of the current carefully before venturing over to Playa Hunku from Playa Porto Marie. The current is usually mild in this area, but generally flows toward the northwest, which means it can be relatively easy to get to Playa Hunku but sometimes challenging to return to Playa Porto Marie. Moreover, divers will require careful air monitoring to explore this site and have enough air to safely return to Playa Porto Marie. If the current is strong, divers and snorkelers have been known to head directly to shore and return to Playa Porto Marie along the cliff edge. However, this can be challenging with heavy dive gear involved.

which is the closest part of the beach to Playa Hunku. Then head along the coast, typically by surface swimming for around 30 minutes. This dive site is better suited to experienced divers and snorkelers if accessed from shore because it requires decent navigation skills and conservative air consumption. Currents are usually mild here, and visibility is usually excellent.

## Description

The reef at Playa Hunku begins about 330 feet (100 meters) from shore and starts to slope gently from a depth of about 15 feet (4.5 meters). The slope is less steep here relative to the reef at nearby Playa Porto Mari, and there is no double reef. The shallower area of the reef supports a good mix of hard and soft corals, while large stretches of sand and patch reefs flow down the slope. Here, divers can find harlequin bass, goatfish and yellowfin mojarra. In the deeper areas of the reef, divers will see large barrel sponges, mahogany snapper and spotted moray eels. Bar jacks and schooling creole wrasses are often spotted above the reef.

33

BANDABOU

# PLAYA PORTO MARI

Difficulty ●●○
Current ●○○
Depth ●●○
Reef ★★★
Fauna ★★☆

Access (boat) about 7 mins from Rif Sint Marie
Access (car) about 30 mins from Willemstad
Access (swim) about 5 mins from shore

**Level** Open Water

## Location

Banda Abou, Curaçao
GPS 12°13.132'N, 69°05.172'W

## Getting there

Head north from Willemstad on Weg Naar Westpunt and turn left on Weg Naar Sint Willibrordus, which is about 1 mile (1.8 kilometers) before the town of Tera Corá. Drive the 3.2 miles (5.2 kilometers) toward Sint Willibrordus, passing Saliña Jan Kok and the Williwood sign on the left-hand side of the road. About 0.3 miles (0.5 kilometers) after the sign, turn left to go around the Church of Sint Willibrordus and then follow the signs for Playa Porto Mari. The gated entrance for Playa Porto Mari appears after approximately 0.4 miles (0.6 kilometers). The sign at the gate indicates that opening hours are between 9:30am and 6:30pm and that a small entrance fee per person must be paid at the beach. Drive an additional 1.8 miles (2.9 kilometers) to the beach from here, where a large parking area provides plenty of space for vehicles. The total distance from Willemstad is approximately 15.5 miles (25 kilometers).

## Access

The small fee required to access Playa Porto Mari must be paid at the beach, so divers and snorkelers must remember to bring cash or a credit card with them if they gear up at their cars. This fee must be paid whether you bring your own gear or rent at the onsite dive center. However, divers are allowed to make use of the rinse tanks and wet area at the dive shop, along with all the other beach facilities as part of their beach access fee, even if they bring their own gear.

Once on the sandy beach, access to the dive and snorkel site involves walking into the water, usually between the pier and the breakwater, and heading southwest toward the floating pontoon. A sandy channel, just to the north of the Reef Ball modules, leads divers into the valley between the two reefs found here. This dive site is suitable for all experience levels. Currents are usually mild here and visibility is usually excellent.

## Description

Playa Porto Mari, also often spelled Porto Marie, is a popular beach for the entire family, not just divers and snorkelers. There is plenty of shade across the wide beach, as well as plenty of lounge chairs for rent. The beach offers facilities, including restrooms, showers, changing rooms and lockers to store personal effects while in the water. Massages can even be booked on the beach and there is even an art studio where you can take classes. For those visitors with an appetite, the bar and restaurant serves a range of refreshments, and the onsite dive center makes exploring the reef much easier. There are several hiking and biking trails available to explore in the surrounding hills, ranging in their degree of difficulty.

The dive and snorkel site at Playa Porto Mari is also called The Valley. It is one of just a few sites in Curaçao where the reef splits in two with a large sandy valley in between. The reef located

## RELAX & RECHARGE

The popular **Porto Mari Bar and Restaurant** is a great place to unwind after diving and snorkeling, and to watch the sunset. The boat-shaped bar serves a range of drinks, from beers, spirits and wines to frozen cocktails. There are sandwiches and bar snacks, as well as ice cream and popsicles for kids. The restaurant is famous for its Indonesian cuisine, particularly their grilled chicken satay and nasi, but they also serve a range of other options, including local dishes and Dutch specialties, such as Kroketten (Dutch croquettes) and frikandellen (sausage). There are also vegetarian options available.

Visit: **PlayaPortoMari.com**

## FEATURED OPERATOR

**Porto Mari Sports** is a PADI 5-Star Dive Center conveniently located at the entrance to the beach. This full-service operator offers a wide range of dive courses, from Discover Scuba to Divemaster internships, as well as gear rental for both diving and snorkeling. The shop is stocked with all your beach essentials, from rash guards and snorkel equipment to beach toys and fish identification cards. The friendly, multilingual staff run daily guided dives on the famous house reef throughout the day, as well as dive trips to other sites around the island, both from shore and by boat.

Tel: +599-9-697-8751
Email: info@portomarisports.com
Visit: **Portomarisports.com**

shoreward of the valley begins at about 15 feet (4.5 meters) and features a line of Reef Balls that runs along the edge of the reef and circles back toward shore at either end. There are 280 Reef Balls in total at Playa Porto Mari, although some of the reefs may have been covered over in sand over the years. These modules provide valuable habitat for a range of reef species, including angelfish, butterflyfish, frogfish, small grouper such as graysbies and coneys, and crustaceans.

A sand chute leads down into the valley and directly to the wreck of a small pontoon barge that sits on a sandy seafloor at a depth of 68 feet (21 meters). The valley is only 100 feet (30.5 meters) wide but runs for over 500 feet (152 meters), roughly parallel to shore. It gradually tapers in width toward the southern end. Several sand chutes cut through the deeper reef taking divers through to the drop-off. Here they may encounter eagle rays, various grouper species, including black, tiger and even Nassau grouper. Divers can explore in either direction along the reef wall. In the shallower areas of the reef, particularly around the Reef Balls, divers and snorkelers can often find frogfish, filefish,

The back reef at Play Porto Mari features many Reef Ball artificial reef modules in which provide shelter for many creatures.

Turtle & Ray ©

scorpionfish, cowfish, drums, trunkfish, hogfish and snapper. It is also common to find sea turtles and stingrays at this site.

## Route

Divers and snorkelers enter the water from the beach. Divers usually head straight for the sand chute that leads to the valley between the two reefs. Most divers will spend some time exploring the wreck of the small barge before heading to the drop-off. Divers can regain some bottom time by exploring the Reef Balls on the way back to shore. There are a couple of established snorkel trails that encompass the Reef Balls at Playa Porto Mari. The visibility at this site is such that most snorkelers can clearly see the wrecked barge from the surface of the water, and those comfortable enough may be able to duck dive to get closer for a better view.

NaturePicsFilm/Shutterstock©

## DID YOU KNOW?

The sheltered bay of Porto Mari, or Puerto Maria as it was known then, was deemed an important strategic location by early Dutch settlers. A lookout post was constructed in the 18th century on the top of Seru Caballe – the hill located on the east side of the bay. This post was later developed into Fort Porto Mari in 1742, along with the addition of 10 cannons. The fort was captured and ultimately destroyed by the British during their invasion of Curaçao in 1805.

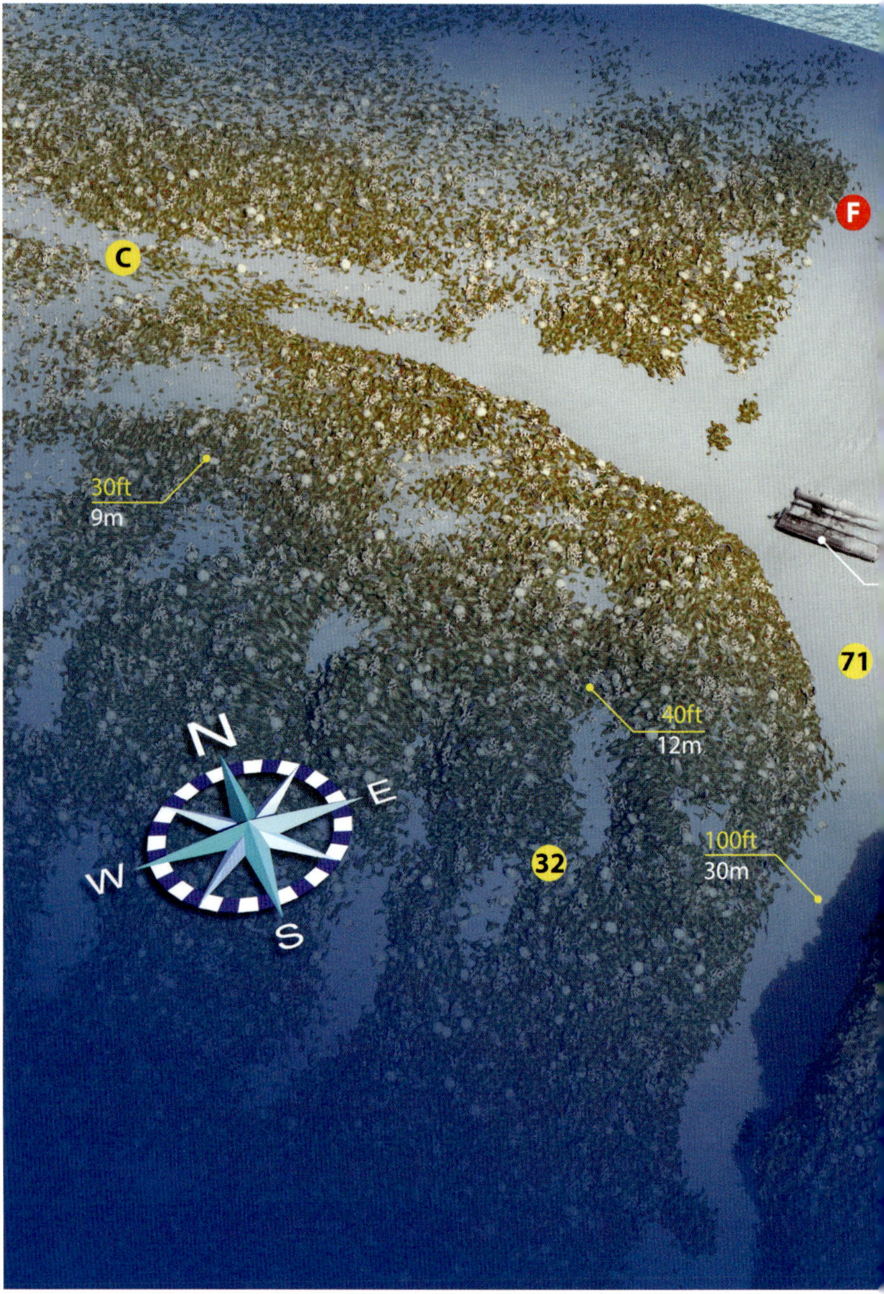
C
F
30ft
9m
71
N
E
W
S
40ft
12m
100ft
30m
32

## DID YOU KNOW?

Visitors to Playa Porto Mari often encounter Willy and Woody – a couple of feral pigs who live on the beach and dine on scraps of foods that are left behind. These surprising residents are not present at other beaches in Curaçao and have become quite the tourism attraction at Playa Porto Mari. They even have their own Instagram page (@willyandwoody) and give the beach its other, slightly tongue-in-cheek, nickname: Playa Porko Mari.

# DAAIBOOI

| | |
|---|---|
| Difficulty | ●○○ |
| Current | ●○○ |
| Depth | ●●○ |
| Reef | ★★☆ |
| Fauna | ★★☆ |

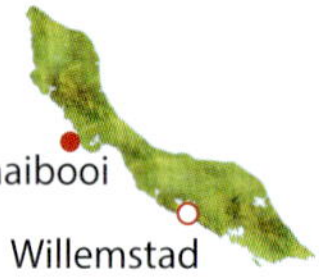


Access (boat) about 5 mins from Rif Sint Marie
Access (car) about 29 mins from Willemstad
Access (swim) about 8 mins from shore

**Level** Open Water

**Location**
Banda Abou, Curaçao
GPS 12°12.723'N, 69°05.089'W

## Getting there

Head north from Willemstad on Weg Naar Westpunt and turn left on Weg Naar Sint Willibrordus about one mile (1.8 kilometers) before the town of Tera Corá. Drive the 3.2 miles (5.2 kilometers) to Sint Willibrordus, passing Saliña Jan Kok and the Williwood sign on the left-hand side of the road. About 0.3 miles (0.5 kilometers) after the sign, turn left to go around the Church of Sint Willibrordus and follow the signs for Playa Daaibooi onto Weg Naar Daaibooi. After a hard left turn in the road, continue for 1.1 miles (1.9 kilometers) to get to the beach. Ignore the left turn into Coral

Estate Rif Sint Marie located just 0.3 miles (0.5 kilometers) after the hard left. The road ends at a large gravel parking lot adjacent to the beach. The total distance from Willemstad is approximately 15 miles (24 kilometers).

## Access

There is no fee required to access the beach at Daaibooi. The dive and snorkel site can be reached by simply walking down the sandy beach and into the water. Many large rocks are scattered across the beach and pose a tripping risk for divers and snorkelers entering the water, so boots are recommended. This dive site is suitable for all experience levels. Currents are usually mild, and visibility is usually excellent.

## Description

There are a number of variations in the spelling of Daaibooi, including Daai Booi, Playa Daaibooi, Daaibooi Bay and Daaibooibaai. It was once a local harbor used to load salt from the neighboring plantations of Jan Kok, Rif and Porto Mari onto ships bound for Willemstad. Today, it is a relaxing beach popular with locals. It features a dive operator, bar-snack counter, a small selection of palapas for shade and beach chair rentals. The beach is recessed, which provides some shelter from the wind and waves and makes this an ideal spot for the entire family. The reef is well worth exploring at this site, although the swim out to the drop-off is about twice the distance than at the neighboring Playa Porto Mari. Divers should head southwest when leaving the beach, as the reef is significantly closer to shore here. Snorkelers often explore the base of the cliffs that extend from either side of the beach. Butterflyfish are particularly common at this site, as are chromis, small grouper species and moray eels. Divers and snorkelers can often find many cryptic species in the back reef, such as shrimp, crabs and flounder.

35

BANDABOU

# WITCHES KITCHEN

Difficulty ●●○
Current ●●○
Depth ●●○
Reef ★★☆
Fauna ★★☆

Access about 3 mins from Rif Sint Marie

**Level** Open Water

## Location

Banda Abou, Curaçao
GPS 12°12.200'N, 69°05.170'W

## Getting there

There is no shore access to Witches Kitchen. The best way to reach this site is through one of the local dive operators located along Curaçao's northwest coast.

## Access

Witches Kitchen is a dive site that is only accessible by boat. Currents are usually moderate to strong here, as the site is located adjacent to a small headland that juts out into the ocean. Visibility is usually excellent. This site is suitable for divers of all experience levels.

## SCIENTIFIC INSIGHT

Sponges have been on Earth for at least 500 million years. They are one of the oldest types of animals on our planet and they have some of the longest lifespans of all creatures on Earth. For instance, the giant barrel sponge *(Xestospongia muta)*, which are common in Curaçao, can live for more than 2,000 years. Next time you see one on the reef, consider the fact that a large individual of more than 6 feet (2 meters) across might have been around since the time of the Ancient Romans.

### Description

Witches Kitchen is located between Daaibooi and the Coral Estate at Rif Sint Marie. The site is named after the large barrel sponges that are scattered along this section of reef, which are said to resemble witches' cauldrons. The constant currents around the headland produce ideal conditions for sponges, which are often home to eels, lionfish and various crustaceans. In the water column above the reef, divers often find black durgon, chromis, creole wrasses, various jack species and occasionally barracuda. Closer to the reef itself , divers often spot sea turtles, eagle rays and schools of snapper that use the large sponges to shelter from the current.

# RIF SINT MARIE & HABITAT

Difficulty ● ○ ○
Current ● ● ○
Depth ● ● ○
Reef ★★☆
Fauna ★★☆

Access about 0 mins from Rif Sint Marie
Access about 32 mins from Willemstad
Access about 5 mins from shore

**Level** Open Water

## Location

Banda Abou, Curaçao
GPS 12°11.890'N, 69°04.742'W

## Getting there

Divers and snorkelers who wish to visit Rif Sint Marie and Habitat from shore must do so through Coral Divers, located at Coral Estate Luxury Resort. Divers are required to rent tanks from the dive center. Guided shore diving tours are also available. Alternatively, these sites can be visited by boat using one of the dive operators based along Curaçao's northwest coast.

To reach Rif Sint Marie and Habitat from shore, head north from Willemstad on Weg Naar Westpunt and turn left on Weg Naar Sint Willibrordus about 1 mile (1.8 kilometers) before the town of Tera Corá. Drive the 3.2 miles (5.2 kilometers) toward Sint Willibrordus, passing Saliña Jan Kok and the Williwood sign on the left-hand side of the road. About 0.3 miles (0.5 kilometers) after the sign, turn left to go around the Church of Sint Willibrordus and follow the signs for Playa Daai Booi onto Weg Naar Daaibooi. After a hard left turn in the road, continue for 0.3 miles (0.5 kilometers) then turn left at the entrance sign for Coral Estate Rif Sint Marie. A security gate is located another 0.3 miles 0.5 kilometers) down the road – visitors will need to show some form of identification to enter, such as a driver's license or passport. Continue down the road for another mile (1.7 kilometers) as it heads down an incline toward the ocean, passing several side roads on the left. At the bottom of the hill, the road turns to the left and runs parallel to the coast. There is a parking lot adjacent to the Coral Estate welcome area located 0.4 miles (0.6 kilometers) after the turn at the bottom of the hill.

Visitors can park here and carry their gear down the hill to the dive center located by the beach. Alternatively, they can drive down the side road that borders the parking lot, veering right to head down the steep incline next to the dive center. There is a small area where cars can turn around at the bottom of the incline, but it is a good idea to scout ahead beforehand to make sure another car or truck is not blocking the way. Once there, visitors can drop off their gear at the dive center before driving back up the very steep incline to the upper parking lot. Cars must be left in the parking lot while divers and snorkelers are in the water. The total distance from Willemstad is approximately 15.5 miles (25 kilometers).

## Access

For shore divers and snorkelers, Rif Sint Marie and Habitat have essentially the same starting point – the concrete steps that lead from Coral Divers dive center directly into the water. Booties can be useful but are not necessary at this site. A thick rope lying flat on the seabed leads the way out to the reef and marks the dividing line between the two dive sites. Once at the reef, divers can head south to explore Habitat or north to explore Rif Sint Marie. The dive center has rinse tanks and

### DID YOU KNOW?

The best place to see flamingos in Curaçao is at the salt pans of Jan Kok in Sint Willibrordus, which is designated a flamingo sanctuary. It is possible to see flamingos in other parts of Curaçao, such as Sint Michielsbaai and the salt pans of Jan Thiel, but it is often harder to get a decent view at these locations. At Jan Kok, however, there is a viewing platform located just east of the town of Sint Willibrordus that provides visitors with the perfect view of the estimated 400 flamingos believed to reside in the saliña. Flamingos have no set breeding season – their reproduction is simply linked to periods of high rainfall that often increases the available food supply. Flamingos form monogamous pairs during breeding and lay a single egg that takes almost a month to hatch. The best time to see flamingos at the salt pans of Jan Kok is usually in the morning or around sunset.

showers on shore, which greatly facilitates the experience of exploring these sites. These dive sites are suitable for all experience levels. Currents are usually moderate, and visibility is usually good.

## Description

Rif Sint Marie and Habitat, also known as Coral Habitat, are contiguous reefs located seaward of Coral Estate Luxury Resort. As such, these two dive sites offer a relatively similar experience for divers and snorkelers. The choice of which site to explore often comes down to personal preference and the strength of the prevailing current.

The reef is only about 250 feet (76 meters) from shore at this location, so it is a relatively simple swim out following the rope that lies along the sandy seabed. There is no need to surface swim, although the seabed is mostly dominated by sand so there is little to see until reaching the top of the reef slope.

The reef slopes gently into deeper water and is relatively featureless in either direction. Numerous coral mounds rise from the substrate, but these are not as large as those at other sites farther north, such as at Mushroom Forest and Kleine Knip. These structures, which are located mainly between 30 and 40 feet (9 and 12 meters), are more numerous along the top of the reef slope at Rif Sint Marie than at Habitat, where the sandy back reef extends slightly farther down the slope.

Divers and snorkelers will find many coral reef creatures hiding beneath and between these coral mounds, including lobsters, moray eels and octopuses. Small grouper, grunts and squirrelfish are also commonly seen here. The density of these nocturnal creatures, and the convenient access to these sites make them ideal for night diving.

Rif Sint Marie and Habitat also support a dense cover of soft corals and sponges, particularly large

Caribbean reef octopuses can be found at these sites, as well as numerous other nocturnal species.

Rich Carey/Shutterstock©

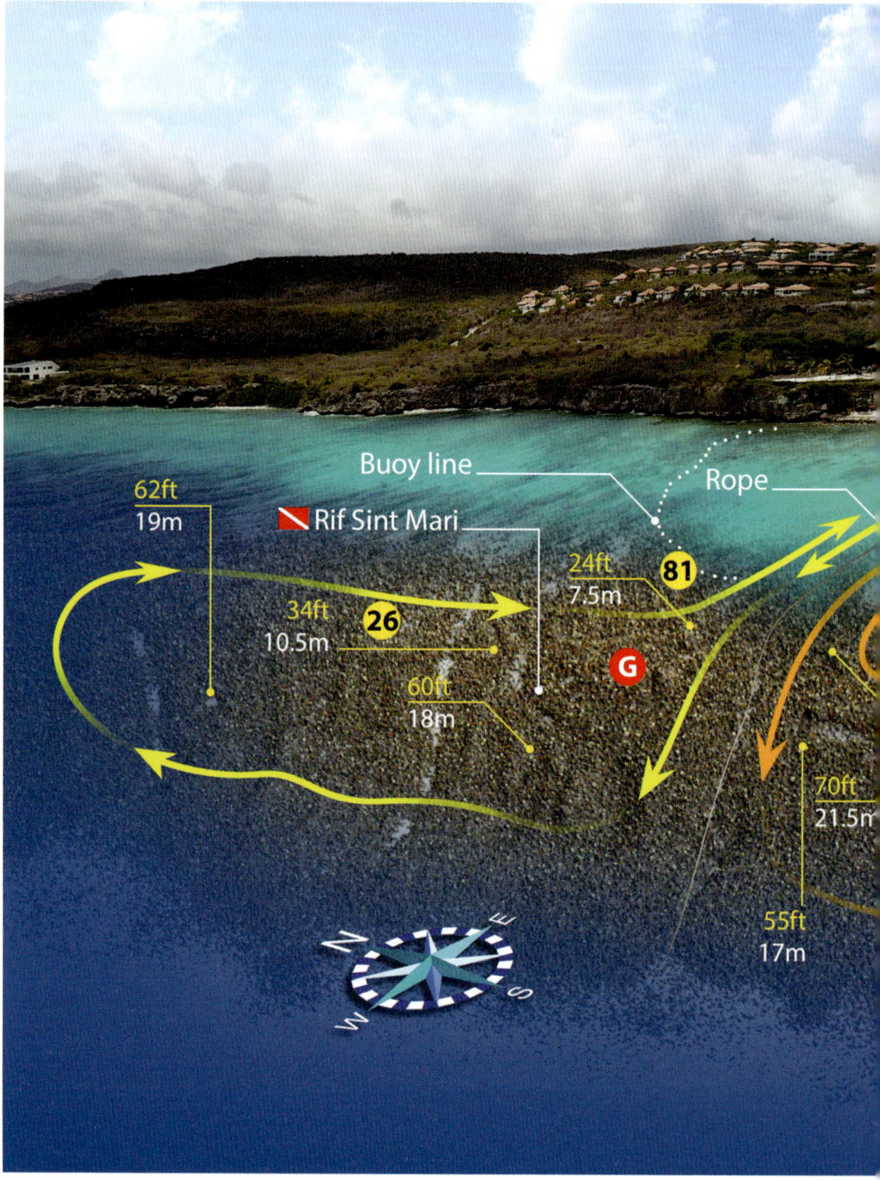


## RELAX & RECHARGE

**Karakter Curaçao** is located just steps from the access point to the Rif Sint Marie and Habitat dive and snorkel sites. This fine establishment offers exceptional toes-in-the-sand dining from 8am until 9pm. The menus, which include breakfast, lunch and dinner, are incredibly varied, ranging from tapas to smoothies. Meals are served on the beach, and dinners are usually accompanied with a stunning Caribbean sunset as the backdrop. Every day there is a new multi-course surprise menu created by the chef, which adds to the wide range of options. Regular features include red snapper, Argentinean Tenderloin with blue cheese beurre blanc, sweet potato Wellington and seafood risotto. There is also an extensive kids' menu. Visit: **Karaktercuracao.com**

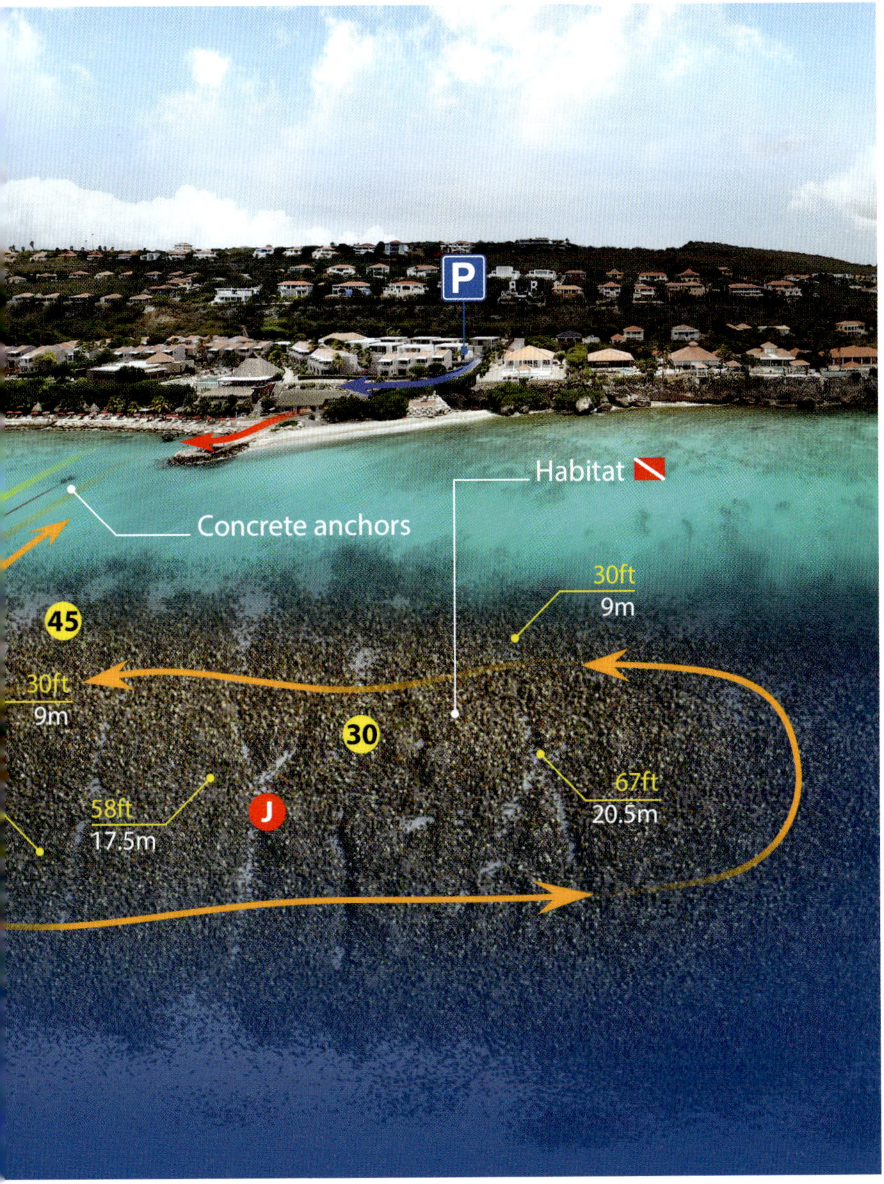


tube sponges. In the deeper parts of the reef, divers may find large parrotfish, schoolmaster snapper, hamlets and green moray eels. The deep edge of the reef transitions to patch reef at about 100 feet (30 meters) and then eventually to sand. In the shallows, divers and snorkelers may encounter sea turtles, barracuda, frogfish, sharptail eels and anemones with their symbiotic crustaceans.

## Route

Most divers navigate out to the reef by following the rope and then continue down the slope to a depth of around 50 to 70 feet (15 to 21.5 meters). From there they can either turn left or right to explore Habitat or Rif Sint Marie, respectively. Navigation is relatively easy, as divers can simply explore along the reef slope until they reach a little more than halfway on their air. They can then turnaround and gradually ascend the slope to explore the shallower parts of the reef. When they encounter the rope that extends down the reef slope, they can turn and follow it back toward shore.

# 38 LIGHT TOWER

Difficulty ● ● ○
Current ● ● ●
Depth ● ● ○
Reef ★★★
Fauna ★★☆

**Level** Advanced

**Location**
Bandabou, Curaçao
GPS 12°11.262'N, 69°03.835'W

Light Tower, also known as Lighthouse and Kap St. Marie, is only accessible by boat. It is located at the southern end of Coral Estate. The lighthouse that gave this site its name does not exist anymore. The current at this site is known to be particularly strong, often resulting in drift dives, and wave action can also be high. Snorkeling is only possible on calm days. The reef here is steep with lots of hard corals, including pillar and elkhorn coral. Sponges are also plentiful, namely elephant ear and vase sponges. Divers often report large barracuda at this site, as well as jacks, eagle rays and large schools of creole wrasses. Nurse sharks often shelter on the reef substrate.

# 39 SELDOM REEF

Difficulty ● ● ●
Current ● ● ●
Depth ● ● ●
Reef ★★★
Fauna ★★★

**Level** Advanced

**Location**
Bullenbaai, Curaçao
GPS 12°11.580'N, 69°03.155'W

Seldom Reef is a spectacular, boat-accessible dive site located in Bullenbaai between Light Tower and Spanish Anchor. The conditions need to be just right to dive this site safely, which is why it is seldom visited, and became known as Seldom Reef. The currents are usually strong here, which means this site is often explored as a drift dive. The reef is also one of the deeper sites in Curaçao, with sheer walls that plummet into the depths. As such, this site is better suited to experienced divers. The reef is packed with large coral formations, both hard and soft, along with sponges growing from the wall in the deeper parts of the site. There are plenty of overhangs where divers may find nocturnal species, such as lobsters, moray eels, octopuses and nurse sharks. Plate-form corals and black corals can be found in the deeper parts of the reef.

NaturePicsFilms/Shutterstock©

# SPANISH ANCHOR

Difficulty ●○○
Current ●●○
Depth ●●○
Reef ★★☆
Fauna ★★☆

**Level** Open Water

**Location**
Bullenbaai, Curaçao
GPS 12°12.017'N, 69°02.663'W

Spanish Anchor is a boat-accessible dive and snorkel site located in Bullenbaai, just west of the oil refinery. Technically, this site can be reached from shore, but access can be challenging, and the remote location of this site makes boat diving preferable. The site is named after the old anchors and chains that can be found on the reef here at a depth of approximately 70 feet (21.5 meters). These date back to when this site was a preferred anchorage for sailing ships in the heyday of the Curaçao salt industry. The back reef contains plenty of healthy blade fire coral, star coral and brain coral. The reef slope supports numerous large sponges and drops off sharply into the depths, hitting sand at the bottom edge. Divers may find chromis, butterflyfish, parrotfish and nocturnal soldierfish and fairy basslets in undercut areas of the reef.

## SCIENTIFIC INSIGHT

The top three threats to corals are: 1) coral bleaching, 2) rising concentrations of dissolved carbon dioxide and 3) coral diseases. Solving these issues requires effort on an international, national and local level, not to mention the efforts of dedicated individuals.

1) Coral bleaching is when a coral's symbiotic algae (known as zooxanthellae) are ejected from their host coral polyp usually in response to heat stress. As the world heats up, so too are the oceans – and that means more frequent bleaching events around the world. Fortunately bleaching is not necessarily a death sentence for the coral, provided the period of extreme heat is brief.

2) Rising carbon dioxide ($CO_2$) in our oceans is causing seawater to become more acidic. Over the past 200 years, the ocean's acidity has increased by over 25%, and it keeps going up at a rate of 5% per decade. When $CO_2$ is absorbed by seawater, it undergoes a chemical reaction, whose byproducts make it harder for corals, and many other important marine organisms, to access the fundamental building blocks of their limestone skeletons (calcium carbonate) and so they must spend more energy to grow.

3) Many diseases affect corals in the Caribbean, including white band, black band, and, most recently, stony coral tissue loss disease (SCTLD). Some of these diseases are caused by bacteria, others by viruses, and some have causes that remain unknown. Unfortunately, as corals spend more energy dealing with frequent bleaching events and ocean acidification, they are increasingly susceptible to the various diseases already present in their environment. And while Curaçao's reefs are remarkably healthy today, if global trends do not improve soon, they may struggle in the near future.

# 41 BULLENBAAI

WILLEMSTAD

Difficulty ●●○
Current ●●○
Depth ●●●
Reef ★★★
Fauna ★★☆

Access about 34 mins from Willemstad

**Level** Open Water

**Location**
Bullenbaai, Curaçao
GPS 12°10.533'N, 69°01.003'W

### Getting there

While Weg Naar Bullenbaai runs literally steps from the shore adjacent to the Bullenbaai dive and snorkel site, there is no way to access to the water from shore at this site. As such, the only way to visit this section of reef is through a local dive operator on Curaçao's central coast.

### Access

There is a typically a mooring buoy at Bullenbaai anchored to the seabed art the southeastern end of the site. The back reef is a narrow ledge at this point, and it extends around 150 feet (46 meters) from shore out to the drop-off. Currents are usually mild at Bullenbaai but can become moderate at times and seas can also be choppy. This site is suitable for divers and snorkelers of all experience levels. However, those with an advanced certification are better able to explore the deeper parts of the wall.

### Description

Bullenbaai is a spectacular dive and snorkel site located just south of the oil refinery in Bullenbaai, hence the site's name. The reef here has a well-defined drop-off that begins at a depth of about 15 feet (4.5 meters) and plummets down a nearly sheer face to extreme depth. The wall lies just a few yards from the mooring ball and initially extends north before bending to the west and finally curving back north at the end of the site as it follows the coastline. The wall features a series of vertical spurs that create a highly scalloped look to the reef. Large shelves extend out from the reef wall and small bays cut back into the face, each approximately 60 to 70 feet (18 to 21 meters) across.

The bays often feature sand chutes cascading down the face of the wall where divers may find goatfish, sand divers and resting grouper. In the areas where the reef extends out from the wall in the form of thick spurs, ledges are often cut into the face of the spurs. These shelves often feature large dome brain corals or elephant ear sponges, surrounded by sea whips and deepwater sea fans. These shelves are often undercut such that divers can find a range of different coral reef creatures hiding in the shadows, including lobsters and moray eels. Blackbar soldierfish, glasseye snapper and fairy basslets are also particularly common under these dark and sheltered overhangs. There are also dense stands of healthy plate-form corals on this reef, particularly at depth. In the water column above the reef, creole wrasses and chromis form large schools to feed on the

## SCIENTIFIC INSIGHT

There are nearly 250 species of black coral in the oceans of the world. Most species resemble small bushes and may be colored in various shades of brown, red, orange or yellow. It is actually the skeleton of the coral that is black, rather than the living polyps. Some species occur in relatively shallow water, less than 150 feet (46 meters), but the vast majority (around 75 percent) are found much deeper, even to depths of 28,000 feet (8,500 meters).

Black corals are well adapted to living in low-light environments because while their tissue is capable of supporting photosynthetic algae, their diet of zooplankton is a much more important source of sustenance. As such, black corals are often found in deep, shady reef areas, like caves, reef channels and beneath overhangs, where other types of corals would have difficulty surviving. Black corals are very slow growing, can live for thousands of years and have virtually no predators.

plankton at this site. These planktivores are often watched closely by solitary barracuda, bar jacks and yellowtail snapper.

It is easy to spend a long time enjoying the stunning reef wall at this site, but divers will need to keep a constant check on their depth and ensure they gradually shallow their profile through the dive. The top of the reef wall is the perfect place for an extended safety stop and supports plenty of life to keep both divers and snorkelers occupied during the swim back to the buoy. Divers and snorkelers regularly see butterflyfish, parrotfish and schools of mahogany snapper along the top of the drop-off. There are also large pillar corals and soft corals along this edge. Lionfish are commonly seen at this site as well, and are subject to regular fishing effort at this site and along the coast up to the pier at the oil refinery.

Wall dives like Bullenbaai provide great photo opportunities for silhouetting divers above.

Drew McArthur/Shutterstock©

## Route

The current at Bullenbaai is gentle, but constant. It often moves along the reef toward the oil refinery to the northwest. Most divers begin by dropping straight down the reef face and moving with the current in the direction, gradually shallowing throughout the dive. If the current is mild enough, both divers and snorkelers will be able to return to the dive boat moored at the southern end of the site. During days when currents are stronger, this site becomes a standard drift dive with divers and snorkelers getting picked up by the dive boat farther along the reef, most commonly to the north.

66
55ft
16.5m
35ft
10.5m
29
17
G
55ft
16.5m

# 42 PESTBAAI

WILLEMSTAD

Difficulty ●●●
Current ●●○
Depth ●●○
Reef ★★☆
Fauna ★★☆

Access about 30 mins from Willemstad
Access about 17 mins from Willemstad
Access about 3 mins from shore
Access about 10 mins from the road

**Level** Advanced

## Location

Vaersenbaai, Curaçao
GPS 12°10.017′N, 69°00.701′W

## Getting there

Turn left onto Weg Naar Bullenbaai from Helmin Magno Wiels Boulevard. Continue past the turning for Blue Bay, which appears on the left after one mile (1.6 kilometers) and continue through the town of Jan Doret. After another 2.5 miles (4 kilometers), the road bends left toward the coast and splits in two, divided by a median. A small sign on the right-hand side of the road, adjacent to the split, indicates Pestbaai/Lover's Beach, the trail for which starts on the opposite side of the road. There is limited parking along the side of the road. The trail, which is officially known as Weg Van Gaans, is a dirt track that is only navigable on foot. It takes about 10 minutes to reach the entry point of the dive and snorkel site. The total distance from Willemstad is approximately 8.7 miles (14 kilometers).

## Access

Pestbaai is one of the most challenging dive and snorkel sites to access from shore. The beach at this site contains virtually no sand and is extremely challenging to reach, involving a climb down the cliff face with heavy dive gear – not to mention scaling the cliff on the way out. The shoreline along this stretch of coast consists of

## SAFETY TIP

There are multiple factors that make Pestbaai challenging from a safety perspective. Besides the long walk and dangerous cliff to scale, the currents here can strengthen rapidly and without much notice. The only place to exit the water at Pestbaai is at the point of entry. Divers and snorkelers may find it difficult to navigate back to the beach if they become disoriented or must swim against a strong current. There are no other decent places to exit the water nearby. If visiting this site from shore, be sure to bring plenty of water and always inform others where you are going and when you plan to return. The safest way to visit this site is through a local dive operator on Curaçao's central coast, which would give this site a one-star rating for difficulty.

large boulders and smaller rocks, some of which can shift underfoot. Currents are usually mild here but can become moderate at times, and seas can be choppy. This site is only suitable for advanced divers and snorkelers when accessed from shore, but suitable for all experience levels when accessed by boat.

### Description

Pestbaai, also known as Lover's Beach, is a beautiful dive and snorkel site located between Bullenbaai and Kokomo Beach. The back reef is often clear and calm, and it supports an abundance of soft and hard corals at an average depth of around 10 feet (3 meters). The sea fans found here often have flamingo tongues on them, while divers and snorkelers may find goatfish, peacock flounders, spotted drums, arrow crabs and anemones in the sandy patches between coral heads. The reef drop-off sits around 350 feet (106 meters) from shore and descends steeply from a depth of about 15 feet (4.5 meters) to well over 100 feet (30 meters). Star, brain and mustard hill corals dominate the top of the slope, along with a range of sponge species. In the deeper parts of the reef, divers may see green moray eels, dog snapper and tiger grouper, along with barrel sponges and sea whips.

# 43 KOKOMO BEACH (VAERSENBAAI & CAR WRECKS)



Difficulty ●●○
Current ●○○
Depth ●●●
Reef ★★☆
Fauna ★★☆

Access (boat) about 28 mins from Willemstad
Access (car) about 16 mins from Willemstad
Access (swim) about 5 mins from shore

**Level** Open Water

**Location**
Vaersenbaai, Curaçao
GPS 12°09.645'N, 69°00.277'W

### Getting there

Turn left onto Weg Naar Bullenbaai from Helmin Magno Wiels Boulevard. Continue past the left turn toward Blue Bay, which appears after one mile (1.6 kilometers) and continue through the town of Jan Doret. The turn toward Kokomo Beach appears on the left-hand side of the road after approximately 1.5 miles (2.4 kilometers) and is well marked. The road becomes a dirt track that terminates at the gravel parking lot for Kokomo Beach after just 0.2 miles (0.32 kilometers). The total distance from Willemstad is approximately 7.5 miles (12 kilometers).

### Access

Kokomo Beach has a large parking lot that is mostly dirt with some gravel sections. Parking is free of charge, as is access to the beach, which is an idyllic spot that the entire family can enjoy. The beach consists mostly of sand and there is a jetty with steps down into the water located front and center. The jetty extends out from shore into waist-deep water and makes entering and exiting the water slightly easier than walking in from the beach. This dive and snorkel site is suitable for all experience levels, but the car wrecks and pontoon barge that are popular attractions for this site are better suited to advanced divers because of their depth and distance from the access point. There is typically a mooring buoy at this site that marks the drop-off above the barge and cars. The currents are generally mild, and visibility is usually good.

### Description

Kokomo Beach, which is also known as Vaersenbaai, is a great spot for both visitors and locals. The beach offers all the amenities needed to make this a pleasant and relaxing day out, including toilets, which are free to use, and showers, which are available for a small fee. There is also a spa, a bar and restaurant, and a dive center where you can rent tanks and rinse your gear down after the dive. Do not forget to try the swings that hang over the water to the left of the jetty.

The reef here is popular with snorkelers who typically explore the shallow areas around the beach and at the base of the adjacent cliffs. Divers usually head straight out to the reef drop-off and then south toward the wreckage of a pontoon barge and the deteriorated chassis of the cars it once carried. This part of the larger Kokomo Beach dive site is sometimes called Off The Road, and it has made this reef site famous over the years. Reaching the pontoon boat requires a swim of approximately 20 minutes and the cars lie farther still to the south.

The sandy back reef at Kokomo extends around

## RELAX & RECHARGE

**Kokomo Beach** has a great bar and restaurant that has a range of tasty food for hungry divers and snorkelers to enjoy. If you feel like stepping beyond a standard burger or cheeseburger, you can try the crispy chicken burger or pulled pork, which are both delicious. There are also barbecued skewers, rib eye and fish and chips, not to mention wraps, paninis, pokè bowls and a range of salads. Drink options include fresh juice blends, like papaya/orange and watermelon/passion fruit. They also have a creative gin and tonic selection. Happy hour is from 5pm and often includes live music as you watch the sun set into the tranquil ocean. There's even a Full Moon Party at Kokomo Beach, which is billed as the biggest monthly beach party in the Caribbean, with drinks galore, DJ music and dancing that goes deep into the night.
Visit: **Kokomo-beach.com**

400 feet (122 meters) from shore. There is a small raft located about halfway between the beach and the drop-off that is anchored to the seabed at a depth of approximately 14 feet (4 meters). A thick rope runs along the seabed from the raft out to the drop-off, which can assist divers when navigating to and from the reef. There is little else in the way of features in the back reef area, but divers and snorkelers may be able to find razorfish, peacock flounders and the occasional mojarra in the open stretches of sand.

The reef at Kokomo Beach is fairly steep, and it supports plenty of healthy habitat. Divers and snorkelers will discover soft corals, hard corals and large sponges scattered throughout the reef drop-off. A particularly large purple tube sponge sits on the reef slope at a depth of approximately 60 feet (18 meters), just south of the rope. The reef ends at a depth of about 110 feet (33.5 meters), where it transitions back to sand and rubble. Divers can find a shark sculpture alongside a large metal frame, which provides structure at the bottom of the reef, at a depth of approximately 120 feet (36.5 meters).

Once on the reef slope, most divers head toward the south to explore the pontoon barge and associated car wrecks. The wreck of the pontoon lies upside down, perpendicular to the reef slope,

The swings in the water at Kokomo are a fun addition to an already entertaining beach.

Gail Johnson/Shutterstock©

## DID YOU KNOW?

Between Kokomo Beach and Boca Sami to the south lies a boat-accessible dive and snorkel site that is often simply known as Halfway. It is so named because it is literally the halfway point along the west coast of Curaçao. It is also sometimes known as Point Halfway and Half Way West. Bar jacks are particularly common in the water column here, as are blue and brown chromis. Meanwhile, spotted drums, scorpionfish and balloonfish are commonly seen near the seafloor. In the deeper parts of the reef, divers may find moray eels, lobsters and tiger grouper.

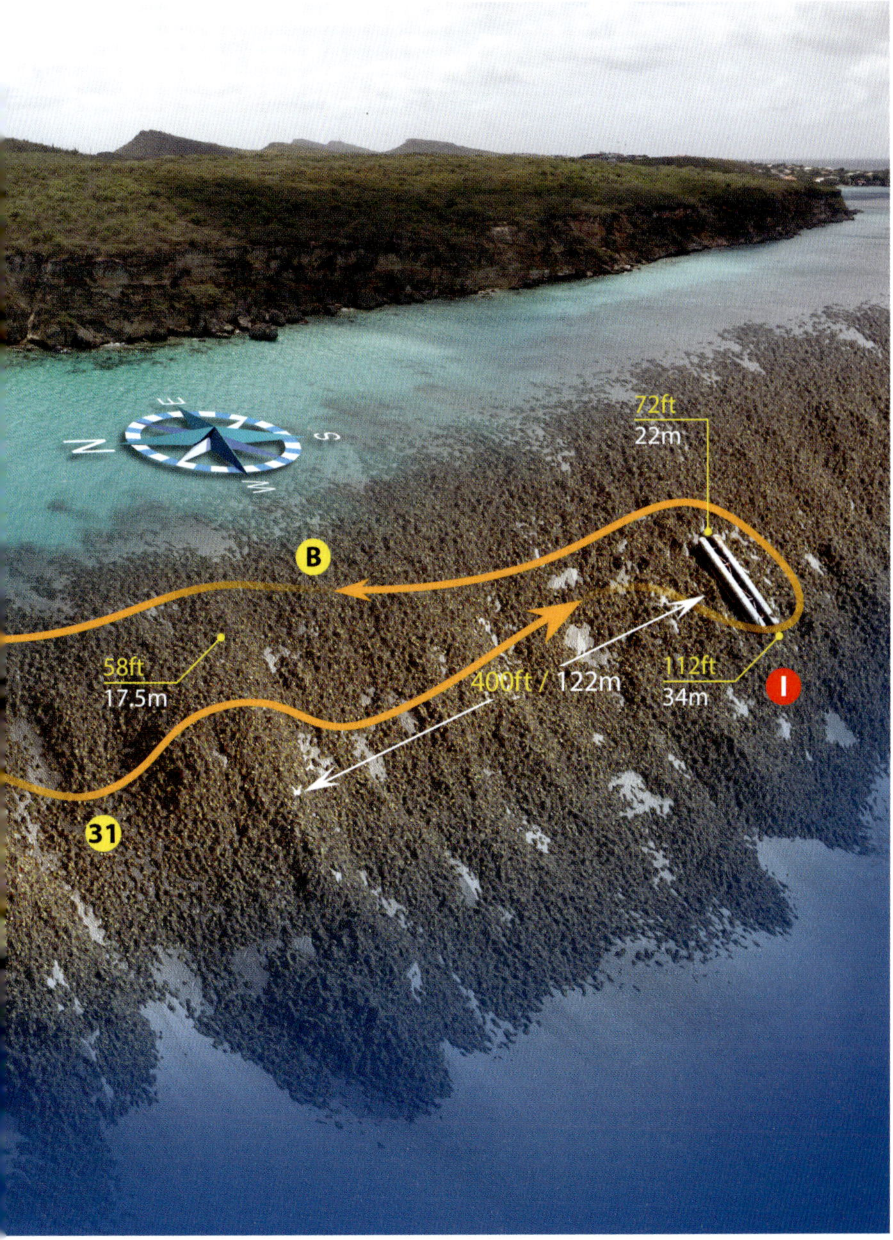


on an east-west axis. Its shallowest point reaches approximately 72 feet (22 meters) and its deepest point sits at 112 feet (34 meters). The structure itself rises 13 feet (4 meters) off the reef and is covered in numerous sea whips (particularly along the deeper section) along with quite a few sponges. The wreck is hard to miss. Not so for the dozens of car wrecks scattered across the reef slope to the south of the pontoon. Many are barely recognizable as cars these days, given that the thin metal shells rust away quickly in the harsh saltwater environment, leaving only the chassis and engine blocks. The wrecks are scattered up and down the reef slope. In addition to the wreckage, divers who venture this far will likely encounter lionfish, porcupinefish, snapper, moray eels, barracuda, greater amberjacks and hawksbill sea turtles.

## Route

There is enough marine life in the shallow

waters near the shore to occupy most snorkelers, particularly those prepared to swim north or south past the beach and along the base of the cliffs, where they will encounter sea fans and plenty of dome-shaped brain corals.

Divers usually swim out to the drop-off before heading in either direction. It is advisable to surface swim initially, in order to consume air and bottom time. The car wrecks and barge are located to the south. Heading in that direction, divers will initially pass over two large coral ridges that extend from the reef into the depths, after which there is a relatively featureless reef slope except for two large coral mounds that rise about 10 feet (3 meters) from

the reef. It usually takes about 20 minutes to reach the pontoon wreck and another five minutes more to reach the car wrecks. Most divers will have only a limited amount of time to explore the wreck and cars before having to ascend into shallower water. Also, most of the cars are near the bottom of the slope, making bottom time even more limited.

The wide sandy back reef is the perfect depth for a prolonged safety stop while heading back toward the beach. Most divers who make it as far as the wreck and cars often cruise back to the beach along the shoreline at the base of the cliffs.

# BOCA SAMI

Difficulty ● ○ ○
Current ● ● ○
Depth ● ● ○
Reef ★☆☆
Fauna ★★☆

Access (boat) about 24 mins from Willemstad
Access (car) about 16 mins from Willemstad
Access (swim) about 4 mins from shore

**Level** Open Water

## Location

Sint Michiel, Curaçao
GPS 12°08.803'N, 68°59.938'W

## Getting there

Boca Sami dive and snorkel site is located next to Boka Sint Michiel – the area of Sint Michiel that is located at the mouth of the saliña. Turn left onto Weg Naar Bullenbaai from Helmin Magno Wiels Boulevard. Continue for 1.4 miles (2.3 kilometers) until just after the town of Jan Doret, and then take a left turn on Kaya Antoine Pijpers, which quickly becomes Kaya Ma Pieternella on the way to Boka Sint Michiel. After approximately 1 mile (1.6 kilometers), the road bends sharply to the right and continues for just over 0.5 miles (0.8 Kilometers) until it reaches the shore. Head right and drive along the shore for about 450 feet (137 meters) to reach Boca Sami Beach. Parking is available along the street. The total distance from Willemstad is about 7.3 miles (11.7 kilometers).

## Access

Accessing this site is relatively simple from shore as the beach is right next to the road ,and the bay is relatively sheltered from waves and currents. There is a set of stairs that leads directly to the beach, as well as a boat ramp that leads directly into the water. The seabed is rocky, however, and there is a noticeable step in the water about knee-depth. There are two dive operators immediately adjacent to this site that can provide equipment rental, rinse tanks and showers, as well as advice about how to explore the site. Visibility is usually

## RELAX & RECHARGE

The **Niffo Huts** is a popular local dining spot located just 250 feet (76 meters) north of the access point for the Boca Sami dive and snorkel site. Open from noon to 10pm every day, the Niffo Huts provide a range of lunch, brunch and dinner options, including burgers, wraps, salads and fish and steak options. For those who have trouble deciding what to eat, there is the Niffo Together Fish and Niffo Together Meat options, which includes a mix of items, with salad and fries on the side. There are also vegan dishes, including a veggie wrap, veggie pasta and a veggie burger. The drink menu offers soft drinks, tea and coffee, beers and spirits, not to mention a wide choice of cocktails, including a twist on several classics and their signature Niffolicious, which contains aged Jamaican dark rum, coconut rum, liquor 43, orange juice, pineapple juice, grenadine syrup and light ground honey.
Visit: **Niffohuts.com**

good and the current is often mild. This dive site is suitable for divers and snorkelers of all experience levels.

### Description

Boca Sami is also known as Sint Michielbaai because it is located adjacent to the town of Sint Michiel in an area known as Boka Sint Michiel. Access from the beach is simple, but the reef slope is about 500 feet (152 meters) from the beach, so surface swimming is recommended to conserve air. The best section of reef to explore is located to the north, toward Halfway. This often means traveling with the prevailing current, so divers should gauge the strength of the current carefully to ensure they have enough air to return to their entry point.

There is a very large mooring buoy for ships, which is anchored on the seabed at about 40 feet (12 meters) on the edge of the drop-off. The access point is roughly due west from here. Boca Sami is known for its smaller cryptic species, such as soapfish, scorpionfish, frogfish and razorfish. Snorkelers will enjoy exploring the back reef, which is wide and shallow and features multiple artificial structures on the bottom, including concrete slabs. Corals have grown on these structures, and they now host many different reef creatures. Sea turtles are often seen in the area close to the beach.

# SNAKE BAY

Difficulty ●●○
Current ●●○
Depth ●●○
Reef ★★☆
Fauna ★★☆

Access (boat) about 21 mins from Willemstad
Access (car) about 16 mins from Willemstad
Access (swim) about 3 mins from shore

## Level Open Water

## Location

Sint Michiel, Curaçao
GPS 12°08.373'N, 68°59.842'W

## Getting there

Turn left onto Weg Naar Bullenbaai from Helmin Magno Wiels Boulevard. Continue for 1.4 miles (2.3 kilometers) until just after the town of Jan Doret, and then take a left turn on Kaya Antoine Pijpers, which quickly becomes Kaya Ma Pieternella on the way to Boka Sint Michiel. After approximately 1 mile (1.6 kilometers), the road bends sharply to the right. Take the left turn immediately after this bend. Continue down this side road for approximately 0.2 miles (0.35 kilometers) and take the third turn on the left. This road bends right and then right again before running parallel to the shore headed in a northerly direction. The public access to Snake Bay is located about 0.1 miles (0.2 kilometers) along this road. A red rock appears on the road adjacent to the free parking lot, which has space for approximately a dozen cars. It is located between Wederfoort Apartments and Bright Sight Villas. The total distance from Willemstad is approximately 7.5 miles (12 kilometers).

## Access

Divers can gear up at the car or use the picnic benches close to the water. A concrete boat ramp leads from the parking lot all the way into the water, adjacent to a very small beach. The area is protected by a small breakwater to the south, so the sea tends to be calm here at the entry point. Even so, divers and snorkelers should be aware that the boat ramp can be a little slippery where it enters the water. The walk out from the beach is predominantly sand, but there are lots of small rocks, so booties are advisable. The drop-off is located about 400 feet (122 meters) from shore. Currents are usually mild but can become moderate at times. This site is suitable for divers of all experience levels. There is a typically a mooring buoy located just south of the breakwater at the midway point between the shore and the start of the reef slope.

## Description

Snake Bay is also known as Slangenbaai and Playa Wachi. The name comes from the many eels that can be found on the reef here. The site has a relatively small back reef that consists predominantly of sand. There are also numerous small coral heads and soft corals scattered throughout the back reef, which occasionally hide trumpetfish and slender filefish. Divers and snorkelers may also see stingrays, goatfish and razorfish here.

The density of these coral patches increases as divers approach the top of the reef slope, which starts to slope downward from a depth of around 30 feet (9 meters). The slope is relatively gentle, descending at an angle of approximately 45 degrees. There are plenty of large star and lettuce corals on the reef slope, as well as barrel and tube sponges, but there is little else in the way of navigable features on this reef.

Large numbers of creole wrasses and chromis fill the water column, which additionally attract jacks and barracuda. As the site name may suggest, morays are quite common at this site, including spotted, green and goldentail morays. Lucky divers may also come across the relatively rare viper moray at Snake Bay. Parrotfish, the favorite prey of moray eels, are also common at this site. Almost all species of parrotfish are represented, including redband, princess, queen, striped, stoplight, redtail and even the rarer rainbow, midnight and blue parrotfish species. This reef also supports a relatively high density of hamlets and lionfish.

## Route

Divers and snorkelers can head in either direction at Snake Bay. Divers should generally head into the current, if any exists. If there is no current, divers can explore both directions in the same dive. Taking a compass bearing before descending may help in navigating back to the access beach at the end of the dive.

The reef in the southern direction has the greatest number of shallow features for snorkelers, including a large stand of pencil coral that covers much of the reef slope. To the north, snorkelers will come across a series of shallow spurs on the reef top, although these do not offer much in the way of profile above the surrounding seabed

A moray eel and sea turtle encounter each other at Snake Bay.

Turtle & Ray©

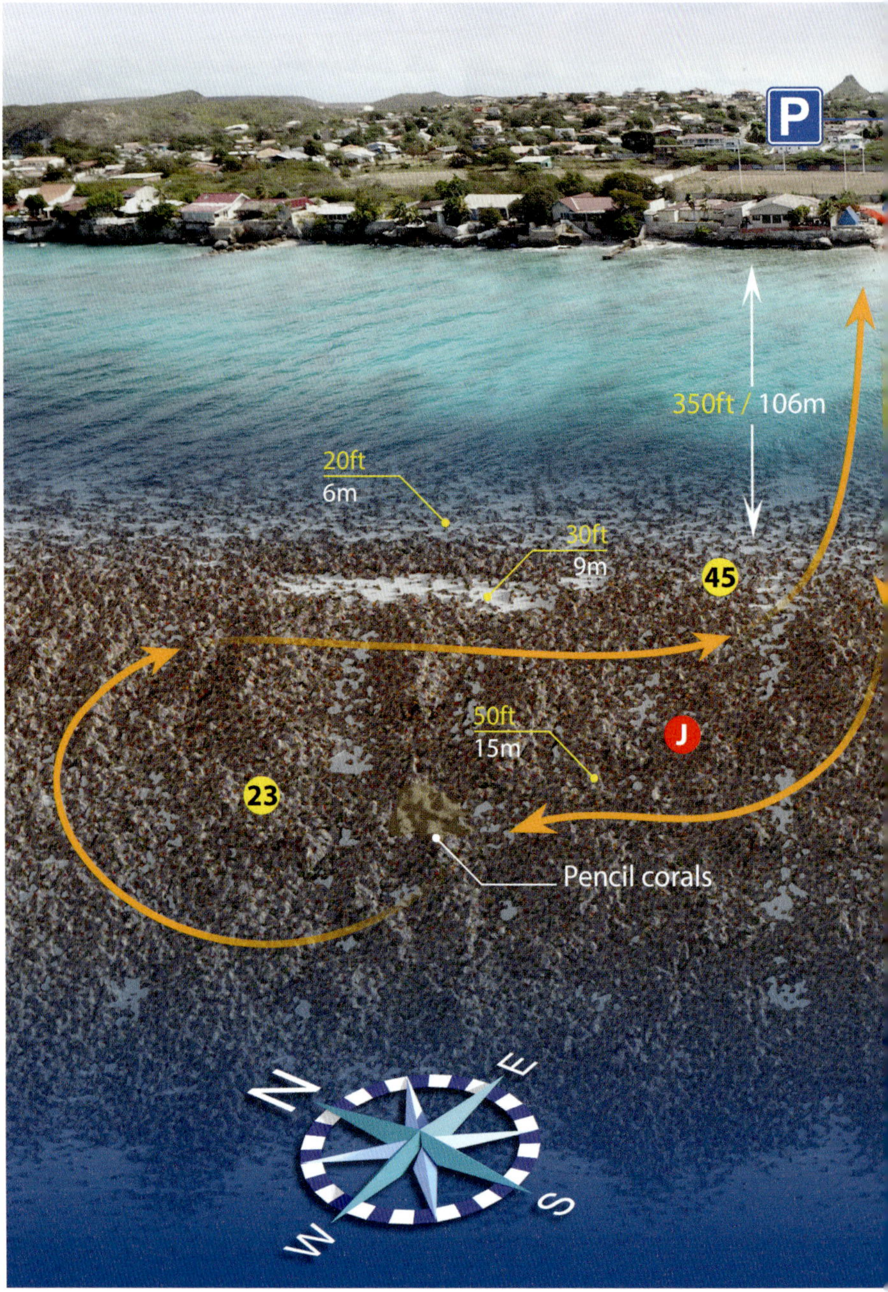
P
350ft / 106m
20ft
6m
30ft
9m
45
50ft
15m
J
23
Pencil corals
N
E
S
W

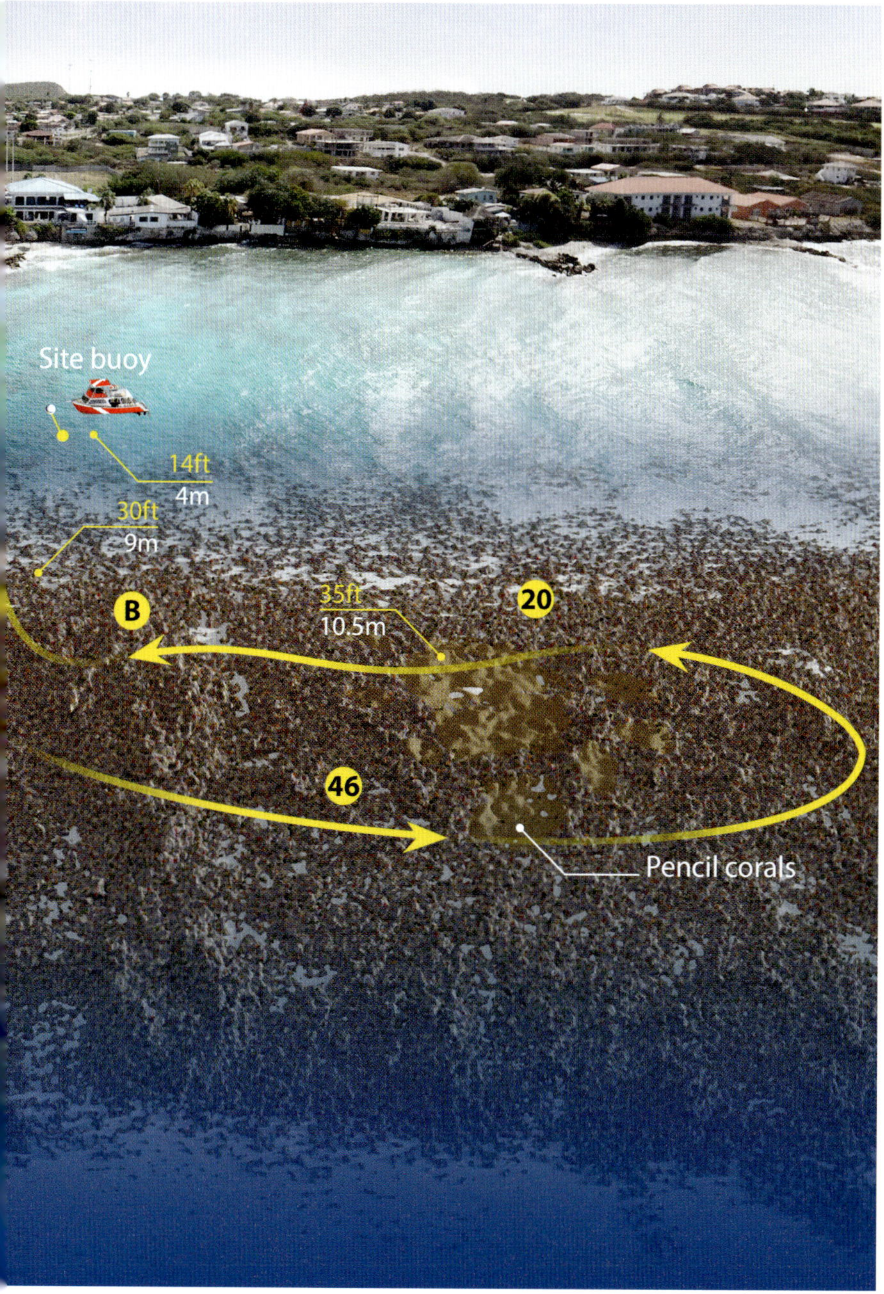
Site buoy
14ft
4m
30ft
9m
B
35ft
10.5m
20
46
Pencil corals

# HOLE NUMBER 6

Difficulty ●●○
Current ●●○
Depth ●●●
Reef ★★★
Fauna ★★☆

Access about 19 mins from Willemstad

**Level** Advanced

**Location**
Sint Michiel, Curaçao
GPS 12°08.142'N, 68°59.545'W

## Getting there

There is no shore access to Hole Number 6. The best way to reach this site is through one of the local dive operators located along Curaçao's central coast.

## Access

Hole Number 6 is a boat-accessible dive and snorkel site that has no permanent mooring buoy installed. Currents can be moderate, and seas can be choppy. This site is better suited to advanced divers and snorkelers.

## Description

Hole Number 6 is also sometimes known as Kaap Mal Meeuw. The site is located at the northern end of Blue Bay Wall, which is the farthest end from the beach. As there is no shore access, and even those with excellent air consumption find it virtually impossible to reach this site from Blue Bay, the only safe way to dive this site is by boat. The name Hole Number 6 comes

## SAFETY TIP

Recognizing your limits is an essential part of diving safely, particularly when shore diving in somewhere like Curaçao without a professional guide. Natural conditions, such as the weather, waves, currents, visibility, temperature, and any shore complexity that can make entering and exiting the water more complicated, are all important parameters to consider before starting your dive or snorkel experience. Divers and snorkelers should also be aware of other conditions, such as the amount of boat traffic in the area. Recognizing your limits is not just related to environmental factors, however, it can also mean your own physical and mental limits. Divers and snorkelers should consider their own level of health and fitness, not just overall, but specifically on the day of the dive. Ask yourself: are you feeling well rested, carrying any recent injury or dealing with any emotional stress? It is never a bad idea to cancel a dive that you are having concerns about before you enter the water. Remember, additional training can always help improve the way you dive or snorkel, as well as help you assess risks and understand how best to handle them.

from the stunning three par hole of the Blue Bay Golf Course that curves around the shore at this location. The back reef features plenty of healthy hard and soft corals, many of which play host to brightly colored flamingo tongues, but the current, surface chop and surge that are commonly seen at this site usually restricts snorkeling. The reef is similar in many ways to the more popular Blue Bay Wall located to the south. Starting at a depth of around 15 feet (4.5 meters), the reef drops down a virtually sheer face to extreme depth. Divers often report finding large snapper and grouper, as well as moray eels and lobsters here.

# BLUE BAY WALL

Difficulty ●●○
Current ●●○
Depth ●●○
Reef ★★☆
Fauna ★★☆

Access (boat) about 18 mins from Willemstad
Access (car) about 16 mins from Willemstad
Access (swim) about 20 mins from shore

**Level** Advanced

## Location

Sint Michiel, Curaçao
GPS 12°08.097′N, 68°59.323′W (reef)
12°08.059′N, 68°59.092′W (shore access)

## Getting there

Turn left onto Weg Naar Bullenbaai from Helmin Magno Wiels Boulevard. After about 0.6 miles (1.7 kilometers), take the left turn adjacent to the large signage marked Blue Bay. A security gate is located approximately 0.3 miles (0.5 kilometers) down this road, marking the entrance to the estate. Drivers will need to show their driver's license and otherwise identify themselves to security personnel at this gate. Continue along this road for another 0.7 miles (1.1 kilometers) and take the right turn that leads up the hill. Continue up and over the hill and then down to the parking lot adjacent to the beach. The roads are not well-signposted inside the estate, so it may be necessary to ask for directions to the dive center and beach. The total distance from Willemstad is approximately 6.5 miles (10.4 kilometers).

## Access

There is a large parking area located next to the beach at Blue Bay with plenty of spaces available. Most divers and snorkelers will need to carry their gear about 500 feet (152 meters) across the parking lot, through the beach entrance and down a small path to the dive center. Blue Bay is a private resort and golf course. As such, a fee must be paid to access the beach, which includes use of the amenities, such as sun loungers, palapas and showers. Visitors will need to rent tanks from the dive center, which also includes access to their rinse tanks. Kayaks and stand-up paddle boards can also be rented. The water just off the beach at Blue Bay is almost always calm because it is sheltered by breakwaters on either side of the beach, which stretches around 400 feet (120 meters) from end to end. Divers and snorkelers just need to walk down the sandy beach and enter the water to access this dive and snorkel site.

Blue Bay Wall is located to the right (northwest) of the beach and requires a swim of approximately 1,400 feet (427 meters), which can take about 20 minutes. The current is usually mild, but can become moderate to strong at times. When it is strong, it can make this swim particularly challenging, especially when returning to the beach since the prevailing currents typically run in a northwestern direction. Thankfully, the onsite dive operator can provide guided boat access to both Blue Bay Wall and Gardens, as well as a number of other dive and snorkel sites nearby. The nature of the current and depth of this dive, make this site better suited to advanced divers, especially when accessing it from shore. The visibility is usually exceptional at this site.

## Description

Blue Bay Wall, sometimes simply referred to as The Wall, is an exceptional dive site that often leaves divers and snorkelers in awe of their experience. The reef is an extension of the cliffs above. They drop into the water and, aside from a narrow plateau just below the surface of the water, they continue to descend in a vertical face for over 100 feet (30 meters). At the base of the cliff, the slope changes and becomes more rubble and sand in nature.

Closer to the beach access point, the drop-off is more like a steep slope, but it becomes increasingly wall-like as divers explore toward the northwest. The reef eventually becomes a sheer wall, with deep undercuts in places, particularly along its base. In the deep areas of the site, where the wall undercuts, divers may find black corals as well as lobsters and green moray eels.

The narrow plateau that sits just below the surface of the water at the top of the wall has an average depth of approximately 20 feet (6 meters). This small plateau hosts an incredibly dense and diverse coral community, including pillar corals, delicate blade fire corals and pencil corals, as well as elkhorn and staghorn corals, soft corals and sponges. This ledge has a couple of large boulders perched at the top of the water that

## DID YOU KNOW?

Blue Bay, or Blaauwbaai as it is known in Dutch, is named after former plantation owner Anno Blaauw, and not after the vivid blue color of the ocean at this popular beach. Anno Blaauw was the owner of Landhuis Blaauw in the 1700s, which now forms part of the Blue Bay Golf and Beach Resort. The plantation once produced citrus fruits, as well as indigo pigment, which was used at the time to dye textiles blue. The product was extracted from the seed pods of two similar looking plants that can still be found growing in Curaçao, which were once exported to Holland. Indigo pigment was big business in the 18th century and was often known as "blue gold."

With its sheer drop-off, Blue Bay Wall is one of the more dramatic sites that can be explored in Curaçao.

Turtle & Ray©

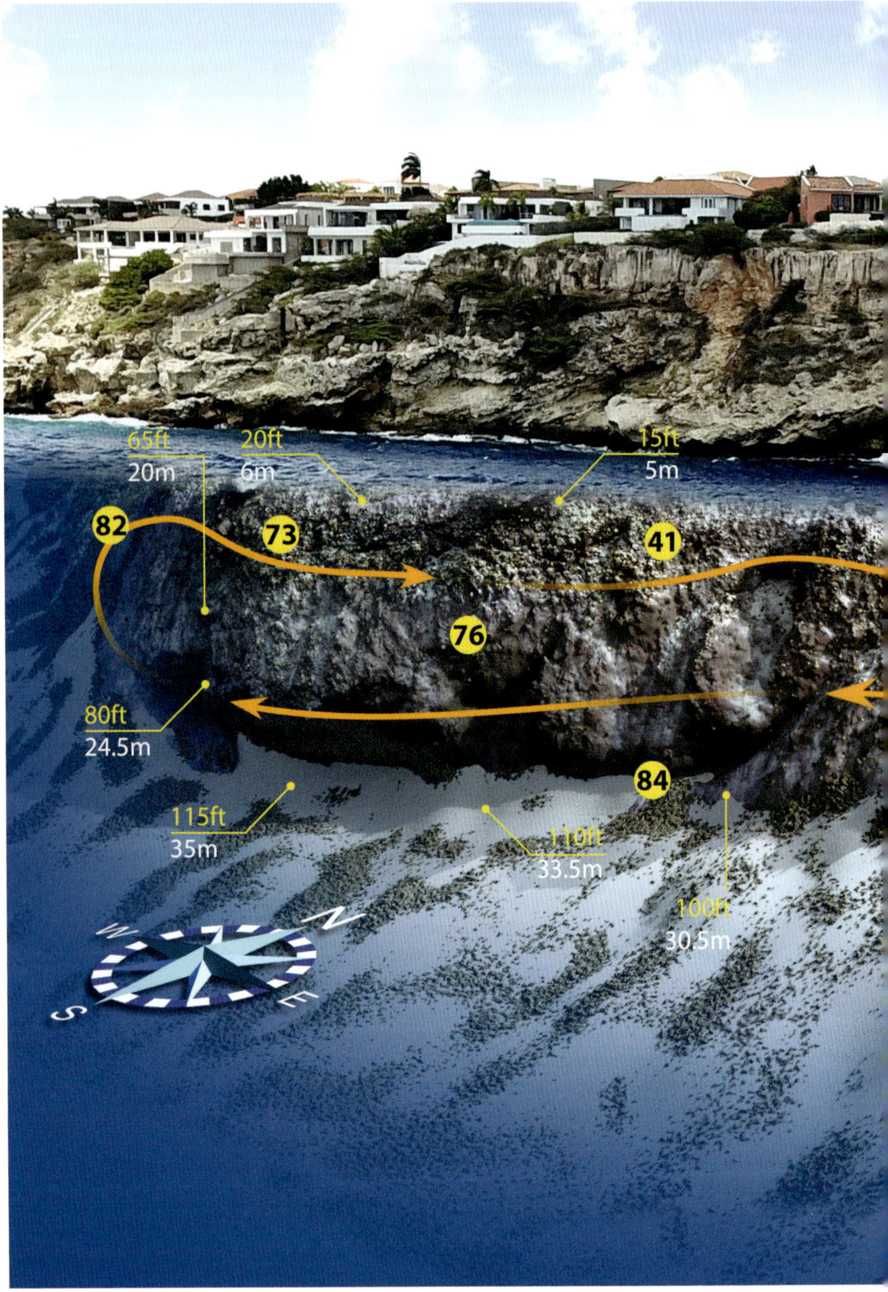


break the surface of the water. These rocks have broken free from the cliff above and fallen onto the plateau to add to the complexity of the site. The quality of the corals and the complex habitat created by the boulders makes the plateau an interesting place to explore, and particularly useful for divers looking to regain some bottom time on their return leg to the beach.

The site supports a diverse assemblage of reef creatures, including large schools of chromis and creole wrasses, barracuda, snapper, grouper, midnight parrotfish, seahorses and frogfish. Divers and snorkelers may also discover sea turtles and eagle rays on this reef, and there are several reports of dolphins being spotted out in the blue. Caution is required when exploring

the plateau, as the shallow area can become turbulent in the presence of wave surge.

## Route

Divers and snorkelers should gauge the current while heading out to Blue Bay Wall. If the current is too strong, it may be worth considering a visit to another site, such as Blue Bay Gardens. The latter site often experiences slightly weaker currents and involves heading into the prevailing current at the start of the dive.

Snorkelers can swim out to the wall by heading out from the bay and around the northwestern breakwater, and then staying close to shore.

There is plenty of marine life to explore along the way, and more than enough to keep snorkelers occupied on the plateau above the wall particularly in the area around the large boulders and the section just beyond these structures. Caution is required in this area as a combination of shallow depth and surge can push divers and snorkelers close to the reef.

Divers should try and remain on the surface until they are outside of the breakwaters and moving along the reef wall, so as to conserve bottom time. The wall is the most interesting area for divers to explore, but the shallow plateau, with its dense coral cover, is also well worth a visit for those with good buoyancy control.

41
23
84
20ft
6m
110ft
33.5m
80ft
24.5m
115ft
35m
N
E
S
W

# 48 BLUE BAY GARDEN

Difficulty ●●○
Current ●●○
Depth ●●○
Reef ★★☆
Fauna ★★☆

Access about 17 mins from Willemstad
Access about 16 mins from Willemstad
Access about 6 mins from shore

**Level** Open Water

## Location

Sint Michiel, Curaçao
GPS 12°07.975'N, 68°59.108'W (reef)
12°08.059'N, 68°59.092'W (shore access)

## Getting there

Turn left onto Weg Naar Bullenbaai from Helmin Magno Wiels Boulevard. After about 0.6 miles (1.7 kilometers), take the left turn adjacent to the large signage marked Blue Bay. A security gate is located approximately 0.3 miles (0.5 kilometers) down this road, marking the entrance to the estate. Drivers will need to show their driver's license and otherwise identify themselves to security personnel at this gate. Continue along this road for another 0.7 miles (1.1 kilometers) and take the right turn that leads up the hill. Continue up and over the hill and then down to the parking lot adjacent to the beach. The roads are not well marked in the estate, so it may be necessary to ask for directions to the dive center and beach. The total distance from Willemstad is approximately 6.5 miles (10.4 kilometers).

## Access

There is a large parking area located next to the beach at Blue Bay with plenty of spaces available. Most divers and snorkelers will need to carry their gear about 500 feet (152 meters) across the parking lot, through the beach entrance and down a small path to the dive center. Blue Bay is a private resort and golf course. As such, a fee must be paid to access the beach, which includes use of the amenities, such as sun loungers, palapas and showers. Visitors will need to rent tanks from the dive center, which also includes access to the rinse tanks. Kayaks and stand-up paddle boards can also be rented. The water just off the beach at Blue Bay is almost always calm because it is sheltered by breakwaters on either side of the beach, which stretches around 400 feet (120 meters) from end to end. Divers and snorkelers just need to walk down the sandy beach and enter the water to access this dive and snorkel site.

Blue Bay Garden is located to the left (southeast) of the beach and requires a swim of approximately 500 feet (152 meters) out and around the southern breakwater, which can take about 6 minutes. The current is usually mild but can become moderate at times. This site is suitable for divers and snorkelers of all experience levels. The visibility is usually good at this site but can be reduced when conditions are windy.

## Description

Blue Bay Garden is a relaxed dive and snorkel site located just south of Blue Bay Beach. The site is also occasionally known as Blue Bay South and Blue Bay Buoy. The reef slope begins just a few yards from the southern breakwater, but then runs slightly seaward, producing a plateau that extends back toward shore with an average depth of 15 feet (4.5 meters). Initially, the

## RELAX & RECHARGE

There are several refreshment options around Blue Bay Beach. **Coach Beach Restaurant** and **Blend Beach** Bar are both located literally on the sand next to the dive center. Coach Beach Restaurant offers breakfast, lunch and dinner, with options to suit every taste, from fresh fish to steaks and vegetarian options, with a view that is hard to beat. Blend Beach Bar shares the same stunning view. Their specialty is beach bites, such as pizzas, burgers and poke bowls, and a wide selection of smoothies and cocktails, which they will serve right to your sun lounger. Both establishments are open until 10pm, so there is plenty of time to soak in the ambiance. On the southeast edge off the beach is **Brass Boer Curaçao**, which has a refined menu that mixes European dishes with a local twist. Chef's specials, including foie gras, caviar, langoustine and sweetbread. There's also a five course chef's menu for those that wish to be surprised. Visit: **Bluebay-curacao.com/food-beverage**

habitat is mostly sand and rubble, but becomes increasingly more complex the farther divers and snorkelers move away from the access point. Despite the low rugosity of the reef close to the breakwater, divers and snorkelers can find all kinds of rare and unusual species, including octopuses, scorpionfish, box crabs and anemones and their symbiotic shrimp. The reef slope descends from the plateau starting at a depth of around 20 feet (6 meters) down to over 150 feet (46 meters) at its base, where it again transitions to rubble and sand.

Distinct ridges or spurs run up and down the reef slope interspersed with sand and rubble chutes. The spurs are dotted with sea fans, sponges and small brain and star corals, and they increase in size and rugosity toward the southern end of the site. There are large undercuts and dramatic ravines in many of the ridges near the turnaround point of the dive.

The reef habitat in Blue Bay Garden hosts numerous cleaning stations, which are often frequented by creole wrasses, chromis and

Spotted cleaner shrimp (*Periclimenes yucatanicus*) and Pederson cleaner (*Ancylomenes pedersoni)* shrimp are often found living within the safety of anemone tentacles, like the ones found in Blue Bay Garden.

NaturePicsFilms/Shutterstock©

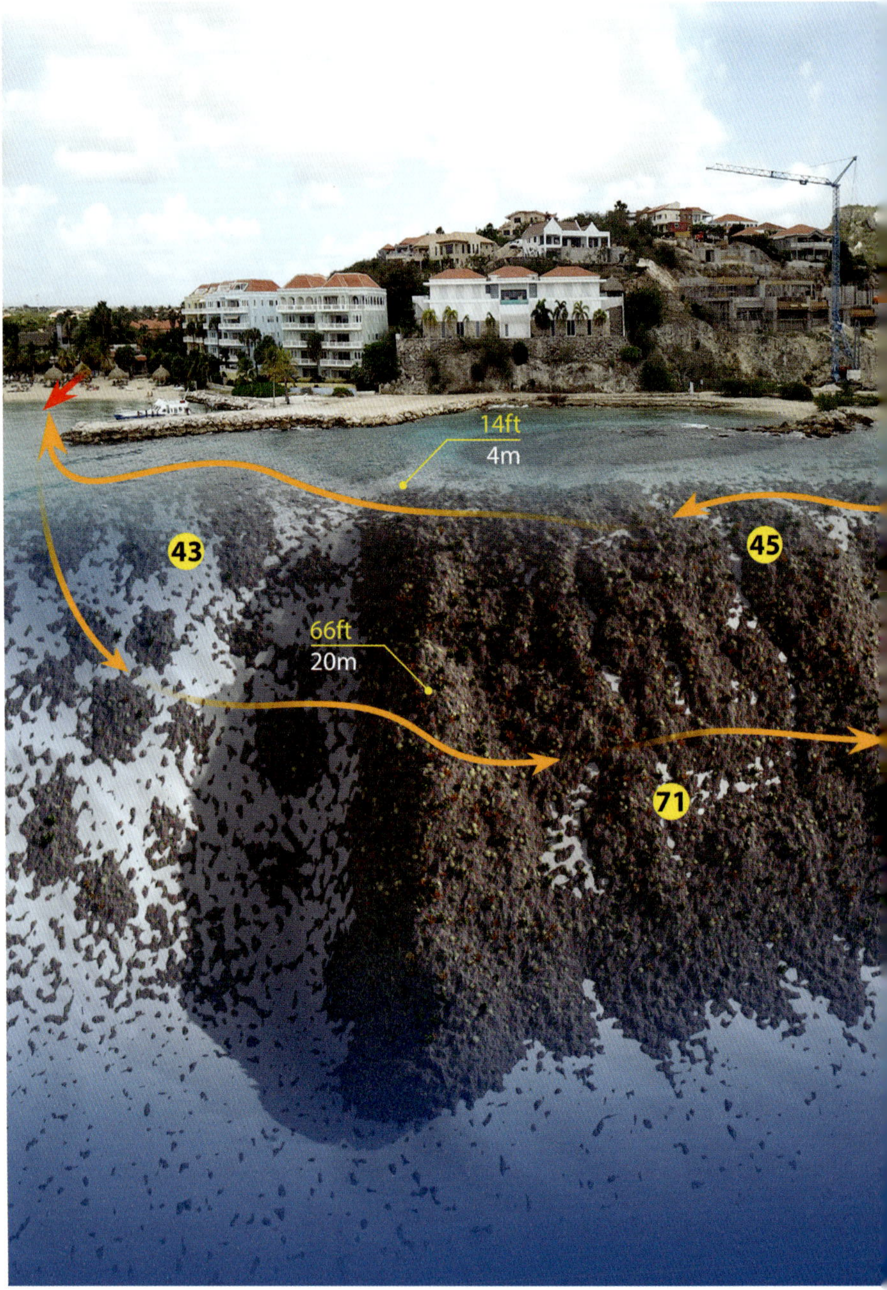


parrotfish. Divers may also find snapper and moray eels, including goldentail moray eels. In the shallow sections of this site there are multiple stands of pillar corals and purple tube sponges located along the top of the reef slope.

## Route

The current at Blue Bay Gardens is usually mild and typically runs from the southeast back toward the beach access point. The prevailing currents make this dive and snorkel site safer to explore than Blue Bay Wall to the north. This site is also much shallower on average than

its neighbor, although divers can take a deep profile if they wish.

Snorkelers often follow the edge of the upper reef slope, adjacent to the plateau, where there is plenty of marine life to explore and the shallow depth makes it easy to observe the reef. A large concrete block marks the top of the plateau approximately three quarters of the way toward the turnaround point at the southern end of this site.

# ROLLING STONES

Difficulty ●●○
Current ●●○
Depth ●●●
Reef ★★★
Fauna ★★☆

Access about 15 mins from Willemstad

**Level** Advanced

## Location

Sint Michiel, Curaçao
GPS 12°07.715'N, 68°58.802'W

## Getting there

There is no shore access to Rolling Stones. The best way to reach this site is through one of the local dive operators located on Curaçao's central coast.

## Access

Rolling Stones is only accessible by boat. The dive and snorkel site typically has a mooring buoy installed. Currents can be moderate, and seas can be choppy. This site is better suited to advanced divers and snorkelers.

## Description

Rolling Stones is a dive and snorkel site located just around the coast from Blue Bay Gardens. It is sometimes called Eighteenth Hole, even though the

## SCIENTIFIC INSIGHT

Fire corals are not true corals. They are hydrozoans of the genus *Millepora*. Like coral however, they are closely related to jellyfish and sea nettles, and they share their relatives' ability to sting. Fire coral can take a few different forms, including branching, encrusting and blade (plate-like), which is the form that is commonly found along many of the reef plateaus and ledges in Curaçao, including at Rolling Stones. A long-term study recently revealed that fire corals are thriving in the Caribbean while true corals species start to disappear. According to the study, fire coral is better able to survive physical damage and water temperatures that are fatal to most corals. As such, they may be important species in maintaining the structural complexity of reefs that so many other organisms depend on.

site is actually located just seaward of the sixteenth hole of the Blue Bay Golf Course. The name stems from the fact that many divers and snorkelers find lost golf balls (rolling stones) on the seabed at this site.

The reef at Rolling Stones can be somewhat exposed to currents and waves, so snorkeling depends on the conditions of the day. These conditions help corals and sponges thrive, however. The back reef extends only 100 feet (30 meters) from the cliff edge, but supports plenty of healthy blade fire coral, elkhorn coral and staghorn coral, as well as soft corals. Squid are common in this area and stingrays are often spotted in the sand patches between the patch reefs. The outer reef is steep, dropping almost vertically to depths in excess of 130 feet (40 meters). Divers report finding tarpon, snapper and grouper here.

# 50 LONG BEACH

Difficulty ●○○
Current ●●○
Depth ●●○
Reef ★☆☆
Fauna ★★☆

Access about 13 mins from Willemstad

**Level** Open Water

**Location**
Piscadera, Curaçao
GPS 12°07.427'N, 68°58.310'W

## Getting there

Although technically accessible from shore via the Jack Evertsberg hiking trail or by swimming from the south side of the channel that leads to Piscaderabaai, these options come with significant challenges. The best way to reach this site is through one of the local dive operators located along Curaçao's central coast.

## Access

Long Beach is a dive and snorkel site that is only accessible by boat. Currents are often mild here but can become moderate at times. Seas can become choppy when windy. Visibility is usually good. This site is suitable for divers and snorkelers of all experience levels.

## Description

Long Beach is a dive and snorkel site located just north of the channel that leads to Piscaderabaai. The site lies immediately seaward of a long sandy and rocky beach, which is why the site is sometimes referred to as Playa Largu or Playa Grandi. It is also sometimes called Piscadera after the adjacent Bay. These alternate names often lead to confusion with some of the other sites located farther north and the site located across the channel.

The focus of this dive site is the gradually sloping reef that bends away from the shore as it extends to the northwest. At the northern end of the site, the reef plateau projects out from shore to form a ridge or spur that is particularly steep in places. Beyond the spur, the reef slope cuts back toward shore and continues uninterrupted toward the northwest. The top of the reef slope is the area of densest coral cover, with large patches of healthy yellow pencil corals and dome-shaped star and brain corals. Many of the coral heads in this area also host busy cleaning stations, frequented by the Queen and stoplight parrotfishes that are abundant along this reef, along with the equally common creole wrasses and blue and brown chromis that are frequently seen in the water column above the reef.

The reef slope has numerous coral ledges cut into its face at depths of around 40 to 50 feet (12 to 15 meters), which are undercut in places. Divers may find lobsters, moray eels and lionfish hiding in these areas, as well as soldierfish and squirrelfish. Small sand patches occur throughout the reef slope, but these start to diminish as divers approach the spur that projects out from the reef slope at the northern end of the site. The reef becomes noticeably steeper here, even becoming wall-like in places. Coral and sponges, including elephant ear sponges, are more common here around this feature.

The wide plateau that extends from the top of the slope back toward the shore averages a depth of around 15 feet (4.5 meters). This area is a complex habitat consisting of sand and patch reef, and divers can find all kinds of creatures, ranging from stingrays to anemones throughout this section of the dive site. Snorkelers may want to focus their attention in this area as well, looking out for the high density of Christmas tree worms that can be found on many of the coral heads on the plateau. Soft corals and fire coral are also found at high density in this shallow region of the reef.

## Route

The most commonly used route for this site is to enter the water near the mooring buoy and then head north, which is where the reef with the most complex structure lies. This route usually follows the prevailing current, which means divers must take into account the fact that the return leg of their dive may take longer as they may be heading up current. For this reason, most divers turn around after passing the large reef spur that is the main feature of this site and return to the dive boat along the shallow back reef plateau. Snorkelers usually spend the majority of their time in the water exploring

Angelfish are often found at Long Beach.

Turtle & Ray©

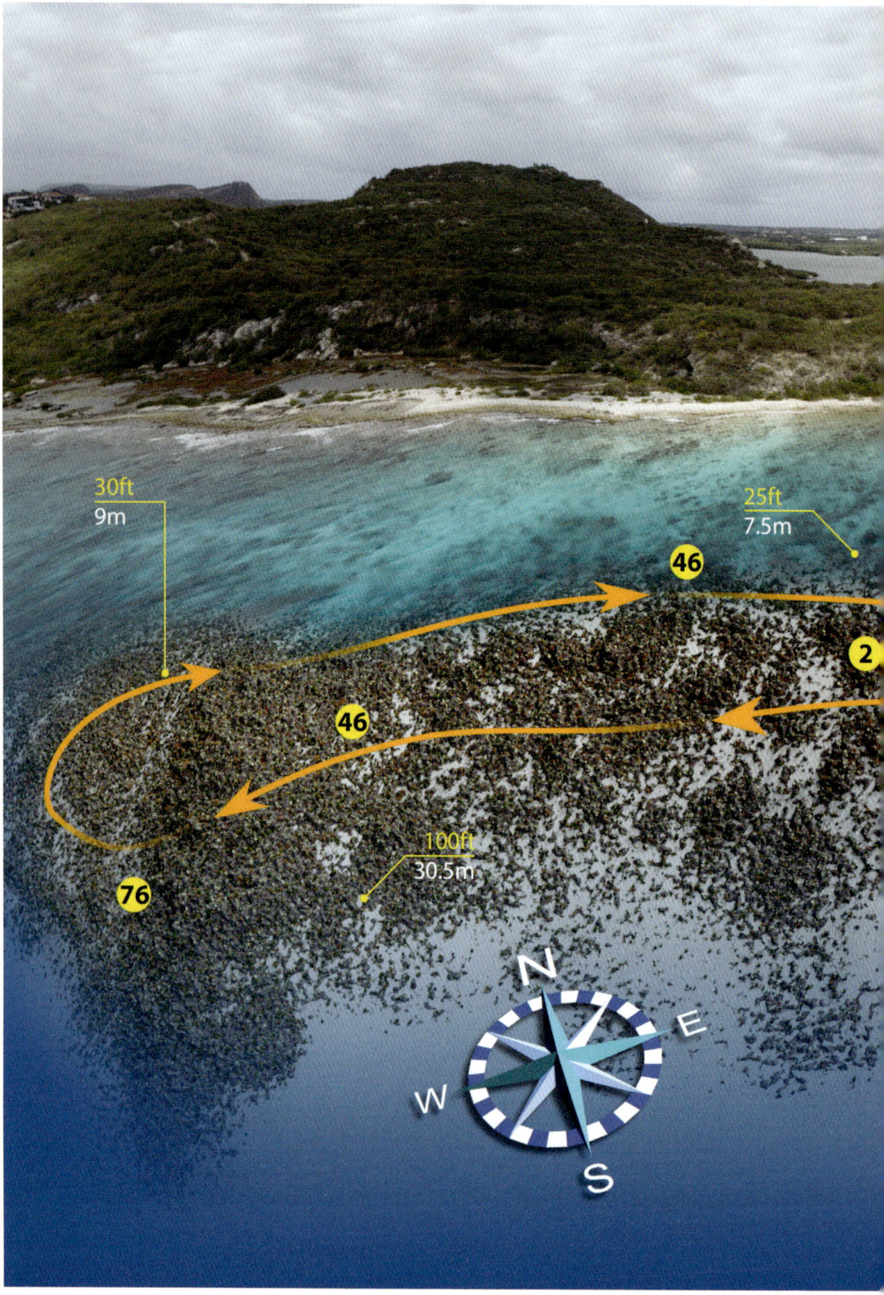


this plateau, which is shallow enough to clearly observe the wide diversity of reef creatures that live here among the corals and sand patches.

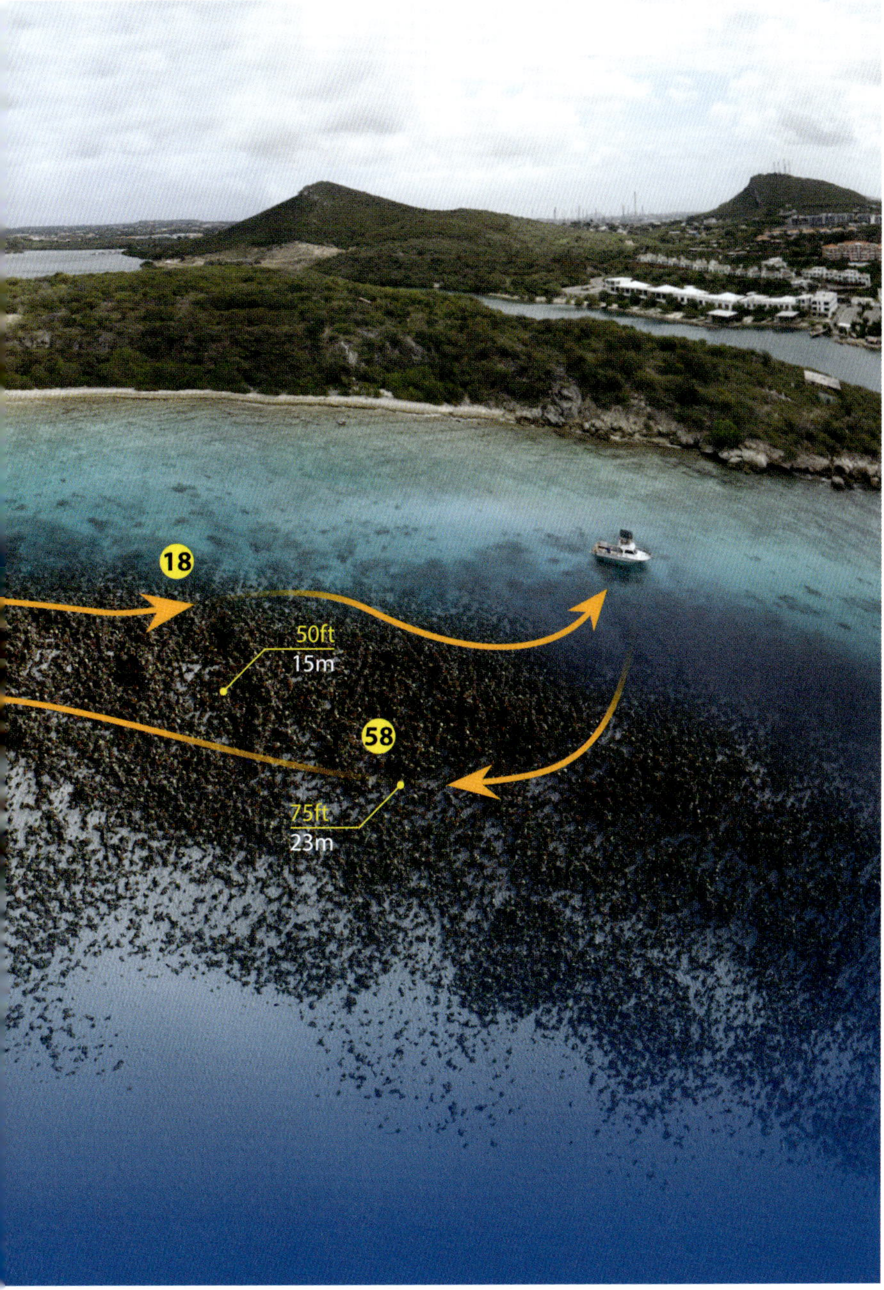
18
50ft
15m
58
75ft
23m

51

# PISCADERA

WILLEMSTAD

Difficulty ● ○ ○
Current ● ○ ○
Depth ● ● ○
Reef ★★☆
Fauna ★★☆

Access about 12 mins from Willemstad
Access about 6 mins from Willemstad
Access about 1 mins from shore

**Level** Open Water

## Location

Piscadera, Curaçao
GPS 12°07.288'N, 68°58.150'W

## Getting there

Head north on Pater Euwensweg from the Otrobanda neighborhood of Willemstad. At the roundabout located 1.9 miles (3 kilometers) down the road, take the left turn onto Piscaderaweg. The road bends to the left and slopes downhill. Turn right at the bottom, and the entrance to Dreams Curaçao Resort Spa & Casino is on the left after an additional 400 feet (122 meters). Alternatively, you can drive another 580 feet (180 meters) and turn left toward Pirate Bay Curaçao, which is located right next to CARMABI. The total distance from Willemstad is approximately 2.5 miles (4 kilometers).

## Access

Divers wishing to access this site are expected to rent tanks from the dive centers at either of the two resorts mentioned above. Access in both cases involves simply walking down the sandy beach and into the water. This site is suitable for divers and snorkelers of all experience levels.

## DID YOU KNOW?

What remains of Fort Piscadera can be found within the grounds of the Dreams Curaçao Resort Spa & Casino. This arrow-shaped fort originally pointed toward the entrance channel to Piscaderabaai when it was constructed in the early 1700s and later redeveloped in the late 1740s. The British took control of the fort during the Napoleonic Wars, when Curaçao fell under British protection and was returned to the Dutch through the Treaty of Paris in March 1815.

Currents are usually mild, and visibility is usually excellent.

### Description

Piscadera is claimed as the house reef for both resorts and their associated dive shops. This site is also sometimes known as Betsy's Backyard, although that name has also been applied to the adjacent site of Marriott Beach. The area directly in front of the beach consists mostly of sand, but divers and snorkelers can still sometimes find stingrays, razorfish and goatfish here.

A collapsed pier has become an artificial reef underwater that attracts more fish than might otherwise be found at this site. Divers and snorkelers often report seeing grunts, parrotfish, surgeonfish, sea turtles and even cryptic species such as octopuses. The natural reef has been damaged in a few places, but it becomes increasingly healthy and wall-like toward the south. The current also increases toward the south, which at times can be too strong to comfortably swim against. In these cases, divers and snorkelers can simply drift back toward the beach and explore the natural reef and artificial structures along their way back to the entry point.

# 52 MARRIOTT BEACH

Difficulty ●●○
Current ●●○
Depth ●●○
Reef ★★☆
Fauna ★★☆

Access (boat) about 10 mins from Willemstad
Access (car) about 5 mins from Willemstad
Access (swim) about 3 mins from shore

**Level** Open Water

## Location

Piscadera, Curaçao
GPS 12°07.000'N, 68°57.890'W (public access)
12°07.108'N, 68°58.063'W (dive center access)
12°07.000'N, 68°58.020'W (Reef)

## Getting there

Head north on Pater Euwensweg from the Otrobanda neighborhood of Willemstad. At the roundabout located approximately 1.9 miles (3 kilometers) down the road, take the left turn onto Piscaderaweg. The road bends to the left and slopes downhill. Turn left at the bottom – a distance of 0.3 miles (0.5 kilometers). The entrance to the public parking lot adjacent to the beach is on the right-hand side, after an additional 0.15 miles (0.25 kilometers). Alternatively, turn right at the end of Piscaderaweg, followed by the first left into the Curaçao Marriott Beach Resort, about 150 feet (45 meters) after the intersection. Divers and snorkelers must inform security that they are visiting the dive center. The total distance from Willemstad is approximately 2.3 miles (3.8 kilometers).

## Access

Marriott Beach is a shore-accessible dive and snorkel site that can easily be reached from the beach on either side of the long rocky breakwater that runs parallel to shore, directly in front of the Curaçao Marriott Beach Resort.

Goby Divers is located at the northwestern end of the beach, which is a great spot to access this side of the site. Divers are expected to rent tanks from this operator in order to access the facilities and can enter the water by stepping off the end of the jetty or walking down the beach. As the site is located on the seaward side of the breakwater, divers will need to loop around the end of the breakwater to reach the main part of the reef – a swim of about 400 feet (122 meters).

Divers and snorkelers can also explore the Marriott Beach site from the public access point at Parasasa Beach at the southeastern end of the reef. Free parking is available here and visitors can gear up at their car in the parking lot before accessing the water by simply walking down the beach. The site is located on the seaward side of the breakwater, so divers and snorkelers will need to loop around the southeastern end of the breakwater in order to reach the main part of the reef – a swim of about 400 feet (122 meters).

Currents are often mild at Marriott Beach but can become moderate at times, and seas may be choppy seaward of the breakwater. Visibility is usually good. This site is suitable for divers and snorkelers of all experience levels, but drift diving this site can be slightly challenging.

## Description

The Marriott Beach dive and snorkel site is sometimes called Parasasa Beach after the public

### SAFETY TIP

There is usually a mild but constant current that moves from the east to the west along the seaward side of the breakwater at Marriott Beach. This current can allow divers and snorkelers to drift the entire length of the breakwater – a distance of approximately 0.26 miles (0.5 kilometers) – and then exiting at the opposite end of the beach, adjacent to Goby Divers. It takes decent air consumption to reach the opposite end of the beach, particularly when the current is mild. As there are no safe passages through the breakwater, divers who run low on air will need to surface-swim to the end of the breakwater to return to the beach. As such, exploring this site from the southeastern (public) end of the beach can be more challenging than from Goby Divers. Snorkelers are advised to explore the water on the shoreward side of the breakwater, unless guided by a professional with boat support.

## FEATURED OPERATOR

**Goby Divers** is conveniently located right on the beach between the Curaçao Marriott Beach Resort and the Dreams Curaçao Resort Spa & Casino. This PADI, SSI and IANTD-affiliated dive center provides a range of shore and boat dives, recreational and technical diving certifications, and support. Their 30-foot (9-meter) island-hopper, *Blue Pearl*, is the perfect transport for divers to access many of the spectacular dive sites along this stretch of coast. Goby Divers also has a range of gear rental options, including nitrox tanks, as well as a free pick-up and drop-off service for guests. Goby Divers is open seven days a week.

Tel: + 599-9-662-2853
Email: info@goby-divers.com
Visit: **Goby-divers.com**

beach that is located adjacent to the beach in front of the Marriott resort. The dive site is also sometimes called Moomba Reef. It is located directly off shore from the Curaçao Marriott Beach Resort. The reef begins to slope about 400 feet (122 meters) from the beach, which is only about 100 feet (30 meters) from the seaward edge of the breakwater. The reef slopes gradually into deeper water, transitioning to sand and rubble at a depth of approximately 100 feet (30 meters).

Toward the southeast end of the site, the top of the reef slope consists largely of sand, but transitions to a complex mix of patch reef, consisting of dome-shaped brain and star corals, as well as soft corals and sponges as it extends north. This complex reef habitat hosts a diverse assemblage of reef fish including parrotfish, wrasses and damselfish, as well as spotted drums, boxfish and filefish. Four cross-shaped structures that resemble large ceiling fans can be found lying flat along the top of the southeastern

Spotted drums are often found hiding on the reef at Marriott Beach.

Denisse Pohls/Shutterstock©

## DID YOU KNOW?

Just to the southeast of the public entrance at Parnasasa Beach lies an area often referred to as The Crash. This is the location of a Vought OS2U Kingfisher float observation plane from World War II. These planes were designed to be catapulted from larger ships, such as cruisers and battleships, where they would provide intelligence on enemy movements or search and rescue efforts. The one located at this site was lost when *USS Erie* was torpedoed by the German U-Boat *U-163* in November 1942. *USS Erie* burned for several days at this spot and was eventually towed to Willemstad to determine whether she could be salvaged. Ultimately *USS Erie* was considered a complete loss and was scuttled in deep water off the coast of Curaçao in 1947. *U-163* moved north to Barbados where she continued to target allied ships before eventually returning to Europe. She was sunk off the northwest coast of Spain four months later by *HMCS Prescott* – a Royal Canadian Navy corvette.

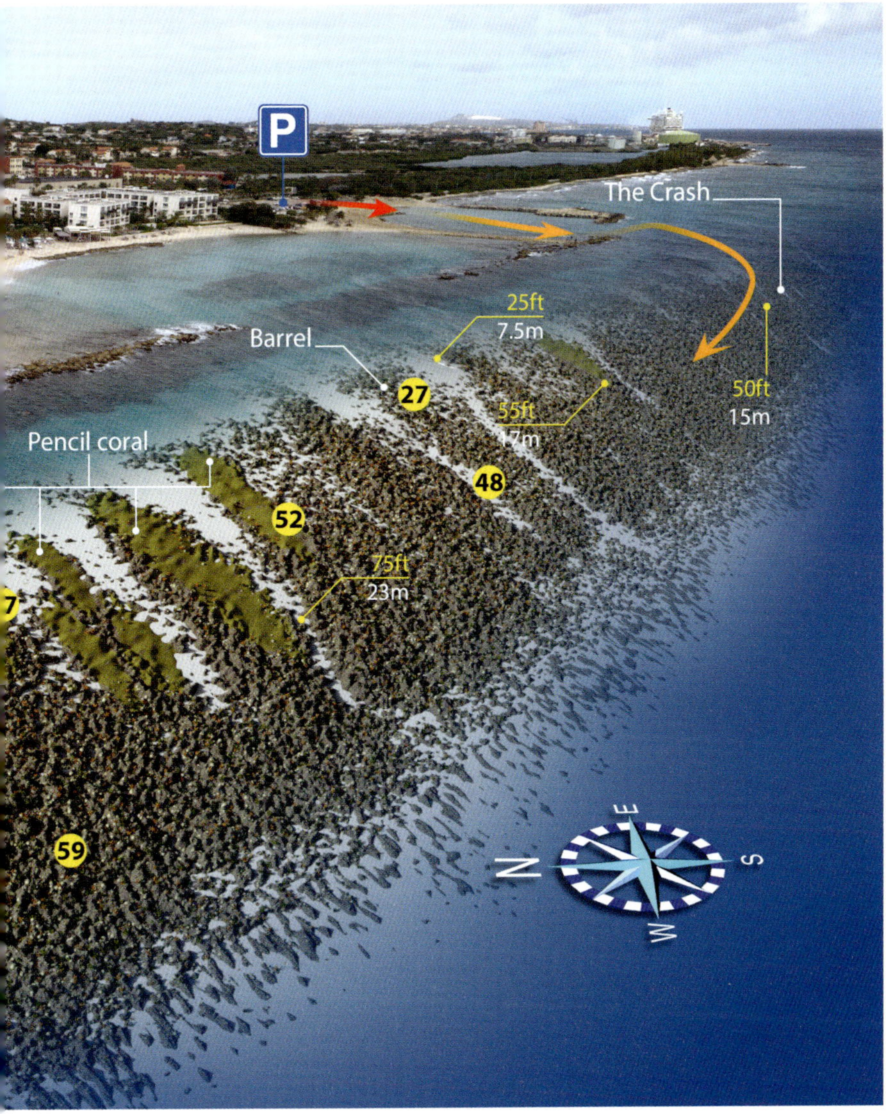


section of the reef slope.

The reef continues toward the northwest, but this slope also includes large expanses of healthy yellow pencil coral, which flow down the reef slope. Meanwhile, the upper areas of the slope are often dotted with pillar corals. Cleaning stations can be found throughout this site, and divers may also discover anemones sheltering their symbiotic shrimp and the occasional seahorse. In the deep areas of the site, divers may find moray eels, lionfish, grouper and snapper.

## Route

Marriott Beach can be explored from the northwestern end of the breakwater, adjacent to Goby Divers, or from the southeastern end of the breakwater, adjacent to the public access point described above. The latter route usually involves a drift dive along the entire length of the breakwater.

When departing from Goby Divers, most divers will start out swimming against the prevailing current. They typically explore the large patches of yellow pencil coral along the top of the reef slope, before looping back toward their point of entry. A rope running along the seabed extends from the reef slope back toward the breakwater to help guide divers back to the beach.

# FISHERMAN'S WHARF

Difficulty ●●○
Current ●●○
Depth ●●○
Reef ★★★
Fauna ★★☆

Access about 5 mins from Willemstad
Access about 4 mins from Willemstad
Access about 4 mins from shore

**Level** Open Water

**Location**
Mundo Nobo, Curaçao
GPS 12°06.572'N, 68°57.225'W

## Getting there

Head north on Pater Euwensweg from the Otrobanda neighborhood of Willemstad. Turn left at the Caribbean Medical University building onto Weg Naar Welgelegen and continue for just over 0.1 miles (200 meters) until you reach the shore. Turn right onto John F. Kennedy Boulevard and drive for about the same distance until you reach the small fishing village located next to the small harbor. Parking is readily available among the fishing huts and restaurants nestled alongside the shore. Parked cars are generally safe here, but it is a good idea to leave valuables at home or ensure that nothing of value is visible in the car when you leave. The total distance from Willemstad is approximately one mile (1.6 kilometers).

## Access

Fisherman's Wharf is also called Fisherman's Hut, Small Harbor and Water Factory. The latter name comes from its proximity to the water desalination plant located just across the road from the fishing village. The best place to enter the water at Fisherman's Wharf is toward the western end of the village. There is a small jetty located here, adjacent to a tiny beach on the outside of the harbor. This beach, which is literally just a few feet in length, is an ideal place to access the water via a gentle slope, although there are a few large rocks for divers and snorkelers to negotiate. Some divers choose to enter the water inside the harbor – either option is possible.

Once in the water, divers and snorkelers must cross the harbor entrance and loop around the western edge of the breakwater to reach the site. This site is also a popular spot for night diving because of the ease of access and well-lit shoreline.

## Description

Fisherman's Wharf dive and snorkel site is a real hidden gem. The quality of this coral reef is exceptional, which is surprising considering it lies immediately adjacent to a busy fishing harbor. Do not be put off by the murky water around the entrance of the harbor – the visibility improves dramatically on the seaward side of the breakwater. The best section of coral reef is located on a small plateau that ranges in depth from about 20 to 25 feet (6 to 7.5 meters). This section is one of the highest diversity reefs on the island, containing a wide mix of hard corals, including elkhorn, staghorn, pillar, lettuce, star and brain coral, and numerous species of soft coral and sponge. Two large stands of elkhorn coral mark the end of the jetty adjacent to the entry and exit point, close to the surface. The plateau, which is located seaward of the breakwater, provides complex habitat for large schools of reef fish, particularly chromis, which attract larger predatory fish such as barracuda, snapper and tarpon.

## RELAX & RECHARGE

For an authentic Curaçao experience, you really cannot go wrong with a meal at one of the local open-air restaurants on the water's edge at Fisherman's Wharf, such as **Kas Di Piskado Purunchi.** These restaurants typically serve the freshest fish you will ever taste, often landed just yards from where you dine. The catch of the day varies, but red snapper, lionfish, jacks and tuna are often on the menu. The fish is usually fried with a side of plantain, funchi (fried corn meal), salad and rice, and you can spice things up with some hot pepper sauce if you wish. This is simple, authentic island cuisine at its finest, and if you feel like hanging out after your meal, the locals are always keen to slam a few dominos with visitors.

## FEATURED OPERATOR

**Dushi Diving** provides outstanding guided dives, from shore or by boat, to all the best sites in Curaçao, such as their house reef Fisherman's Wharf. This operator is a **5-star Instructor dive academy** affiliated with IDD Worldwide & PADI and they provide a great diversity of training options from bubble maker to instructor level, and all the way up to Course Director. Dushi Diving also offers a wide selection of specialties, including Nitrox, Lionfish hunt, Wreck, Deep, Boat diving, among others. They aim to provide a personalized dive experience, and ensure small groups, which provides a relaxed experience for their guests and gives those taking courses the time they need to succeed. Wouter Goudswaard, the owner of Dushi Diving (and a former Navy diver), has many years of experience working with children and has personally taken over 3500 kids on their first dive. They provide special equipment for all children.

Tel: +599-9-515-6170
Email: dushidiving@gmail.com
Visit: **Dushidiving.com**

Just below the plateau, about midway along the reef, divers will find a sloping sandy ledge, bordered by large patches of yellow pencil coral. A particularly large barrel sponge is located at the edge of this ledge. Divers can often find large parrotfish, porcupinefish, angelfish, butterflyfish and spotted drums in this area. To the east, separated by a sand chute, the reef transitions to a small wall that drops vertically from about 25 feet (7.5 meters) at the top to around 50 feet (15 meters) at its base. Fairy basslets cover this wall and divers may also encounter moray eels, lobsters and hamlets.

### Route

Divers and snorkelers can head in either direction at Fisherman's Wharf, but the best reef is located east of the entry point, in front of the breakwater.

The shallow plateau located just seaward of the Fisherman's Wharf breakwater supports a thriving coral reef.

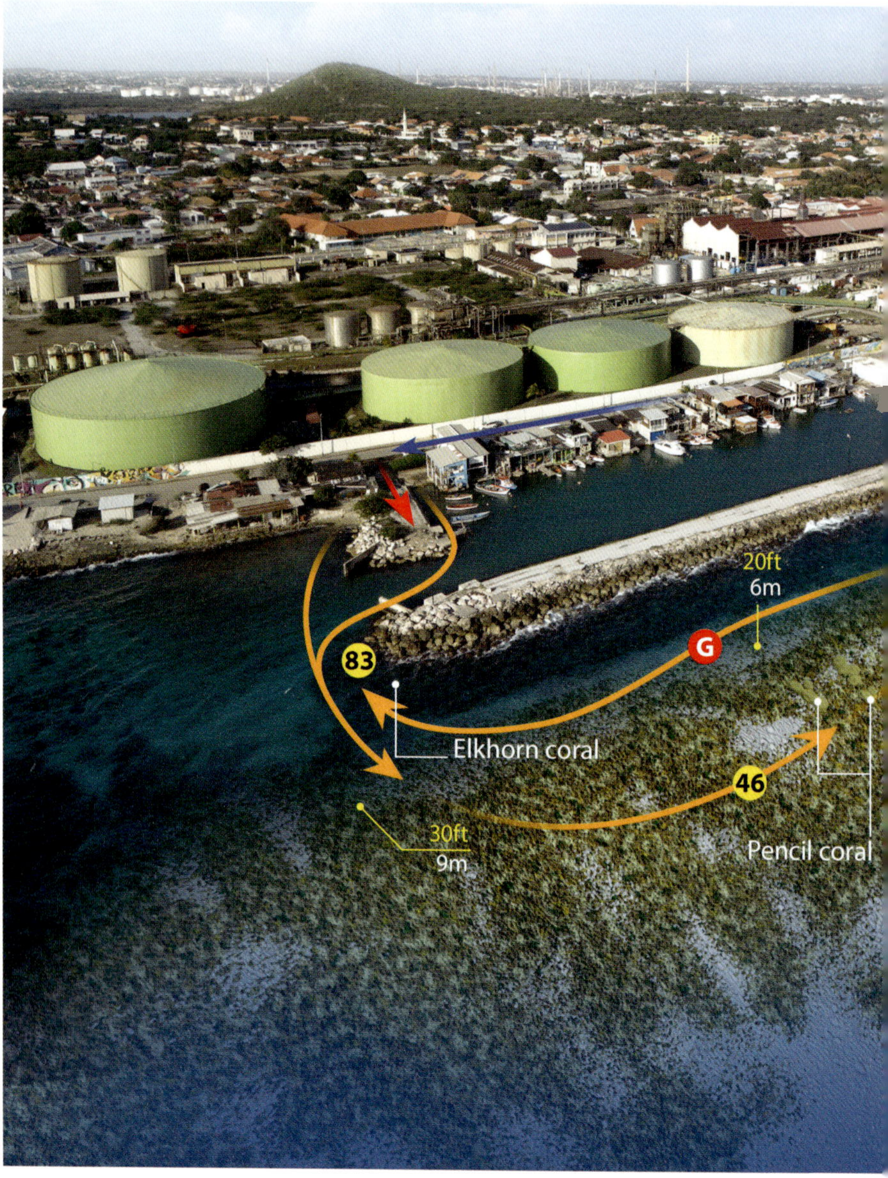


## SAFETY TIP

Fisherman's Wharf is located alongside an active fishing community, which means boats are often passing through the area and particularly through the harbor entrance. Divers and snorkelers should carry a dive flag whenever possible and should carefully listen and watch for boat traffic before surfacing. The current at this site can also vary significantly from day to day, ranging from no current to one that is extremely strong. Do not be afraid to cut your dive short if you find the current is too strong to swim against as you clear the breakwater and head east. In these conditions, the only way to safely explore Fisherman's Wharf is to drift dive from the eastern end of the site,

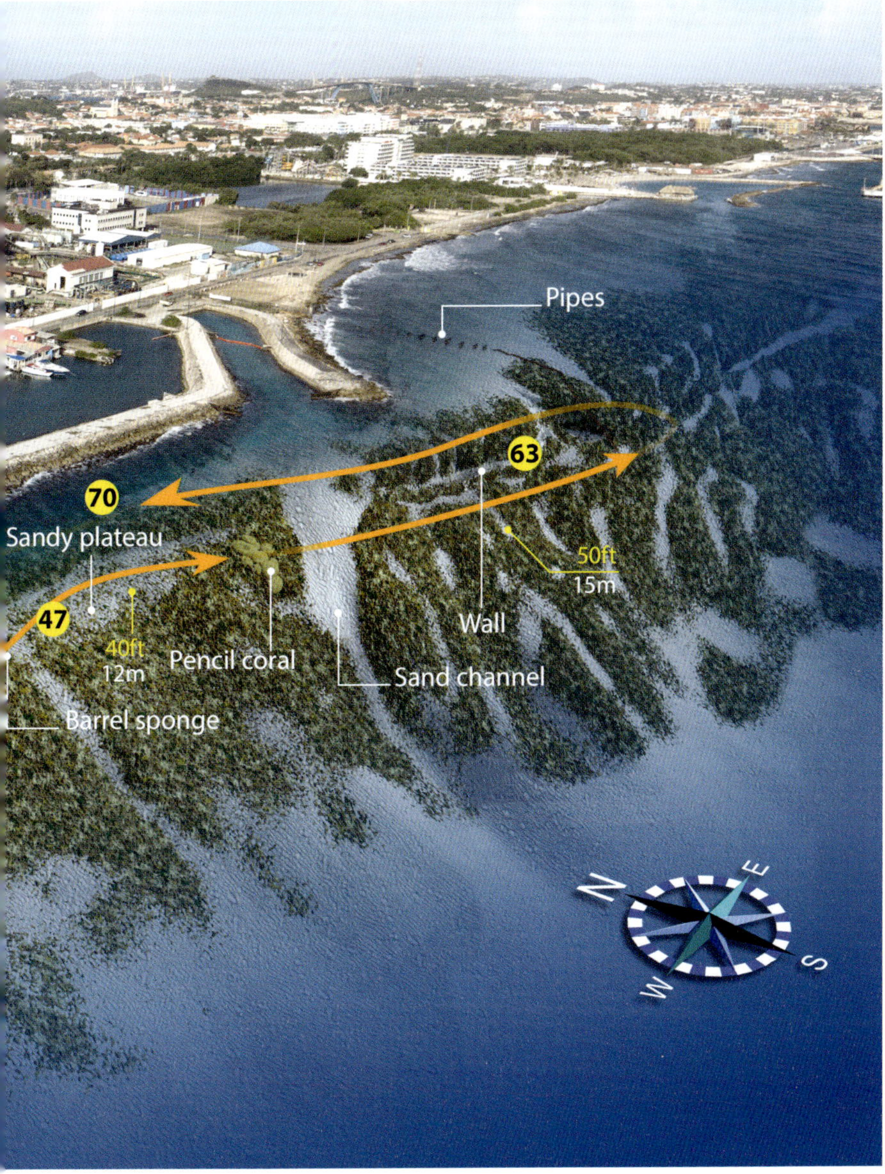


The prevailing currents generally run east to west, which means most divers typically start out heading into the current. Snorkelers usually focus their time on the shallow plateau, which has exceptional coral cover that is readily visible from the surface. Divers usually head down the reef slope and explore the sandy ledge before continuing east to the small wall. The pipe located at the eastern end of the site is often a good spot to turn around, but divers with good air consumption can usually move beyond this point, especially if the current is mild.

# DOUBLE REEF

Difficulty ●●○
Current ●●○
Depth ●●○
Reef ★★☆
Fauna ★★★

Access (boat) about 4 mins from Willemstad
Access (car) about 4 mins from Willemstad
Access (swim) about 5 mins from shore

**Level** Open Water

## Location

Otrobanda, Curaçao
GPS 12°06.473'N, 68°56.872'W

## Getting there

Head north on Pater Euwensweg from the Otrobanda neighborhood of Willemstad. Turn left at the Caribbean Medical University building onto Weg Naar Welgelegen and continue for just over 0.1 miles (200 meters) until you reach the shore at the junction of John F. Kennedy Boulevard. A gate blocks vehicles from accessing Park Lucha pa Libertat to the east, but there are plenty of parking spots adjacent to the gates that divers can use when visiting this site. The total distance from Willemstad is approximately 1 mile (1.6 kilometers).

## Access

It is best to enter the water in the shallow lagoon close to the Freedom monument, located at the eastern end of John F. Kennedy Boulevard. Unfortunately for divers, the only way to get there is to walk through Park Lucha pa Libertat with their gear – a distance of just over 0.1 miles (200 meters). The lagoon is relatively protected from waves and currents, but there are a lot of rocks in the water, which can make entering and exiting challenging. The water shallows to a small berm that runs across the mouth of the lagoon, before dropping off again toward the sea. The current is usually mild at Double Reef but can be moderate to strong at times. Visibility is usually good. This site is suitable for divers of all experience levels.

## Description

Double Reef is a relatively deep dive site located between the *Superior Producer* wreck to the east and Fisherman's Wharf to the west. The site gets its name from the two reefs that are the central feature of the site: a shallow reef slope separated from a deep bank reef by a wide sand channel. Double Reef is known for its abundance of sea turtles, and divers often encounter both green sea turtles and hawksbills at this site, usually on the deeper, second reef.

Most divers descend to the bottom when they are approximately level with the breakwater in front of Corendon Mangrove Resort. The seabed here consists of scattered dome-shaped star and brain corals at a depth of around 12 feet (3.5 meters). Heading due south, divers will pass several car tires and a large square block of concrete on the bottom before the reef starts to descend to the wide sand channel that separates the shallow reef from its deeper counterpart.

A collection of debris consisting of old outboard engines, a street sign, pipes and a shopping cart with bottles, is located in the middle of the sand channel at a depth of around 80 feet (24.5 meters). The shoreward reef is patchy in nature and divers can often find giant anemones in this area. The

## DID YOU KNOW?

Park Lucha pa Libertat, or Fight for Freedom Park as it is known in English, was established to commemorate those involved in the Curaçao Slave Revolt of 1795. The leader, Tula Rigaud, often simply known as Tula, led a group of up to 50 enslaved people in a month-long revolt that began at the Knip plantation in the west of the island. The revolt progressively gained steam as the rebels moved south through Santa Cruz toward Willemstad, freeing additional slaves while en route. The uprising was eventually suppressed, and Tula was executed, along with numerous other slaves, including Bastian Karpata and Louis Mercier who are also commemorated in this park. Tula is still revered as a freedom fighter and champion of human rights in Curaçao today. He was tortured to death at this spot, on October 3rd, 1795. Slavery was not abolished in Curaçao until 1863 – almost 70 years after the initial slave revolt.

## FEATURED OPERATOR

**Soul Divers** is a small, full-service dive operation run by a friendly and knowledgeable Dutch couple. With their personalized approach, they ensure that scuba diving is a relaxing experience for every guest. Soul Divers organizes daily introduction dives and guided shore & boat trips. Diving at Curaçao's best dive sites, from east to west, including their personal favorite Double Reef. They also offer a wide range of dive courses for those who want to start their scuba adventure or for those who want to take their diving to the next level. Soul Divers is open seven days a week.

Tel: +599-9-664-8000
Email: info@soul-divers.com
Visit: **Soul-divers.com**

deeper reef contains a much higher density of corals and sponges. At its highest point, it rises up to about 65 feet (20 meters) before dropping to an extreme depth on its seaward side.

Fish life is also much denser and more diverse on the deeper seaward reef. Beyond the sea turtles that are often encountered here, divers may also see moray eels, parrotfish, snapper and large schools of creole wrasses. The sand channel that separates the two reefs is about 65 feet (20 meter) wide on average, but it widens and narrows in several places along its length. A white porcelain toilet is also located in the sand at around the midpoint of the site. Divers often find southern stingrays in this sandy area, as well as Queen conch and sand tilefish.

As divers head west, the deep reef flattens slightly and the shallow reef becomes increasingly patchy, until the two merge into a single reef slope dotted with large barrel sponges and tall pillar corals. A school of large tarpon is often found here. Farther west, the reef transitions to a small wall starting at about 65 feet (30 meters) depth. Just beyond this feature sits a bay with significant amounts of yellow pencil coral. The two pipes that mark the end of Double Reef and the start of Fisherman's Wharf are located here.

### Route

Divers enter the water at the eastern edge of the site and surface swim for the first couple of minutes until they are roughly adjacent to the breakwater in front of the Mangrove Beach Corendon Curaçao Resort. After descending to the bottom, divers should head roughly southward, down the reef slope toward the wide sandy plateau. Most divers explore the small artificial reef before following the sand channel

Sea turtles are often seen at Double Reef.

©NaturePicsFilms/Shutterstock

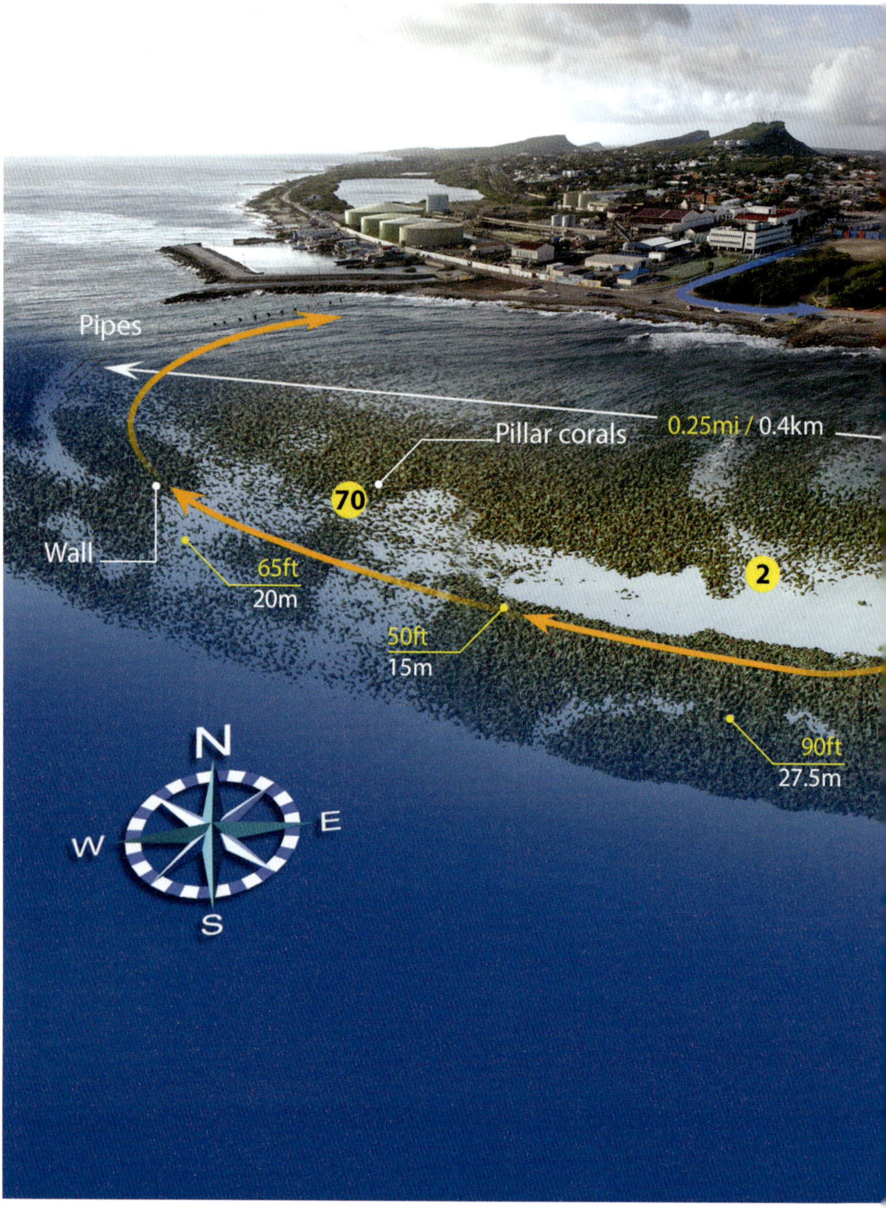


## SAFETY TIP

At Double Reef, hugging the bottom of the sandy plateau will produce a dive profile with a maximum depth of around 80 feet (24.5 meters). Most dive tables allow for a bottom time of only 30 minutes at this depth, which makes for a particularly short dive. Use of a dive computer will likely extend bottom time, especially in the latter stages of the dive, as the reef gradually shallows to the west. In the first half of the dive, where the reef is deepest, divers may want to consider hovering 10 to 15 feet (3 to 4.5 meters) above the habitat to extend their bottom time and get the most out of their dive.

west, checking out both the deep reef and the sand plateau.

The route gradually shallows toward the western end of the site. Most divers return to shore soon after the shallow and deeper reefs merge. Divers with good air consumption may reach the pipes that mark the start of the Fisherman's Wharf dive site, however. While currents generally move in a westerly direction at this site, they are often weaker at depth. If a current does exist, divers can use it to enjoy a drift dive that could take them all the way through both Double Reef and into Fisherman's Wharf, when conditions allow.

## DID YOU KNOW?

Several wrecks are located in the Willemstad area in addition to the *Superior Producer*. The two most prominent of these wrecks include the *Alphen* and the *Mediator*. What remains of these wrecks lies in the deep, low-visibility channel known as Sint Annabaai, which is not open to diving or snorkeling. The *Alphen* was a Dutch naval frigate commissioned in 1763. She spent a decade patrolling the Mediterranean before moving into the Caribbean. While at anchor in Sint Annabaai in September 1778, she exploded when her powder stores ignited, blowing the ship apart and killing 205 of her crew.

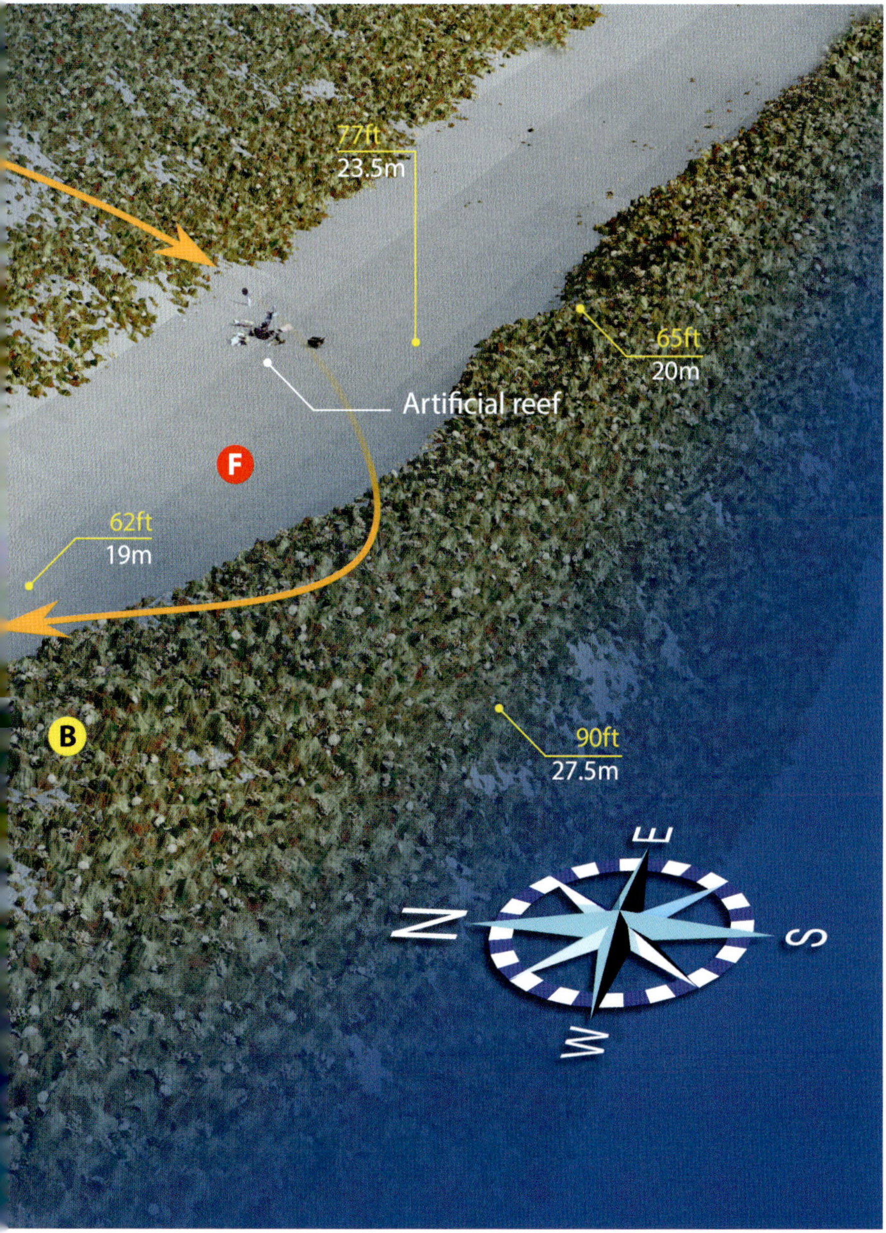


*SS Mediator* was a passenger steamship constructed in Liverpool in 1872. For four years, she carried passengers and goods between England and India under the name *Dahlia*. She was sold to new owners in 1876 and her name was changed to *Mediator*, and she soon started to sail to the Caribbean. In July 1884, while at anchor in Sint Annabaai, she was stuck by the German steamer *Thuringia* and sank slowly enough that everyone on board could be evacuated and some of the cargo salvaged.

# SUPERIOR PRODUCER

Difficulty ● ● ●
Current ● ● ●
Depth ● ● ●
Reef ★★★
Fauna ★★★

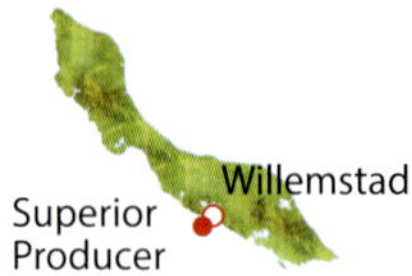


Access about 2 mins from Willemstad
Access about 4 mins from Willemstad
Access about 3 mins from shore

**Level** Advanced

## Location

Otrobanda, Curaçao
GPS 12°06.288'N, 68°56.653'W (wreck)
12°06.352'N, 68°56.672'W
(service pier access point)

## Getting there

Head south on Baden Powellweg from the Otrobanda neighborhood of Willemstad. Turn right onto Gouverneur van Slobbeweg and take the first left at the security kiosk for the port. Divers must register with port authority security before diving the *Superior Producer* from shore and are required to leave behind official ID, usually a driver's license or passport, which they can pick up again after the dive. Once cleared by security, divers must drive to the farthest cruise ship pier to the west. There is usually plenty of parking available since this site is only diveable when there are no cruise ships at the terminal. The total distance from Willemstad is approximately 0.6 miles (1 kilometer).

## Access

*Superior Producer* lies between the two cruise ship piers, about 510 feet (155 meters) from shore. The wreck is much closer to the western pier, so divers tend to enter the water from here, even though reaching the wreck from here usually requires swimming into the current for a few minutes. Divers usually set up their gear at their vehicle. After walking onto the main pier, divers will notice a small service pier to the right, less than 150 feet (45 meters) from shore. This service pier has a ladder at the end that provides easy access to the water. Alternatively, experienced divers can use a giant stride-entry from the pier into the water.

Once in the water, move rapidly away from the pier structure. There is often current and swell in this location, so it is advisable to pass beneath the pier and head in the direction of the wreck as rapidly as possible. Divers should take a bearing that is slightly east of south, or approximately 160 degrees. A heading of due south may result in divers missing the wreck if the current is strong.

It is only permitted to dive the *Superior Producer* when there are no vessels docked at either of the two mega pier ships terminals. This occurs only on about seven days each month, so be sure to check the schedule on the Curaçao Ports Authority website, visit: **Curports.com** and click on the cruise ships tab, to plan your visit to Curaçao's most famous wreck. For more information, contact the Curaçao Ports Authority on Tel. (5999) 434 5999 or email **info@curports.com.** This dive is suitable for advanced divers only.

## Description

*MV Superior Producer* is one of the most popular dive sites in Curaçao, not to mention one of the most famous. This wreck is also regarded as one of the premier wreck dives in the Caribbean because of its simple shore-accessibility, incredible coral growth and colorful history.

*Superior Producer* was a cargo ship constructed in the Netherlands in 1957. She was originally named *MV Andromeda* and was based out of Rotterdam. She changed ownership in 1962 and her name was changed to *Superior Producer*. In 1971, she changed ownership again, as well as location, moving across the Atlantic to Panama City. She changed hands one more time, several years later, in 1973 to new Panamanian owners.

On the morning of September 30, 1977, *Superior Producer* was docked at Sint Annabaai in Willemstad. She was considerably overloaded with a mix of consumer goods bound for retailers in the Venezuelan island of Margarita for the upcoming Christmas shopping season. The weather had started to turn, causing increasingly rough seas that shifted the cargo inside to ship, unbalancing the entire vessel. The ship started to list. A crewmember allegedly left a porthole open, which exacerbated the situation. Frantic attempts were made to stabilize the ship, but it was to no avail. It was clear that the *Superior Producer* could not be saved, so she was moved away from the shore to her current position and allowed to sink. *Superior Producer* settled upright on the mostly sandy seabed at a depth of 110 feet (33.5 meters) with her bow facing west.

**SAFETY TIP**

Entering the water adjacent to the cruise ship pier can be challenging, particularly if there is swell. The drop from the main pier is dangerously high, so always enter from the lower service pier. The ladder can be slippery when wet, especially for divers carrying gear, so take your time, moving one rung at a time, and always maintain several points of contact. Divers using a stride-entry from the pier should first make sure their equipment is streamlined before entering the water. Snagging a regulator or console on the pier as you jump can caused serious injury, not to mention equipment damage. Only experienced divers should attempt this. While the depth of the water is fine for a stride entry, try to time your entry so that you land on the peak of a wave in order to minimize the distance of the jump. Once in the water, move rapidly away from the pier so you are not pushed into the structure by a rogue wave.

Divers explore one of Curaçao's most iconic dive sites: *Superior Producer*.

Turtle & Ray©

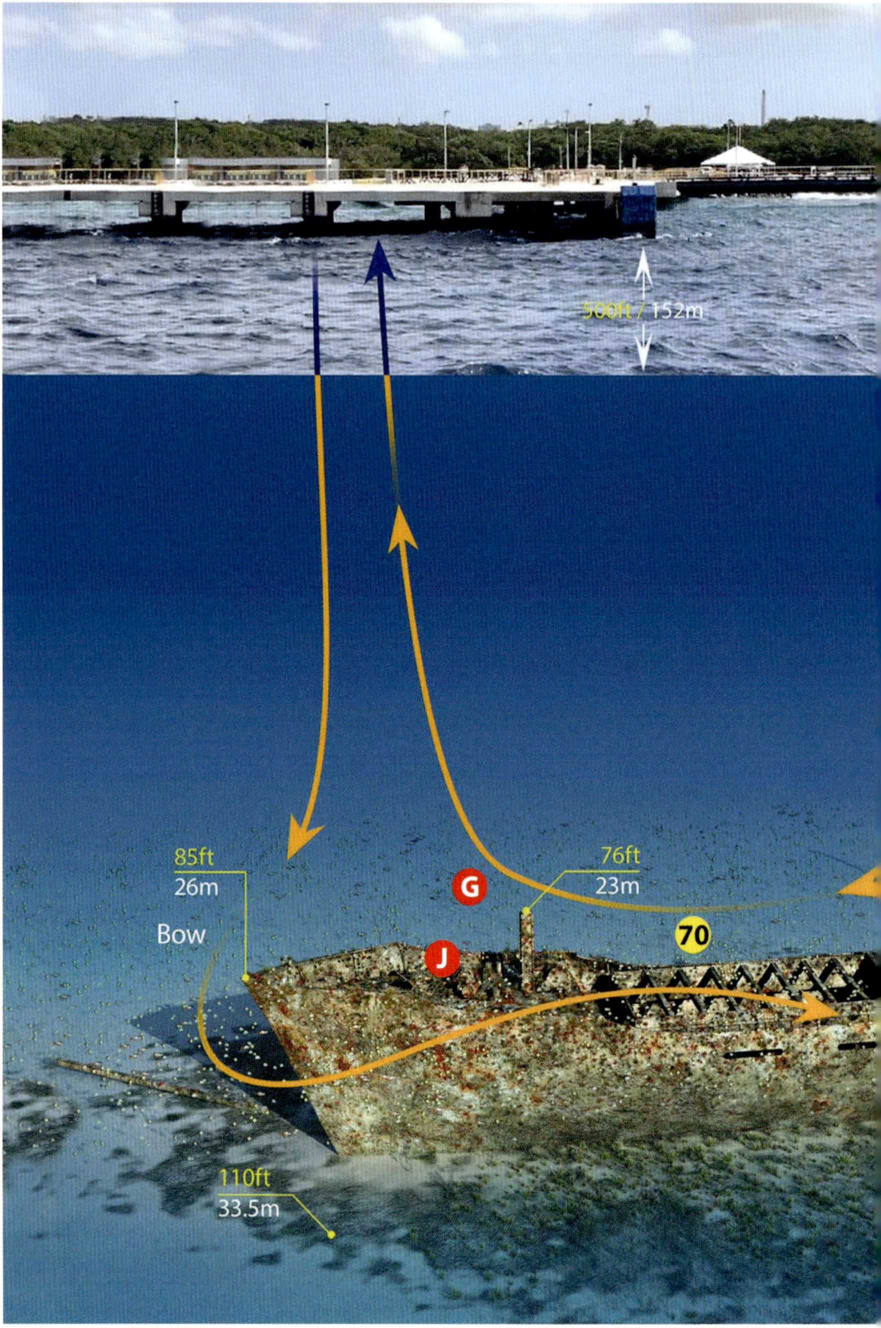


In the days after the ship sunk, her cargo was ransacked by divers brave enough to enter the cargo bays of the unstable wreck. Divers surfaced with all manner of loot, ranging from bottles of whiskey and perfume to clothing, shoes and handbags. According to some sources, dozens of Dallas Cowboys football shirts were on board the wreck when it sank, and for a period of time after the wreck went down, many locals could be found walking the streets wearing these shirts.

Today, *Superior Producer* is a stunning artificial reef with only minor damage, including a bent starboard railing near the stern and a loading mast

**Name:** *MV Superior Producer*
**Type:** cargo freighter
**Previous names:** *MV Andromeda*
**Length:** 165 ft (50.3m)
**Tonnage:** 400 grt
**Construction:** Kootstertille, Netherlands (1957)
**Last owner:** Pan-Ven Line Sa, Panama City
**Sunk:** September 30, 1977

that lies askew the wreck, crossing the aft hold and angling down to touch the sand off the port side. The wreck is covered in corals and sponges, including deepwater sea fans, sea whips, tube sponges and orange cup corals. The wreck has open and accessible cargo bays where divers can explore. Tarpon and barracuda are common on the wreck, as well as various species of snapper and jack. Caribbean spiny lobsters are often found in the hold. Parrotfish, French and Queen angelfish and scorpionfish are commonly seen around deck level, and a large green moray eel is often found around the winch near the bow. Sea turtles are also frequent visitors to the wreck.

## Route

Divers following the access directions mentioned earlier usually arrive at the *Superior Producer*'s

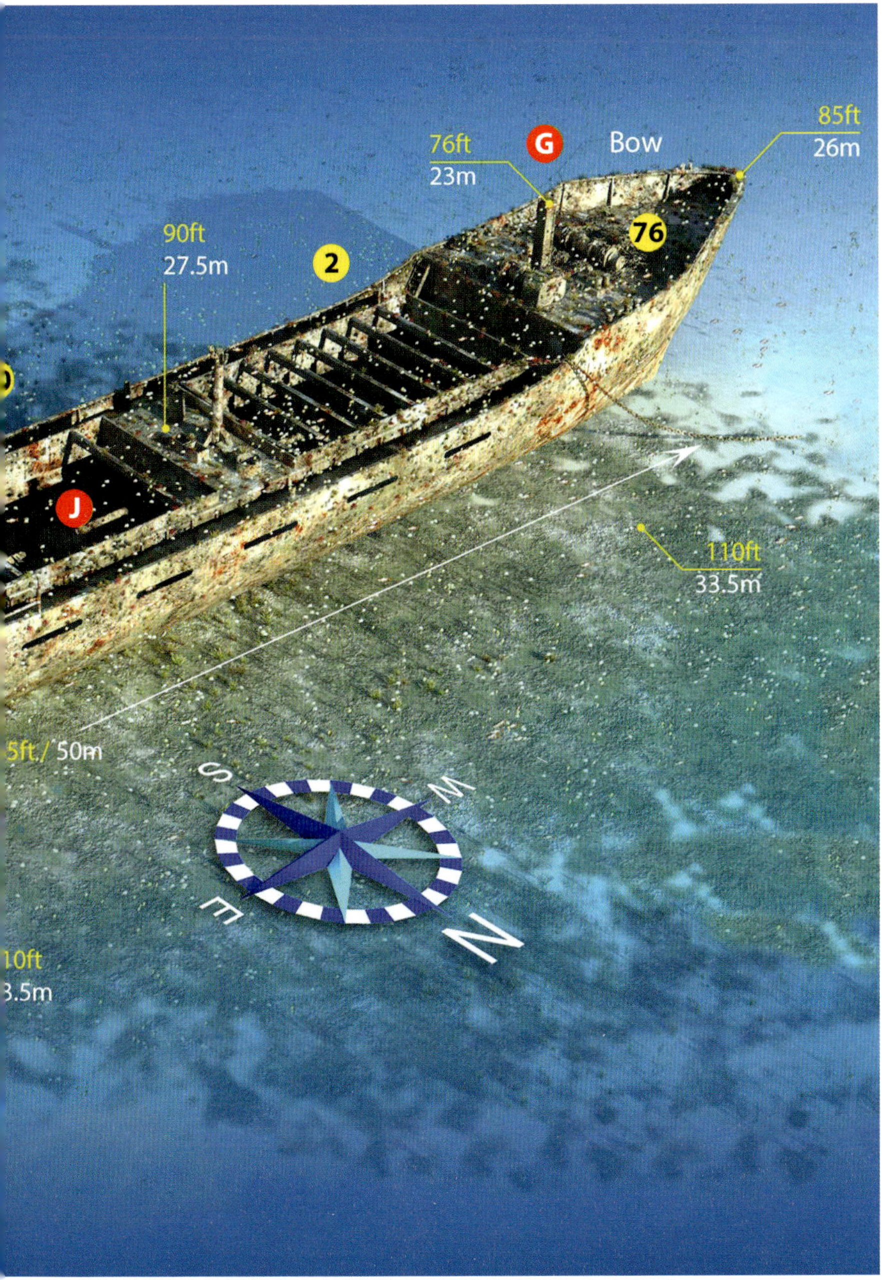


bow, which is a decent spot to start exploring the wreck. Unless visibility is very poor, the wreck should be visible before leaving the reef slope adjacent to the pier.

Most divers like to check out the open holds initially, as they represent the deepest part of the wreck. Due to entanglement risks, most local operators do not endorse divers entering any part of the ship aside from the hold, regardless of certification and experience. From there, divers usually transition to the superstructure in the stern area of the ship, which rises to around 75 feet (23 meters) in depth – the shallowest part of the site. It is important that shore divers leave plenty of air to return to the jetty and complete their safety stop exploring the reef at the base of the pylons before exiting the water.

# 56 TARPON CITY

| | |
|---|---|
| Difficulty | ●●● |
| Current | ●●○ |
| Depth | ●●○ |
| Reef | ★☆☆ |
| Fauna | ★★☆ |

Access (boat) about 0 mins from Willemstad
Access (car) about 3 mins from Willemstad
Access (swim) about 3 mins from shore

**Level** Advanced

## Location

Punda, Curaçao
GPS 12°06.177'N, 68°55.945'W

## Getting there

Head into Willemstad on Abraham Mendez Chumaceiro Boulevard. Loop around Waaigat, turning left on Theaterstraat and then right on Pietermaai. A large parking lot used to be located adjacent to this beach-accessible site, but recent coastal development in the area has made it challenging to access. Divers and snorkelers should still be able to find plenty of paid street parking near the beach.

## Access

The south facing Punda Beach Curaçao, also known as Playa De Los Venezolanos, is the best way to access Tarpon City. The Marichi Pier, which extends from the shore before cutting west, provides protection from the waves and currents, making it easy to get in and out of the water here. Divers and snorkelers should enter the water as close to the jetty as possible to avoid stepping on

**SAFETY TIP**

The swim out to see the tarpon usually involves swimming with the prevailing current. It is therefore important that divers conserve enough air to return to the beach while swimming against the current. This can be challenging if the current is strong, so it is recommended that divers assess the current carefully before committing to the dive. Do not be afraid to abort the dive if the current is too strong.

the rubble and reef area that runs along shore at northwestern side of the beach. A small channel, approximately 70 feet (21 meters) wide, runs due west between the beach and the jetty, providing access to the reef. The current is usually moderate at Tarpon City and visibility can become poor – these conditions make this site better suited to advanced divers and snorkelers.

## Description

Tarpon City is a shore-accessible dive and snorkel site located in the Punda neighborhood of Willemstad, which is why it is also sometimes referred to as Punda. The site is also sometimes referred to as Waterfort, which was a military fort that once existed adjacent to shore and is now home to the Plaza Hotel Curaçao. This site is famous for the school of tarpon that are often found here, sometimes numbering as many as two dozen individuals. The steep reef slope starts only 200 feet (61 meters) from shore and runs due west to the Sint Annabaai channel. Divers and snorkelers are not permitted to pass the channel marker. The entire dive site is therefore only about 1,300 feet (396 meters) in length. The tarpon are often found on the reef around 20 minutes into the dive, or a distance of less than 1,000 feet (300 meters) from the beach, at a depth of around 40 feet (12 meters). Divers and snorkelers may also find barracuda, porcupinefish, angelfish and parrotfish at this site.

# 57 DIVE CITY

Difficulty ●●○
Current ●●○
Depth ●●○
Reef ★★☆
Fauna ★★☆

Access (boat) about 3 mins from Willemstad
Access (car) about 3 mins from Willemstad
Access (swim) about 3 mins from shore

**Level** Open Water

**Location**
Punda, Curaçao
GPS 12°06.110’N, 68°55.62’W

### Getting there

Head into Willemstad on Abraham Mendez Chumaceiro Boulevard. Loop around Waaigat and turn left onto Johan van Walbeeckplein, followed by a right on Plasa Smeets and a left onto Kaya Wilson Godett. The public access to the dive and snorkel site is located on the right side of the road after an additional 50 feet (15 meters). Street parking is available throughout this neighborhood of Willemstad.

### Access

The access point is via a small, gently sloping rubble beach that is only about 50 feet (15 meters) across. The beach sits to the east of a wall/breakwater that houses a pipe. The breakwater only extends out a few feet from shore before submerging beneath the surface, so it offers little in the way of protection from waves or surge. Divers and snorkelers can expect to get pushed around as they enter and exit the water at this site, making boots essential. The current is usually mild to moderate at Dive City and visibility is usually decent. This site is suitable for all divers and snorkelers, except when the current is strong and the surface of the water is choppy.

### Description

Dive City is a shore-accessible dive and snorkel site located adjacent to Dive Center Pietermaai. The site is also known as Dive Center Pietermaai House Reef. The stone wall/breakwater that sits adjacent to the beach continues along the seabed and down the reef slope to a depth of approximately 50 feet (15 meters). Here the wall stops abruptly, but the pipe contained within continues down the slope to a depth of approximately 75 feet (23 meters). The upper part of the wall/breakwater is dominated by fire coral, but transitions to larger brain corals in deeper water.

The main focus of this dive site lies to the southeast of this pipe. The reef slope descends steeply from the sandy plateau adjacent to the beach, featuring large patches of pencil corals as well as a high density of brain corals. The slope here is steeper than it is to the west of the pipe, and it is broken up by narrow sand channels that run down its face.

Continuing to the southeast, the reef slope eventually gives way to a short wall that projects out from the slope, bottoming out in a curved sand patch. Continuing along the slope, divers will come across a second wall with lots of small ledges and associated undercuts, followed by a third, smaller wall. The walls bottom out at an average depth of around 70 feet, where the reef slope resumes, this time featuring mostly sand and rubble habitat that descends into the depths.

To the west of the pipe, the reef slope is attractive but relatively featureless. The reef slopes less steeply here than in the opposite direction, and it features a greater number of sand patches on its slope and a higher density of soft corals.

Meanwhile, the back reef plateau extends roughly 260 feet (80 meters) from the beach and makes for an interesting area of exploration for most snorkelers, as well as divers who wish to extend their bottom time at the end of a dive. The area is mostly sand, rubble and patch reef, but there are interesting features to explore, such as the large elkhorn coral that sits in a sandy patch in shallow water near the wall/breakwater. At a depth of between just 20 and 30 feet (6 and 9 meters), this plateau gets a lot of light and is shallow enough for most snorkelers. Divers and snorkelers should be aware that there is a decent amount of boat traffic along the coast here, so the use of a surface marker buoy (SMB) is recommended.

Dive City hosts plenty of fish life, including lots of sergeant majors, Spanish hogfish, chromis, butterflyfish, parrotfish and squirrelfish. Keen-eyed observers will also be able to find trunkfish, trumpetfish and filefish hiding within

## FEATURED OPERATOR

**Dive Center Pietermaai,** located in the historic Pietermaai District of Willemstad, is a PADI 5-Star IDC Dive Resort. Their highly skilled and multilingual dive staff provide a range of training and guiding options from beginner to professional level. With their Scuba Bus, they are able to access the best shore diving spots around the island, even the beautiful beaches and reefs of West Punt. They also offer night dives, lionfish hunt dives and snorkeling trips.

Tel: +1 599-9-699-8877
Email: diving@scubalodge.com
Visit: **Divecenterpietermaai.com**

the soft corals at this site. Bar jacks, mahogany snapper and schoolmaster snapper are also quite common.

### Route

Divers and snorkelers can head in either direction on this reef, but the area to the southeast of the pipe is generally considered to have the more interesting habitat to explore, with its steeper reef and undercut areas. Exploring in this direction generally involves swimming into the prevailing current, which also makes this direction the safest route. At the southeastern end of the site, the reef slope curves back toward shore with a heavy undercut at its base. This marks a good spot to turn around and head back to the beach, gradually shallowing and exploring the sandy back reef plateau at the end of the dive.

Schooling creole wrasses are common at Dive City.

Turtle & Ray©

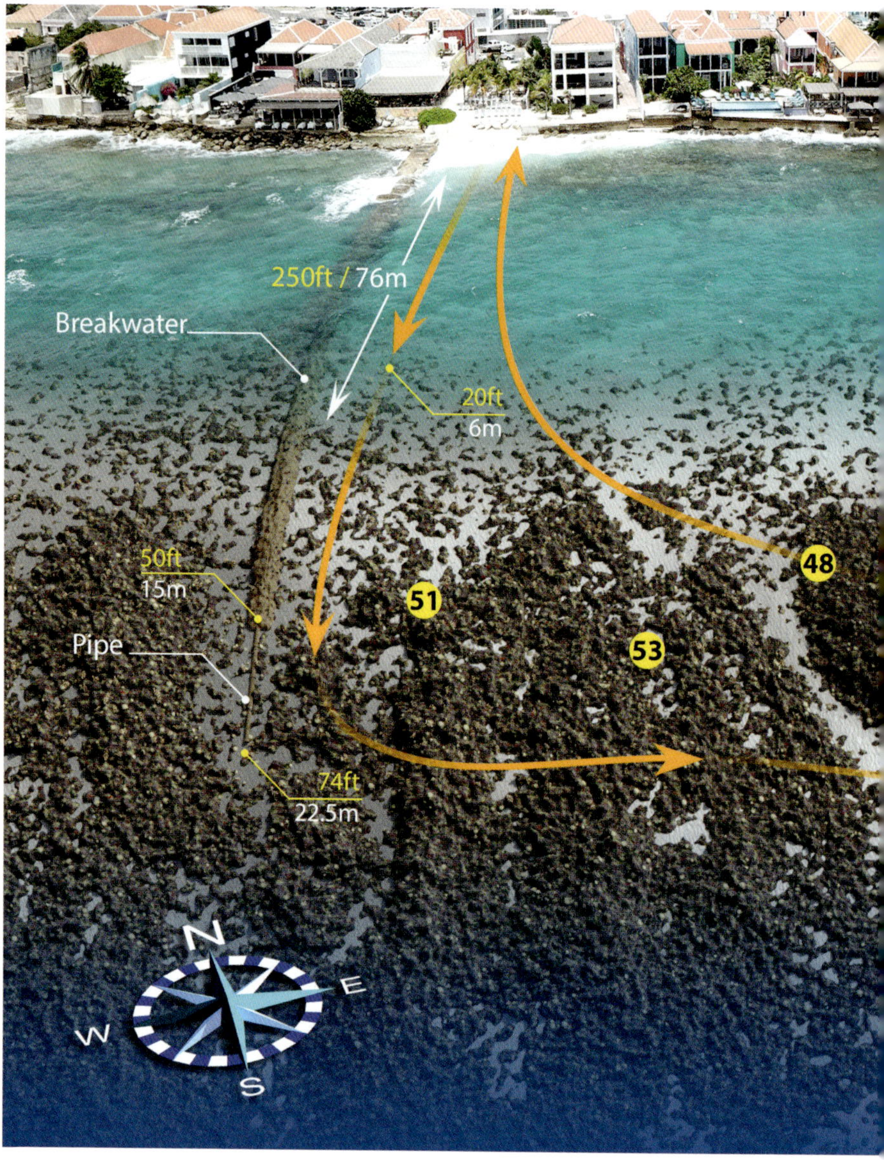


## RELAX & RECHARGE

**La Boheme** is a family-run restaurant in downtown Willemstad. This restaurant specializes in arepas – a South American dish that originates in the region now occupied by Columbia, Panama and Venezuela. It consists of ground maize dough stuffed with a filling. At La Boheme, the filling ranges from beef tenderloin to chicken curry to tuna and surimi salad, among others. As most arepas cost less than $5 USD, you can try many different types, all of which are delicious. There are also salads, sandwiches, wraps and a selection of desserts. To wash down these South American delicacies, there is a range of fruit smoothies, as well as beers, mocktails and cocktails, including a mango mojito, a Punda's punch with homemade strawberry syrup and of course, the classic Curaçao Blue Lagoon. La Boheme is also open for breakfast.
Visit: **Labohemecuracao.net**

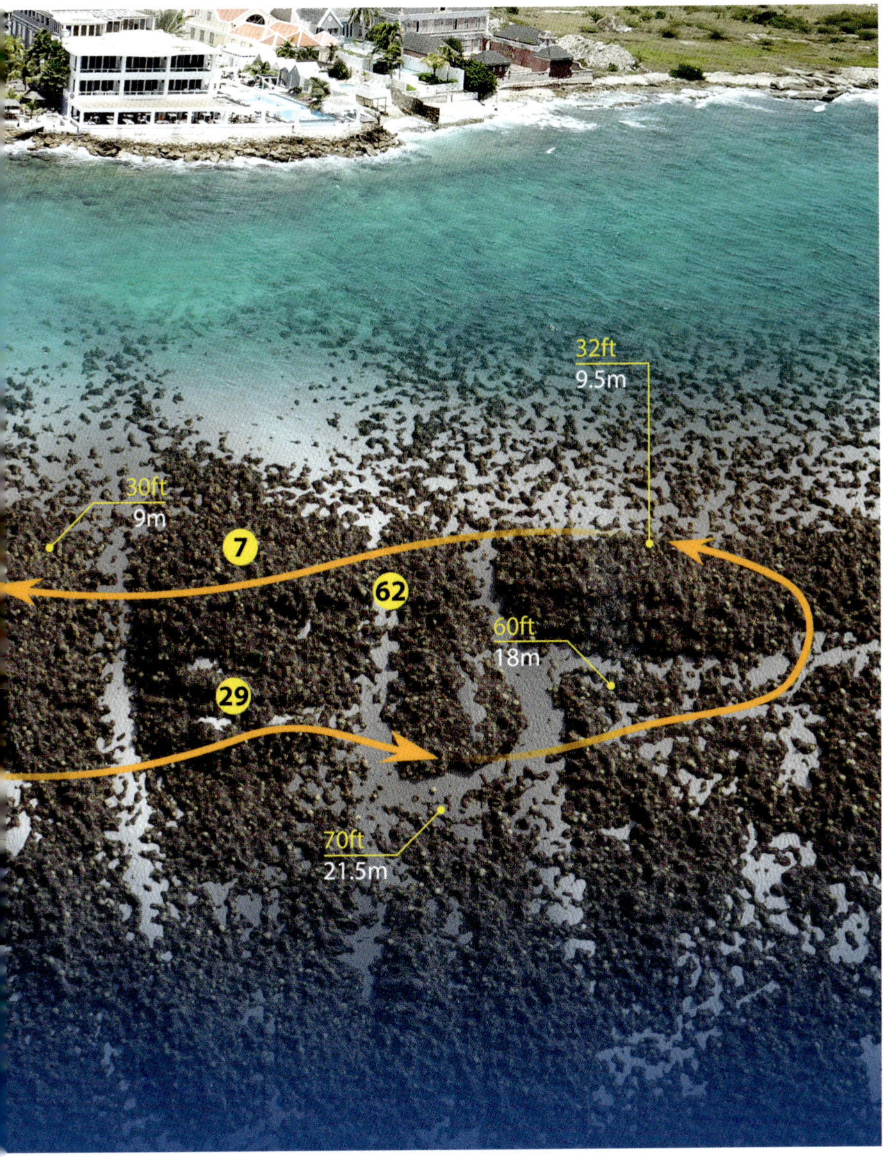


## RELAX & RECHARGE

**De Heeren at Sea** is a popular restaurant with a great atmosphere, located in Scuba Lodge, just steps from Dive City. The terrace has wonderful ocean views and fantastic food and service. The lunchtime menu has a range of options, including delicious paninis and sandwiches, including a salmon wrap, crisp pork belly sandwich and tenderloin carpaccio. For dinner, there are salads, burgers, schnitzel, steaks, fish, and even Thai green curry. Their pasta options are particularly popular, especially the truffle beef fettuccine and the seafood pasta, which includes lots of local fish, clams, shrimps and mussels. Happy hour is daily from 5 to 7pm – the perfect time to enjoy a nice cool drink while watching the sun slowly sink into the tropical ocean.

Visit: **Deheerencuracao.com**

# BOCA SIMON

Difficulty ●●○
Current ●●○
Depth ●●○
Reef ★★☆
Fauna ★★☆

Access (boat) about 6 mins from Willemstad
Access (car) about 2 mins from Willemstad
Access (swim) about 2 mins from shore



**Level** Open Water

## Location

Willemstad, Curaçao
GPS 12°05.792'N, 68°54.905'W

## Getting there

Leave Willemstad on Penstraat, which becomes Dr. Martin Luther King Boulevard. After a drive of about 0.8 miles (1.3 kilometers), turn right onto Scheveningenstraat. The Boca Simon dive and snorkel site is located at the end of the road, which is only 130 feet (40 meters) in length. The total distance from Willemstad is approximately 0.8 miles (1.3 kilometers).

## Access

Boca Simon is a small beach located close to the main road. A stone jetty curls around the beach on the southeast side of the site, providing protection from waves and currents. The beach is a mix of sand and rock, so boots are recommended. The current is usually mild and the visibility is usually good. This site is suitable for divers and snorkelers of all experience levels.

## Description

Boca Simon is not an official Curaçao dive site, but like its neighbor to the southeast, it is considered a real hidden gem in Curaçao's busy southern Willemstad area. Divers and snorkelers can explore to the left or right of this site, with both directions featuring plenty of healthy reef to explore. The reef slope at both Boca Simon and Atlantis is very similar, with a dense mix of corals and sponges. Hamlets, grunts, butterflyfish and parrotfish can be found on the reef. Brown and blue chromis fill the water column above the reef and large patches of garden eels can be found in the sand at the bottom of the reef and the back reef plateau. A popular option for visiting both these sites is for divers and snorkelers to swim between the two, usually with the prevailing currents, which tends to flow from Atlantis to Boca Simon – a distance of approximately 1,200 feet (366 meters). Navigation skills are essential for this.

# ATLANTIS

Difficulty ●●○
Current ●●○
Depth ●●○
Reef ★★☆
Fauna ★★☆

Access (boat): about 7 mins from Willemstad
Access (car): about 4 mins from Willemstad
Access (swim): about 2 mins from shore

**Level** Open Water

## Location

Willemstad, Curaçao
GPS 12°05.702'N, 68°54.748'W

## Getting there

Leave Willemstad on Penstraat, which becomes Dr. Martin Luther King Boulevard. After a drive of about 1 mile (1.6 kilometers), turn right onto Drielstraat. The Atlantis dive and snorkel site is located at the end of the road. It is best to park close to Dr. Martin Luther King Boulevard and walk the approximately 350 feet (107 meters) distance to the shore. The total distance from Willemstad is approximately 1.1 miles (1.7 kilometers).

## Access

Like its neighbor to the northwest, Atlantis has a simple public access point, which involves wading out from a small well-protected beach, just steps from the access road. The shoreline berm occupied by Baoase Luxury Resort Curaçao extends into the water by about 300 feet (91 meters) immediately to the southeast providing a nice calm environment for divers and snorkelers to enter the water. The beach is a mix of sand and rock, so boots are recommended. The current is usually mild at this site and the visibility is usually good. This site is suitable for divers and snorkelers of all experience levels.

## Description

Atlantis is not an official Curaçao dive site, but like its neighbor to the northwest, it is considered a real hidden gem in Curaçao's busy southern Willemstad area. Divers and snorkelers can explore to the left or right of this site, with both directions featuring plenty of healthy reef to explore. The reef juts outwards slightly to the southeast, in front of the Baoase Luxury Resort Curaçao. This results in a sandy plateau in the shallows with an average depth of around 20 feet (6 meters). This is a decent spot for snorkelers to find soft corals with trumpetfish and slender filefish in their branches, as well as anemones and their symbiotic shrimp and goldentail morays.

The reef slope at both Atlantis and Boca Simon is very similar, with a dense mix of corals and sponges. Small parrotfishes, such as princess and redband parrotfish, are extremely common, as are butterflyfishes, angelfishes and surgeonfishes. Brown and blue chromis fill the water column above the reef and large patches of garden eels can be found in the sand at the bottom of the reef and the back reef plateau. A popular option for visiting both these sites is for divers and snorkelers to swim between the two, usually with the prevailing currents, which tends to flow from Atlantis to Boca Simon – a distance of approximately 1,200 feet (366 meters). Navigation skills are essential for this.

### DID YOU KNOW?

About a mile or so inland from these dive and snorkel sites is a former plantation known as Landhuis Chobolobo. This site is now home to the Curaçao Liqueur Distillery, which creates the world-famous Blue Curaçao Liqueur. The drink is flavored with the dried peel of the bitter orange fruit known as laraha. Spanish explorers introduced the bitter Seville orange to the island in the 1500s and it is believed that this fruit was the progenitor of the laraha.

# PIERBAAI & CAR PILE (PLAYA MARIE PAMPOEN)

Difficulty ●●○
Current ●○○
Depth ●●● (Car Pile)
Reef ★★★
Fauna ★★★

Access (boat) about 10 mins from Willemstad
Access (car) about 6 mins from Willemstad
Access (swim) about 4 mins from shore

**Level** Open Water (Pierbaai)
Advanced (Car Pile)

## Location

Marie Pampoen, Curaçao
GPS 12°05.422'N, 68°54.283'W

## Getting there

Leave Willemstad on Penstraat, which becomes Dr. Martin Luther King Boulevard. After a drive of about 1.6 mile (2.7 kilometers), pull off to the right side of the road into a small gravel parking lot located just before the Sunscape Curaçao, Resort, Spa & Casino. This is the public beach access for Playa Marie Pampoen, which lies just the other side of the restaurants. The total distance from Willemstad is approximately 1.6 miles (2.7 kilometers).

## Access

Pierbaai & Car Pile is located adjacent to Playa Marie Pampoen. This beach is sheltered by several breakwaters, which produce calm water within this small bay even on the windiest day. This coupled with the free access, public showers, and gently sloping sandy beach to the water, are just some of the reasons that this dive and snorkel spot is so popular. The other reasons all lie beneath the surface. The Marie Pampoen Jetty is the large curved structure that loops around the beach. The jetty has a finished concrete walkway on top and a wooden platform located on the shoreward side toward the end. Divers and snorkelers can enter the water on either side of this structure, either at the main beach adjacent to the restaurants, or on the other side, next to the wall that runs down the eastern side of the site. Seaward of the breakwater, the current at this site is usually mild to moderate and the visibility is usually exceptional. This site is suitable for divers and snorkelers of all experience levels, although divers who wish to visit the car wrecks should only do so if they have advanced certifications due to their depth.

## Description

Pierbaai & Car Pile is also known as Playa Marie Pampoen because of the beach where the site is located. This is an incredibly popular spot, located just south of Willemstad and surrounded by numerous dive operators. The site is also sometimes called Dive Bus House Reef – the dive operator located literally across the street who adopted this dive site from PADI's Project AWARE Adopt a Dive Site Program.

Part of this site is known as Car Pile because of the presence of a barge and numerous car wrecks scattered along the reef. The barge, which has a collapsed crane on top and other assorted beams, is located at a depth of just over 100 feet (30 meters). The cars, some of which date back to the 1940s, can be found scattered around the barge at a depth of around 120 feet (37 meters) and deeper. Very little remains of the cars apart from their chassis and engine blocks.

## RELAX & RECHARGE

**Seaside Terrace** is located right on the water's edge at Playa Marie Pampoen. It has been serving up delicious seafood for 30 years, so you know you are getting quality when you visit this unique establishment. The restaurant is small and wide open – most of it is outdoors – so you can see the food being expertly prepared before your eyes and savor the delicious aromas as you enjoy an ice-cold beer with your feet in the sand. There is a wide selection of fresh fish, including red snapper, mahi mahi and lionfish, as well as conch, shrimp and lobster. Those who simply can't decide, can order the seafood mix deluxe, which includes a pretty much everything. There is chicken and beef, and a vegetarian dish, for those who desire a land-based option.
Visit: **Facebook.com/seasideterracecuracao**

Dozens of beams and other metal debris can be found strewn down the reef slope at the western end of the site, starting at a depth of approximately 50 feet (17 meters), and continuing to the bottom of the reef slope. These artificial reef structures were deployed in the 1960s and are now heavily encrusted with corals and sponges. A coral restoration project managed by Reef Renewal Curaçao lies just beyond the reef to the west. Divers should consider checking out the coral trees on their way back to shore.

The reef at Marie Pampoen starts to slope downwards at about 350 feet (107 meters) from shore. There is plenty of dense coral cover in the shallows, including elkhorn, staghorn, fire coral, lettuce coral and yellow pencil corals. Meanwhile, divers will see large tube sponges, soft corals and brain and star corals in the deeper parts of the reef.

Divers and snorkelers can find yellowtail snapper, schoolmaster snapper, rainbow parrotfish and large tarpon on this reef. On the substrate, stingrays, scorpionfish and flying gurnards are often present, as well as moray eels. Pierbaai is also an excellent spot for night dives given its easy access and well-lit shoreline.

### Route

Divers and snorkelers usually access this site from the public beach at its western end

The car wrecks at Pierbaai are a wonder to explore.

Sascha Caballero/Shutterstock©

# PIERBAAI & CAR PILE (PLAYA MARIE PAMPOEN)

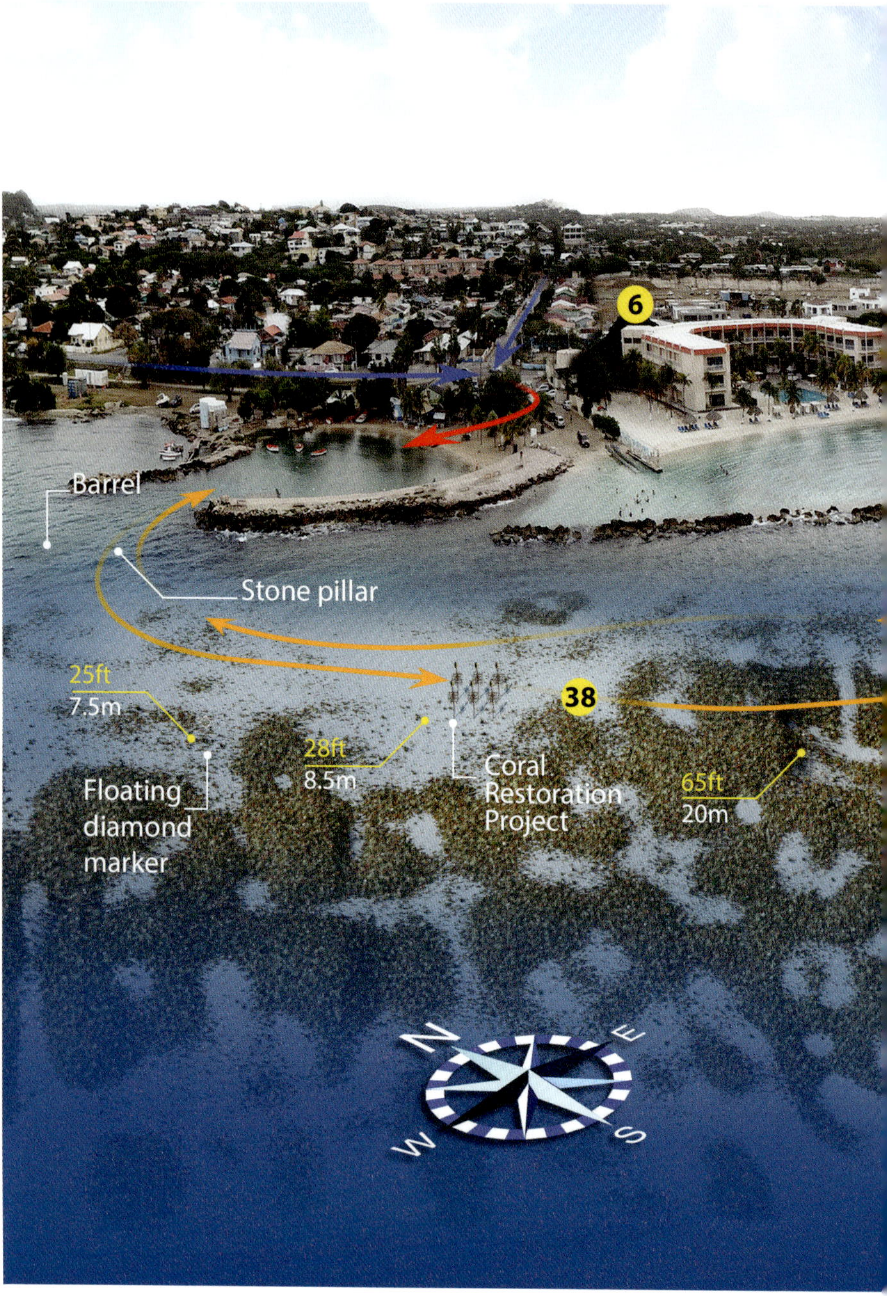


## SAFETY TIP

It is easy to get carried away while exploring all the features of Pierbaai & Car Pile. So it is very important to keep a close eye on your depth if you head down to the car wrecks at the bottom of the reef. The reef slopes gradually in this area and it is possible to drop into water that is deeper than anticipated.

before heading out on either side of the paved breakwater. Those visiting the barge and car wrecks should do so at the beginning of the dive, heading east and dropping deep, before circling back toward the west. There is plenty of opportunity to regain bottom time while exploring the stunning back reef, with its delicate branching corals and coral restoration project.

**DID YOU KNOW?**

This site can also be explored by drift diving or snorkeling from the adjacent site known as Oswaldo's Drop Off (page 192), which features reefs that are just as healthy as at Marie Pampoen. There will not be enough bottom time to explore the barge and car wrecks when accessing the site from this side, but there are numerous other structures worth exploring in the shallower areas of the reef, including large metal beams and

a car wreck located shallower than the rest at 55 feet (17 meters). Playa Marie Pampoen is the best place to exit, so divers should use the coral restoration project as a landmark to indicate when to turn north to head into the beach.

# OSWALDO'S DROP OFF

Difficulty ●●○
Current ●●○
Depth ●●○
Reef ★★★
Fauna ★★★

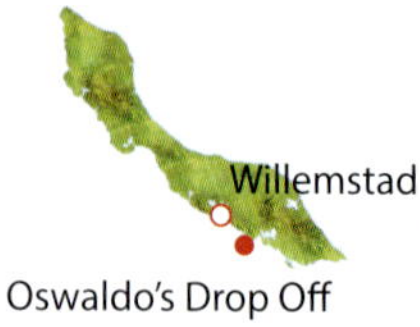


Access (boat) about 11 mins from Willemstad
Access (car) about 6 mins from Willemstad
Access (swim) about 2 mins from shore

**Level** Open Water

## Location

Marie Pampoen, Curaçao
GPS 12°05.250'N, 68°54.142'W

## Getting there

Leave Willemstad on Penstraat, which becomes Dr. Martin Luther King Boulevard. Pass Playa Marie Pampeon and enter the Sunscape Curaçao Resort, Spa & Casino, located 0.2 miles (0.3 kilometers) beyond Playa Marie Pampoen. The total distance from Willemstad to Sunscape Curaçao Resort, Spa & Casino is 2.1 miles (3.4 kilometers).

## Access

Ocean Encounters at Sunscape Curaçao Resort, Spa & Casino is the only safe way to access Oswaldo's Drop Off. Divers and snorkelers should enter the resort, purchase a resort pass if desired, and walk to the dive center located at the southeastern end of the site. Divers and snorkelers can enter the water via the beach or the jetty located next to the dive center, and then head out through the channel to the dive site, which represents a distance of about 200 feet (61 meters). The current is usually mild to moderate at this site but can become strong at times. Visibility is usually good. This site is suitable for divers and snorkelers of all experience levels.

## Description

Oswaldo's Drop Off was named after a local diver who popularized diving and snorkeling at this site. The site is also referred to by some as the Sunscape House Reef and Kon Tiki Beach Reef after the nearby resorts, and Breezes and Princess Beach, which reference resorts that were previously located at this site.

The site has a narrow back reef that extends just 100 feet (30 meters) from the breakwater that runs in both directions at this site. The reef slope is populated by large fields of yellow pencil corals close to the mouth of the southeastern channel, as well as dome-shaped star corals and blade fire corals. Some of the most complex and diverse habitat can be found within a depth range of 30 to 70 feet (9 to 21.5 meters).

Divers who head west out of the channel may encounter a traffic sign anchored in the reef at a depth of about 40 feet (12 meters). It points the way down the reef slope toward the adjacent site of Car Pile (page 186), and it is often surrounded by schools of chromis and creole wrasses. The reef continues to slope to a depth of over 100 feet (30.5 meters), where it transitions to sand and rubble.

Schools of grunts are common at this site, often mixed with mahogany and schoolmaster snapper. Large parrotfish species, including stoplight and rainbow parrotfish, dart through the site. Honeycomb cowfish are one of the rarer fish that seem to be common at this site, along with rock beauties and yellowtail hamlets. Black durgon, bar jacks and Bermuda chub are often present above the reef. Chain morays can be found in the deeper parts of the reef.

## Route

From the Sunscape Resort divers usually start out swimming west once they exit the channel , and then descend into deeper water. They typically follow a large, looping route that involves heading deep first and then gradually shallowing while swimming back along the slope toward the east, which is usually into the prevailing current. They then finish off by drifting back west along with the current in the shallower part of the reef on their way back to the entry point.

For snorkelers, the sheltered bay located shoreward of the breakwater provides a calm and relaxing

> **SAFETY TIP**
>
> Boats regularly access the channels at either entry point at this site. It is therefore essential that divers and snorkelers swim out to the reef and return to shore on the surface, so they are visible to boat traffic at all times.

## DID YOU KNOW?

Day passes can be purchased for **Sunscape Curaçao Resort, Spa & Casino**, which provides access to the resort's amenities, including unlimited food and drinks. There is often family-friendly fun to be had in the evenings, so it's worth staying after sundown or even considering a night dive or snorkel.



Divers descend the outer reef slope at Oswaldo's Drop Off.

Turtle & Ray©

## RELAX & RECHARGE

There are nearly 20 different bars and restaurants located along the 0.65-mile (1-kilometer) stretch of Mambo Beach between Playa Maria Pampoen and Stella Maris Reef. That is far too many to list here. This densely packed beach area is great fun to visit for the entire family and these establishments, which are virtually all high quality, will cater to absolutely every taste and style.

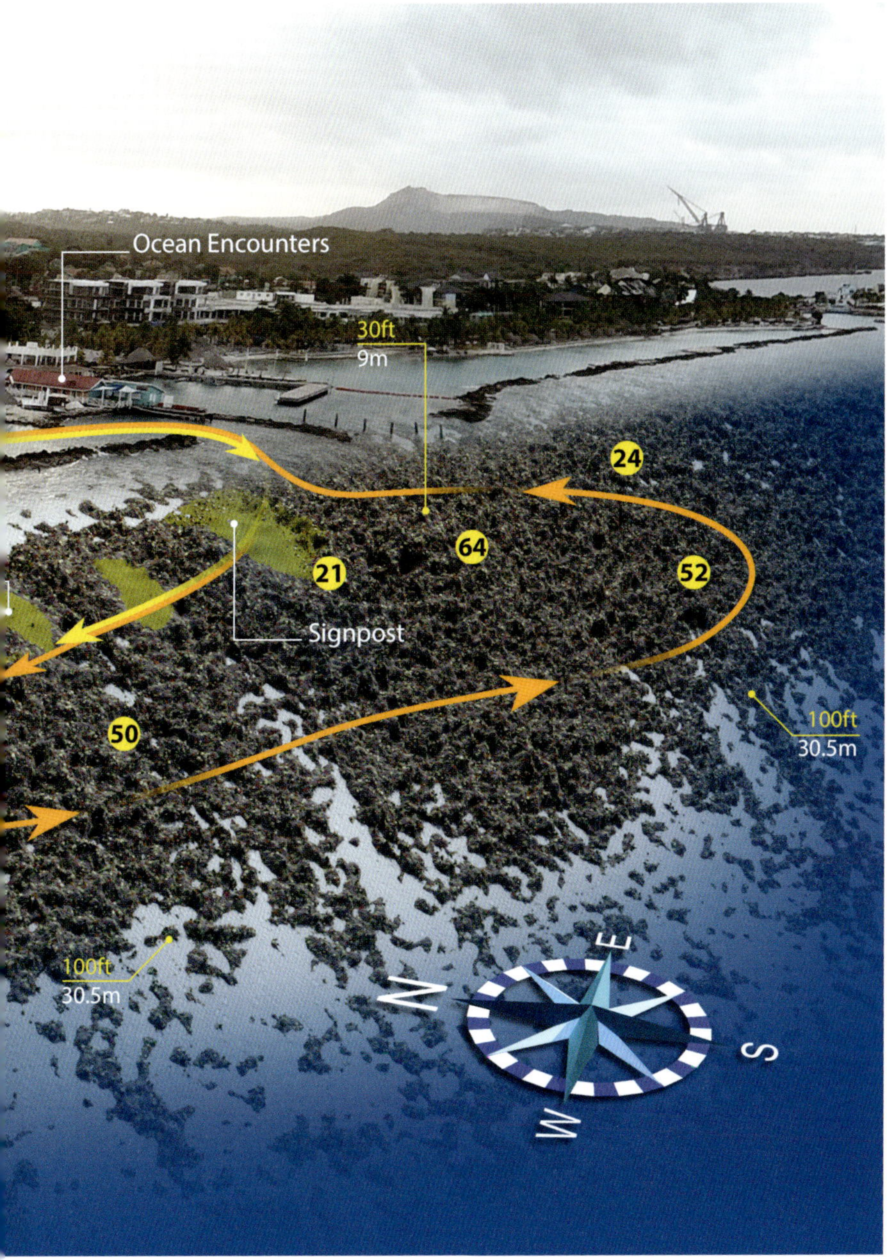


area to explore. Many coral reef fish species can be found here, but the bottom consists largely of sand and rubble. More advanced snorkelers can venture out beyond the breakwater, but tend to stay relatively close to the breakwater where they can explore the shallow coral patches.

If the current is moderate to strong, divers and snorkelers may find it possible to drift all the way along to the adjacent site of Plerbaai and exit the water at Playa Marie Pampoen. That exit also allows access to the Sunscape Resort lagoon, and offers a sheltered route back to the entry point. There is not enough bottom time to explore the barge and car wrecks when following this route, but divers can explore a shallow car wreck located at a depth of 55 feet (17 meters) and some metal beams, as well as the coral trees from the Reef Renewal coral restoration project location just off the beach at Marie Pampoen.

# STELLA MARIS REEF

Difficulty ●●○
Current ●●○
Depth ●●○
Reef ★★★
Fauna ★★★

Access about 12 mins from Willemstad
Access about 7 mins from Willemstad
Access about 5 mins from shore

**Level** Open Water

**Location**
Bapor Kibra, Curaçao
GPS 12°05.115′N, 68°53.965′W

## Getting there

Leave Willemstad on Penstraat, which becomes Dr. Martin Luther King Boulevard and then Bapor Kibra just after Playa Marie Pampoen and the Sunscape Curaçao Resort, Spa & Casino. The road runs roughly parallel to the coast for about 2.2 miles (3.5 kilometers) before taking a sharp right turn just after Mambo Beach, followed by a sharp left. Turn into LionsDive Beach Resort. The total distance from Willemstad is 2.35 miles (3.8 kilometers).

## Access

LionsDive Beach Resort provides simple access to Stella Maris Reef through the onsite dive operator, Ocean Encounters. There is a simple beach access point adjacent to the Hemingway restaurant, or divers and snorkelers can simply walk down the steps in front of the dive center. From here, divers and snorkelers pass through the channel in a westerly direction to reach the reef – a distance of about 550 feet (167 meters). The current is usually mild to moderate at this site but can become strong at times. Visibility is usually good. This site is suitable for divers and snorkelers of all experience levels.

## Description

Stella Maris Reef is named after the wreck located in extremely deep water off the seaward edge of the reef. It also is sometimes referred to as the LionsDive House Reef or Sea Aquarium. The site has a narrow sand plateau that extends just 100 feet (30 meters) from the breakwater that runs for nearly 0.3 miles (0.45 kilometers) to the northwest, toward the Sunscape Resort. This plateau is dominated by sand but has large patches of reef that are wonderfully lit from the surface. These patches host plenty of healthy corals, including elkhorn, staghorn, yellow pencil coral, blade fire coral and even some pillar coral. The abundance of coral is helped along by the constant currents that carry clear, clean water through this site and of course by the effort of the Reef Renewal Curaçao project located here.

The reef starts to slope at a depth of about 30 feet (9 meters) and continues down to a depth of approximately 130 feet (40 meters), where the habitat transitions to sand and rubble. Schools of blue tang, surgeonfish and doctorfish can often be found at this site, as well as bluestriped and French grunts. Banded butterflyfish and foureye

NaturePicsFilms./Shutterstock©

### ECO TIP

The **Reef Renewal Curaçao** project located at Stella Maris Reef is the most extensive on the island. Divers can enjoy a tour of this nursery and restoration site through Ocean Encounters, which started the project and remains the organization's largest donor. Their PADI Coral Restoration Curaçao specialty course brings the science of reefs to life and allows divers to receive hands-on training to maintain the coral nurseries, propagate new corals and outplant corals back onto the reef, providing a living and lasting legacy to Curaçao's shallow water reef system. The course is perfect for families, single divers, vacationers, school groups, and more.

Email: info@reefrenewalcuracao.org
Visit: **Reefrenewalcuracao.org**

Reef Renewal Curaçao

### SAFETY TIP

Boats regularly access the channel at this site. It is therefore essential that divers and snorkelers swim out to the reef and return to shore on the surface, so they are visible to boat traffic at all times.

The Reef Renewal Curaçao Project at Stella Maris Reef is quite the attraction for both divers and snorkelers

butterflyfish are also common, and divers and snorkelers can often find spotted drums, soapfish and moray eels hiding in the reef. Blue and brown chromis fill the water column and bar jacks and yellowtail snapper are also regular visitors.

## Route

From the channel at LionsDive Beach Resort, divers and snorkelers can explore the reef in either direction as long as the current permits. There is a rope that leads divers out of the channel and down onto the reef. From there, most divers follow a counterclockwise loop dropping down the reef slope and then swimming with the prevailing currents toward the northwest.

After using half a tank, divers can then shallow up and circle back to return along the edge of the drop-off and reef plateau, pausing to check out the coral trees that are part of the Reef Renewal coral conservation project. Snorkelers generally stay closer to the breakwater during their exploration. The option of drift dive all the way to Sunscape Resort and the start of Oswaldo's Drop Off is also possible when currents are favorable.

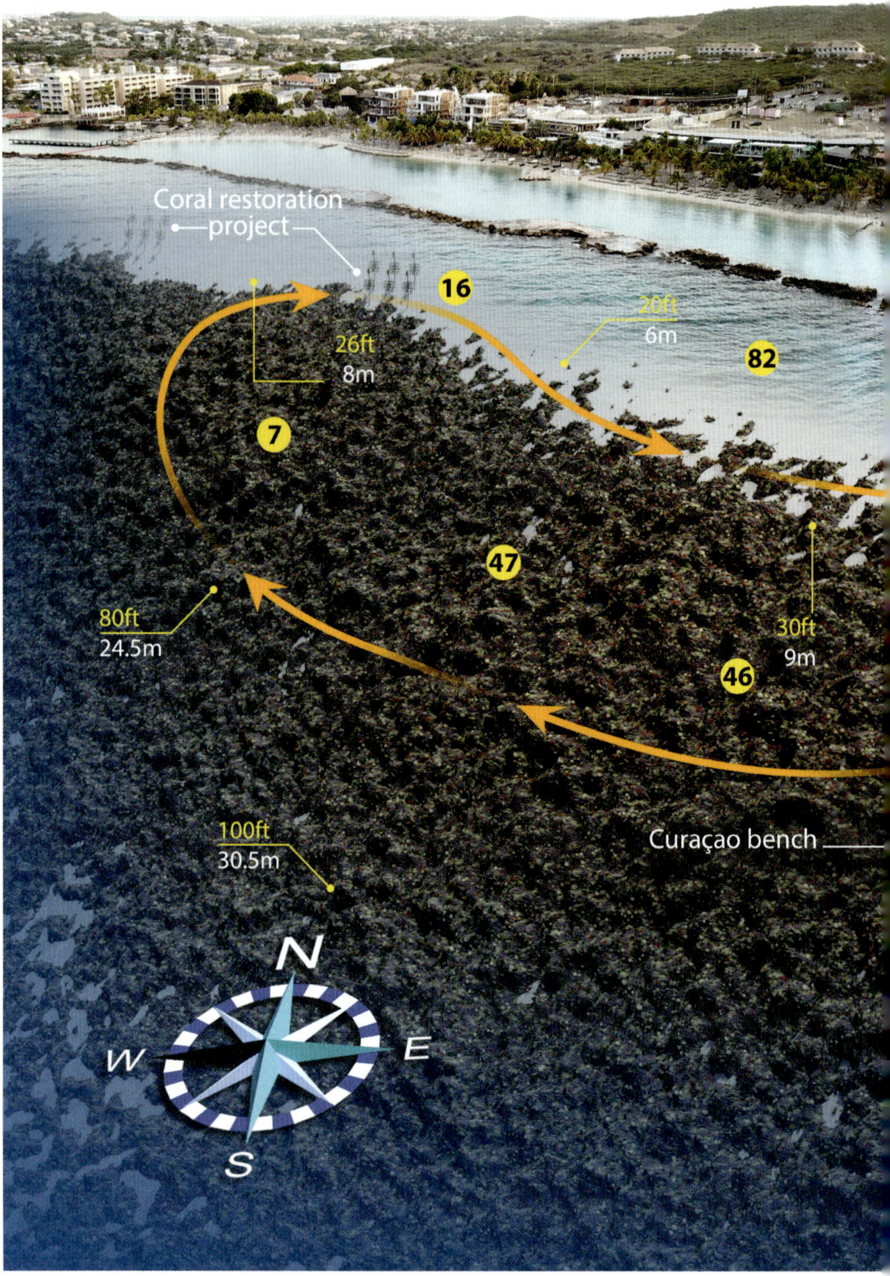


## DID YOU KNOW?

The wreck of the *Stella Maris* is located in the southeastern part of the site that bears its name. She was a 300-foot (90-meter) freighter that was confiscated by the authorities for drug trafficking and sunk as an artificial reef in the mid-1980s. As she sank beneath the waves, the ship slid into waters too deep for recreational diving and was lost for several decades. The *Stella Maris* was rediscovered in 2006 by a team of

STELLA MARIS REEF

technical divers. She lies on her starboard side at a depth of over 400 feet (122 meters). While the wreck is too deep for recreational divers to visit, she can be explored through Substation Curaçao, located near the Sea Aquarium. The Curasub is capable of taking five people to a depth of 1,000 feet (300 meters) and has been in operation since 2011.
Visit: **Substation-curacao.com**

# SHIPWRECK POINT

Difficulty ●●○
Current ●●●
Depth ●●○
Reef ★★★
Fauna ★★☆

Access about 13 mins from Willemstad
Access about 7 mins from Willemstad
Access about 5 mins from shore

## Level Open Water

## Location

Bapor Kibra, Curaçao
GPS 12°04.954'N, 68°53.724'W

## Getting there

Leave Willemstad on Penstraat, which becomes Dr. Martin Luther King Boulevard and then Bapor Kibra just after Playa Marie Pampoen and the Sunscape Curaçao Resort, Spa & Casino. The road runs roughly parallel to the coast for about 2.2 miles (3.5 kilometers) before taking a sharp right just after Mambo Beach, followed by a sharp left. Turn into LionsDive Beach Resort. The total distance from Willemstad is 2.35 miles (3.8 kilometers).

## Access

LionsDive Beach Resort provides simple access to Shipwreck Point through the onsite dive operator, Ocean Encounters. The site is technically accessible from shore, but it can be challenging to reach, especially when conditions are rough and the current is strong, which is common at this site. It is therefore safest to access the dive and snorkel site via boat through one of the local dive and snorkel centers located in this part of Curaçao. Visibility is usually good, and the site is suitable for divers and snorkelers of all experience levels.

## Description

Shipwreck Point is a wide fringing reef, roughly triangular in shape, located immediately off shore of the Curaçao Sea Aquarium, which is why the site is also occasionally known by this name. The name Shipwreck Point originates from the large number of ships that have been wrecked at this location over the years, including the *Stella Maris* described on page 198.

Shipwreck Point is widely regarded as one of the more pristine dive and snorkel sites in Curaçao. The current is often strong at this site creating great conditions for corals and sponges, as well as planktivorous fishes, such as blue and brown chromis. Divers and snorkelers may also discover French and grey angelfish, midnight and blue parrotfish and nurse sharks, as well as lobsters and green moray eels in the deeper parts of the site.

While generating great conditions for marine life, the current at Shipwreck Point can be tricky for divers and snorkelers, as it pushes up onto the reef plateau from the east and splits in two directions. When active, this diverging current can cause some degree of disorientation for divers as they navigate the drop-off.

The reef plateau, which is one of the main features of Shipwreck Point, is densely covered in corals, including large stands of pencil corals and a large elkhorn coral. Divers can explore a large prop and anchor located on the plateau, along with another prop and anchor located in the sand channel that sits on the western slope of the plateau. The triangular plateau gives way to a relatively steep reef slope across all sides. The transition between plateau and slope takes place between 30 and 40 feet (9 and 12 meters) and the slope itself is cut through by multiple sand channels and outcrops that add complexity to the habitat. Divers with technical training also have the opportunity to explore the deeper parts of the reef slope where they will find two tugboats located at a depth of around 165 feet (50 meters).

## Route

Most dive boats tie into the large prop that sits

### DID YOU KNOW?

One of the most famous ships to have been wrecked off Shipwreck Point is the *SS Oranje Nassau* – a steamship that was built in 1884 and owned by the Dutch West Indies Company. She grounded during a storm in 1906 and until recently, its boiler could be found in the channel between the Sea Aquarium and the Royal Sea Aquarium Resort.

in a sand patch at the center of the reef plateau. After entering the water and descending the line, divers can explore the plateau, looking out for the large anchor that sits next to a stand of elkhorn coral to the northwest of the prop. The channel that shelters the second anchor and prop offers a convenient way to transit the plateau and head over to the drop-off. From there, most divers head south along the slope, staying relatively shallow along the drop-off to see the dense corals and large schools of chromis. As they round the corner at the southern edge of the site, divers may notice that the current switches direction. Divers typically switch to drifting with the current as it carries them along the slope before returning up onto the plateau to finish off their dive. Divers who were hot-dropped onto the plateau can instead drift along into Corneliusbaai, and then signal for pickup by their dive boat.

Divers and snorkelers can use the propeller located on the reef plateau at Shipwreck Point as a navigational aid.

NaturePicFilms/Shutterstock©

## DID YOU KNOW?

The northeastern part of Shipwreck Point is considered a separate site by some, often referred to as Cornelius Bay. Elkhorn corals extend along the shoreline at this location and divers and snorkelers can often find seahorses sheltering among the large sea fans at this site.

## DID YOU KNOW?

The **Curaçao Sea Aquarium** is located adjacent to the breakwater that marks the northern edge of Shipwreck Point. This facility was opened in 1984 with the vision of sharing a passion for the sea with the general public. The facility initially consisted of only a handful of aquaria, but over the years there have been numerous additions to the park, including the Dolphin Academy, Animal Encounters, Ocean Lens

and Substation, each featuring unique and interactive programs with a focus on marine education.
Visit: **Curaçao-sea-aquarium.com**

# TUGBOAT SABA

Difficulty ●○○
Current ●○○
Depth ●○○
Reef ★★☆
Fauna ★★☆

Access about 15 mins from Willemstad

**Level** Open Water

**Location**
Jan Thiel, Curaçao
GPS 12°04.817'N, 68°53.382'W

## Getting there
There is no shore access to *Tugboat Saba*. The best way to reach this site is through one of the local dive operators located along Curaçao's southeast coast.

## Access
*Tugboat Saba* is only accessible by boat. There is typically a mooring buoy anchored to the seabed just next to the wreck site. Currents at this dive and snorkel site are often mild, but seas can be choppy at times. This site is suitable for divers and snorkelers of all experience levels.

## Description
*Tugboat Saba* is a dive and snorkel site located just seaward of the Jan Thiel salt flats. The central focus of the site is the wreck of a small tugboat. It is very similar to the tug located on the Caracasbaai peninsula (page 228), but slightly less famous because of the more challenging access.

Sometimes simply called the *Saba Tug*, this wreck was sunk deliberately as an artificial reef. The wreck now sits with a strong list to its port side in a patch of sand on a shallow reef plateau. The wreck sits at a maximum depth of just 21 feet (6.5 meters) and rests a mere 75 feet (23 meters) from the edge of a relatively steep drop-off. The highest point of the wreck is its starboard bow, which reaches 16 feet (5 meters) in depth, which makes this site ideal for snorkelers. The tug's bow points along the coast toward Willemstad with a northwestern heading.

The shallow nature of the wreck has taken a toll on the small tug, and its superstructure has detached and currently lies next to the hull off its port side, closer to the bow than the stern. The deck has deteriorated as well, and large holes in the deck allow divers and snorkelers to peer into the hidden confines of the hull, albeit without any opportunity to actually penetrate. Thankfully the outside of the wreck provides plenty of opportunity for exploration as the complex habitat is thoroughly overgrown with a dense covering of corals and sponges, including fire corals and domed brain corals, which provide habitat for a wide variety of coral reef organisms. Divers and snorkelers can often find lobsters, moray eels, scorpionfish, yellowtail snapper and large schools of blue chromis, creole wrasses and grunts near the wreck.

The reef plateau and drop-off also offer plenty

## SCIENTIFIC INSIGHT

Artificial reefs deployed in shallow waters must withstand a lot of energy from currents and waves. This energy is often enough to cause extensive damage and even physically move artificial reefs some distance from their initial position. The reason for this is that as a wave passes over the surface, the energy sets water particles into orbital motion immediately below. The size of the orbital diameter decreases with increasing depth, which means shallow artificial reefs are hit with greater wave energy. In the case of the *Tugboat Saba*, the tall, narrow wheelhouse that originally sat atop the deck would have had to withstand the greatest amount of wave energy, considering its shallow position. By comparison, the wreck of the *Superior Producer* (page 172) sits in much deeper water and is therefore buffered from the energy of waves that pass above it.

for divers and snorkelers to explore once they get tired of exploring the small wreck. Snorkelers can check out the plateau with its large coral heads, including brain and lettuce corals as well as fire corals. Meanwhile, divers may want to explore down the reef slope. The slope is more like a wall in many places, with deeply cut sand channels and large coral mounds providing complex habitat that supports a wide range of coral reef creatures, including barracuda and snapper.

### Route

Divers can choose to visit the wreck and the surrounding reef from a boat tied to the mooring buoy located here, or they can opt to drift dive the plateau. The latter allows a greater chance to fully explore the reef here given that most divers would be hard pressed to expend their entire

The bow of *Tugboat Saba* is covered in various corals and sponges.

NaturePicsFilms/Shutterstock©

bottom time on just the small tugboat, as iconic as it is. Divers looking to drift can follow the edge of the plateau as it heads west away from the tug before the reef curves around to a more northwestern direction. Currents are generally mild to moderate here, so divers are unlikely to drift far enough to reach Corneliusbaai before they run out of air and need to surface.

Snorkelers typically stay near the wreck and explore the reef plateau that surrounds the tug. Visibility is often good despite the shallow nature of the plateau, and so snorkelers should find it relatively easy to maintain their bearings as they explore.

# TUGBOAT SABA

| | | | |
|---|---|---|---|
| **Name:** | *Saba* | **Last owner:** | n/a |
| **Type:** | tugboat | **Sunk:** | n/a |
| **Previous names:** | n/a | | |
| **Length:** | 51 ft (15.5m) | | |
| **Tonnage:** | n/a | | |
| **Construction:** | n/a | | |

# SANDY'S PLATEAU

Difficulty ●○○
Current ●●○
Depth ●●○
Reef ★★★
Fauna ★★☆

Access about 18 mins from Willemstad

**Level** Open Water

**Location**
Jan Thiel, Curaçao
GPS 12°04.705′N, 68°53.165′W

**Getting there**
There is no shore access to Sandy's Plateau. The best way to reach this site is through one of the local dive operators located along Curaçao's southeast coast.

**Access**
Sandy's Plateau is a boat-accessible dive and snorkel site. Currents are often mild along this stretch of the coast, but they can become moderate at times. Seas can also be choppy at times, in part due to the shallowness of the plateau here. This site is suitable for divers and snorkelers of all experience levels.

**Description**
Sandy's Plateau is a dive and snorkel site located just seaward of the Jan Thiel salt flats and slightly

## SCIENTIFIC INSIGHT

Atlantic trumpetfish (*Aulostomus maculatus*) engage in what is known as "aggressive mimicry." This behavior is where a predator attempts to mimic the shape, pattern, and/or movement of another organism, usually one harmless to the mimic's intended prey, in order to hide its intentions. In the case of trumpetfish, they often float along with their head pointed down, mimicking a harmless piece of algae floating in the current. They are also often seen hiding in forests of soft corals, waiting for unwary prey to swim by. To make it even harder for them to be spotted, trumpetfish also have pigmented cells called chromatophores in their skin. They can use these cells to subtly alter their coloration to enhance the effect of their mimicry.

closer to Jan Thiel Beach than to *Tugboat Saba* (page 204). The site is also sometimes known as Boka Di Sorsaka. The slope along this section of reef is quite steep and is even undercut in numerous places. Divers commonly encounter Caribbean spiny lobsters, channel clinging crabs and green morays in the nooks and crevices of the undercut areas, while the reef slope itself has a dense covering of soft and hard corals. Large tube sponges and barrel sponges are common, further adding to the complex reef habitat.

The upper reef area consists of a shallow plateau that supports lots of soft corals and blade fire coral. Flamingo tongues are often found attached to sea fans in this shallow area of the reef, while trumpetfish and slender filefish are often seen hiding among the branches of the soft corals. Foureye and banded butterflyfish are also common at this site, and divers and snorkelers are likely to spot Spanish hogfish, smooth trunkfish, rock beauties and honeycomb cowfish in this area.

NaturePicsFilms/Shutterstock©

# 66 JAN THIEL/SWEET BOTTOM

Difficulty ●○○
Current ●○○
Depth ●●○
Reef ★★☆
Fauna ★★☆

Access (boat) about 18 mins from Willemstad
Access (car) about 16 mins from Willemstad
Access (swim) about 3 mins from shore (to *Strea* wreck)
Access (swim) about 8 mins from shore (to the reef)

**Level** Open Water

## Location

Jan Thiel, Curaçao
GPS 12°04.558'N, 68°52.820'W (wreck)

## Getting there

Head south on Schottegatweg Zuid from Willemstad. Take the exit onto Kaya C. Winkel and the second exit at the roundabout onto Caracasbaaiweg. Follow this road for 3.8 miles (6.1 kilometers) and turn right at the roundabout on the water by Caracasbaai onto Kaya Indiko. After 0.4 miles (0.6 kilometers), turn left onto Kaya Adriatiko. Continue for 0.5 miles (0.8 kilometers) and then turn right at the roundabout and then take the first left into Papagayo Beach Plaza & Beach Club. Entrance to the beach is free of charge for those exploring the dive and snorkel site through the featured operator. The total distance from Willemstad is approximately 6.4 miles (10.3 kilometers)

## Access

The beach at Jan Thiel, which is sometimes known as Zanzibar, is mostly sandy, which makes access simple. Also, the bay itself is relatively enclosed, which helps protect the water here from currents and waves that could make diving and snorkeling challenging. Visibility can be poor within the bay, although it is usually good along the reef outside the bay's inlet. There are plenty of amenities available near the access point, including showers and washrooms. This site is suitable for divers and snorkelers of all experience levels.

## Description

Jan Thiel Bay and Jan Thiel Reef (the common name for the reef located just beyond the mouth of the bay) are popular dive and snorkel sites located close to the busy Jan Thiel Beach area. The bay itself features a slight depression in the middle, which drops in depth sharply from around 10 feet (3 meters) down to 30 feet (9 meters) in the center. It rises back up to 10 feet (3 meters) toward the mouth of the bay. The seabed in the middle of the bay consists of sand and is mostly featureless except for the wreck of a sailboat, known as the *Strea*, which sank in 2003. The wreck lies on its side with its bow pointing east. The shallowest point is about 12 feet (3.5 meters) deep, so this wreck offers plenty of opportunity for exploration by both divers and snorkelers, but particularly the latter. While there is not much coral life on the wreck, there are plenty of fish hanging around the area. Squid are often found here as well.

The best section of reef for divers to explore is out beyond the 500-foot-wide (152-meter) mouth of Jan Thiel Bay. Divers must swim out to the bay's inlet, but can then head in either direction once they reach the outer reef slope, which starts at a depth of 33 feet (10 meters). The area of reef immediately to the northeast of the mouth of the bay is often referred to as Sweet Bottom and contains a coral restoration project. This site can be reached from Jan Thiel Beach, but only by divers with exceptional air consumption. Sweet Bottom is easier to reach by boat than by shore.

In either direction along the reef slope, divers will encounter a wealth of biodiversity that can include parrotfish, trumpetfish, butterflyfish, grunts and snapper, including schoolmaster and mahogany snapper. Sea turtles are also often spotted along the reef here. Blue and brown chromis are particularly common in the water column above the reef, along with barracuda, while small grouper, such as graysbies and coneys, frequent the reef below.

### SAFETY TIP

Boats are common within the bay at Jan Thiel, and they regularly pass through the mouth of the bay at all hours of the day. It is therefore essential that divers and snorkelers use a surface marker buoy (SMB) while exploring this site.

## FEATURED OPERATOR

**Dive Center Scuba Do** is perfectly located for divers and snorkelers to take advantage of the stunning reefs and wrecks located around Jan Thiel Bay. Located literally on the shore, this PADI 5-star Dive Resort has easy access to the house reef, where they conduct daily guided tours as well as trips to other nearby diving hotspots, such as *Superior Producer*, Director's Bay, *Tugboat* and Marie Pampoen. They also provide the opportunity to dive Curaçao's east point by boat. Dive Center Scuba Do offers all PADI certifications and many specialty courses, and through their onsite dive shop, they also have you covered for any diving or snorkeling rental needs or new equipment purchases for your time in the water.

Tel: +599-9-525-0332
Email: info@scubadoCuracao.com
Visit: **ScubadoCuracao.com**

DIVE CENTER
SCUBA DO
CURAÇAO

### Route

Most divers head straight for the reef slope, which is the most interesting area to explore for divers. They typically circumnavigate the side of the depression as the center of the bay offers little in the way of landmarks or interest. The reef slope to the northwest is generally considered better, including the coral restoration project if divers can make it that far. Divers do not need to go deep to encounter dense fish life, however. This also means that the outer slope can be an area of interest for adventurous snorkelers. Even so, most snorkelers are content to stay within the bay where the currents and waves are virtually absent and where the wreck of the *Strea* can be an entertaining feature to explore. Most divers explore this wreck on their way back during their safety stop.

The wreck of the sailboat *Strea* lies in Jan Thiel Bay.

Turtle & Ray©

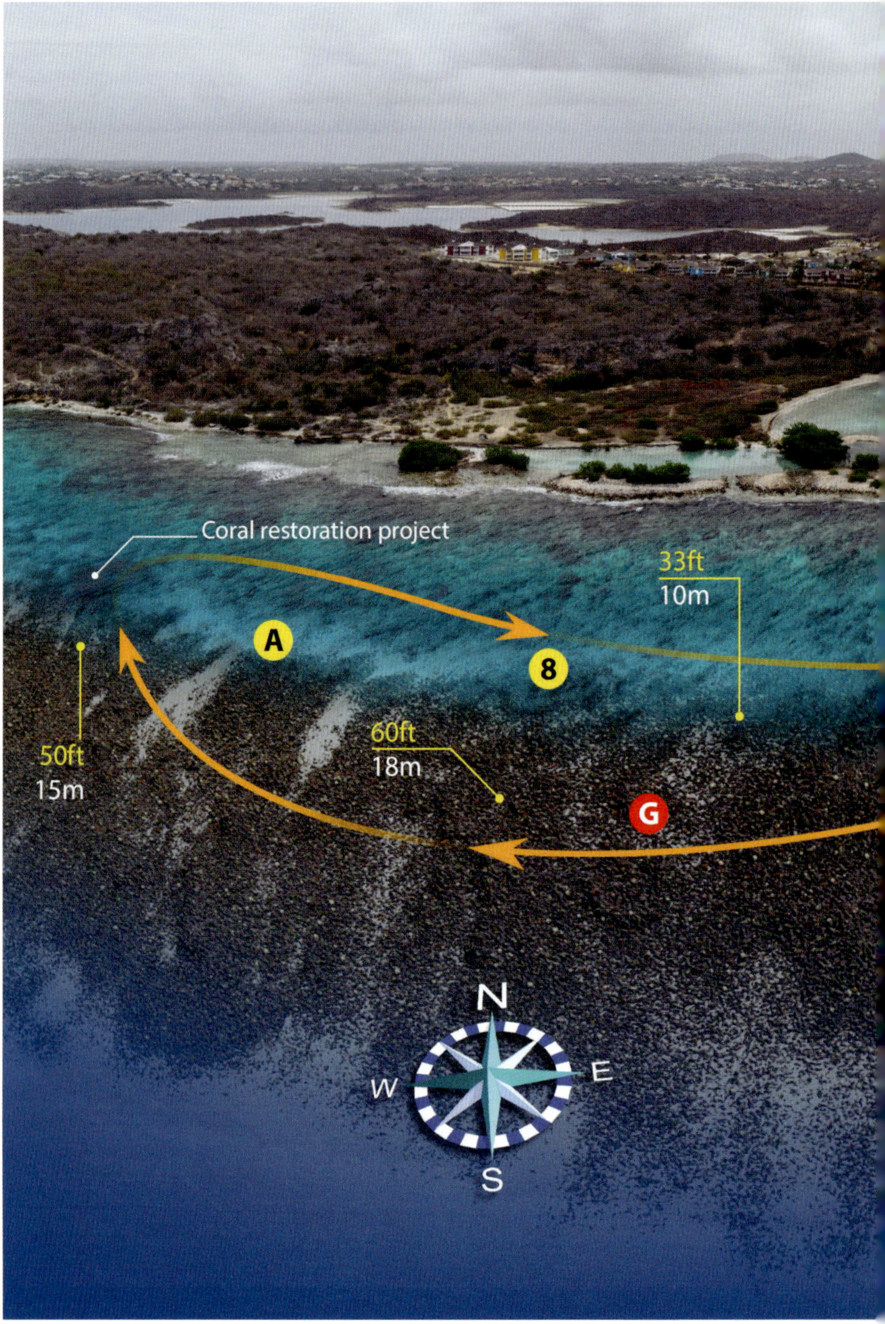
Coral restoration project
33ft
10m
A
8
50ft
15m
60ft
18m
G
N
W
E
S

NaturePicsFilm/Shutterstock©

| | | | |
|---|---|---|---|
| **Name:** | *Strea* | **Last owner:** | n/a |
| **Type:** | sailboat | **Sunk:** | 2003 |
| **Previous names:** | n/a | | |
| **Length:** | n/a | | |
| **Tonnage:** | n/a | | |
| **Construction:** | n/a | | |

# DIVER'S LEAP

Difficulty ●●○
Current ●●○
Depth ●●●
Reef ★★☆
Fauna ★★★

Access about 20 mins from Willemstad

**Level** Open Water

**Location**
Jan Thiel, Curaçao
GPS 12°04.333'N, 68°52.625'W

### Getting there

Diver's Leap is a boat-accessible dive and snorkel site. Fundiving Curaçao, located on the shore close to Jan Thiel Beach, can provide access to the northwestern part of the site, which allows divers and snorkelers to reach Diver's Leap when the prevailing current is mild. The best way to reach this site is through one of the local dive operators located along Curaçao's southeast coast.

### Access

Currents are often mild at Diver's Leap but can become moderate at times. Seas can also be choppy at times. This site is suitable to divers and snorkelers of all experience levels, although the deeper parts of the wall can only be explored by advanced divers.

### Description

Diver's Leap is a steep wall dive located between Jan Thiel Beach and Beacon Point. Some say the name Diver's Leap comes from the fact that divers used to access this site by leaping from the adjacent ironshore ledge, back before the Papagayo Beach Resort was constructed there. Others say the name stems from the feeling that divers get as they drift over the edge of the steep wall that makes this dive so spectacular. The site is also sometimes known as Piedra Sombre, or Stone Hat in English. This name references the hat-shaped rock located along the shoreline, which divers and snorkelers once used to help locate the site before GPS (and shoreline development) made it easier to locate.

The main feature of Diver's Leap is a series of steep scalloped walls that run parallel to shore, although the densely covered reef plateau offers divers a bounty of coral habitat to peruse, including elkhorn, staghorn, brain, lettuce, and fields of gorgonians. Some particularly impressive examples of pillar coral can be found at this site, particularly at the southeastern end of the plateau close to the neighboring site of Beacon Point, where most boat-access dive and snorkel experiences begin.

The shallow back reef plateau at Diver's Leap has particularly healthy examples of pillar coral.

By comparison, soft corals dominate the wall, interspersed with hard corals and sea whips, while pencil corals form large fields that cascade down the slope in between the various wall sections. The largest section of wall is located in the southeastern part of the site, and it projects out into the blue, dropping from around 27 feet (8 meters) adjacent to the back reef plateau, down to approximately 100 feet (30 meters). A massive barrel sponge is located at a depth of about 87 feet (26.5 meters) in the middle of the wall. Below the wall, the reef transitions back into a slope of sand and coral rubble that descends into the depths.

Near the center of the site, the wall begins to flatten somewhat and starts to look more like a slope, although the slope stops abruptly at a depth of around 120 feet (36.5 meters) with a heavy undercut area that is deeper that most recreational divers will be able to explore given bottom time and air constraints. The slope then gives way once again to a series of smaller walls by the northwestern end of the site. Divers who are exploring the site as a drift dive are usually shallowing at this point, however, and typically join any snorkelers on the shallower back reef plateau.

There are many large reef species that divers are likely to encounter at this site, particularly along the wall sections. For example, barracuda, mackerel, tarpon and jacks are often seen up in the water column, while grouper and moray eels are found in the deeper parts of the reef. Diver's Leap is also known for its seahorses,

Turtle & Ray©

which are regularly found along the top of the wall and on the coral-filled plateau. The average depth along the plateau and the top of the drop-off is around 20 feet (6 meters), which is perfect for conducting a safety stop.

### Route

When the current is moderate to strong, most divers and snorkelers explore this reef by drifting from the mooring at Beacon point, exploring the scalloped walls and moving to the back reef plateau as the walls transition to a steep slope. The site can be explored from the northwestern side of the site, but prevailing currents can make this challenging at times and can limit the extent to which divers can explore the site.

## DID YOU KNOW?

In Curaçao, currents generally flow from east to west. These are largely driven by the trade winds that blow steadily in the same direction, in the region just north of the Equator. This large-scale flow of surface water is part of the North Atlantic gyre, which rotates clockwise, moving water from North Africa to the Caribbean and then northwards along the east coast of North America via the Gulf Stream, which then carries the warm water back toward Europe.

Because of the incredible quantity of water moved by ocean currents, a special unit of

measurement, namely the Sverdrup (sv), was created early in the 20th century by the famous oceanographer Harald Sverdrup. One sverdrup equals a flow of one million cubic meters per second. If you have a hard time wrapping your mind around such a large volume, think about it this way: the flow is enough to fill the New Orleans' Superdome in just two seconds.

While the general direction of the current in Curaçao moves from east to west, on a smaller scale, currents may be driven by local conditions, such as shoreline topography and weather patterns. Depending on the factors involved, currents can change from one day to the next and even over the course of a single dive. This is why local knowledge is so important when planning for a dive, and can help make diving and snorkeling so much safer.

To learn more about ocean currents (and marine science in general) check out another book by Reef Smart Guides called Beneath the Blue Planet. Available in all good bookstores and many dive centers, as well as online.

# BEACON POINT

Difficulty ●●●
Current ●●●
Depth ●●●
Reef ★★★
Fauna ★★★

Access about 21 mins from Willemstad



**Level** Advanced

## Location

Jan Thiel, Curaçao
GPS 12°04.230′N, 68°52.375′W

## Getting there

Beacon Point is only accessible by boat. This dive and snorkel site is located on the southern tip of the Jan Thiel area. The best way to reach this site is through one of the local dive operators located along Curaçao's southeast coast.

## Access

Currents are often moderate to strong at Beacon Point and the visibility is usually good. Seas can be choppy at times. This site is better suited to advanced divers and snorkelers.

## Description

The Beacon Point dive and snorkel site is named after the lighthouse that once stood there, which is why it is also sometimes known as Jan Thiel Lighthouse. The site also sometimes goes by Kabes Di Barankas, which translates as "head of the rock." It is known for its steep wall and spectacular reef plateau, which hosts some large patches of elkhorn and staghorn coral and is known to have some of the most extensive pillar coral formations in the Caribbean.

The currents at this site generally come from the southeast, and they often diverge when they hit the point. As a result, Beacon Point can be used as a starting point to visit the two sites on either side, namely Diver's Leap (page 214) and Lost Anchor (page 219). Large jacks, snapper, tarpon and barracuda are often seen here, as well as the occasional eagle ray.

# LOST ANCHOR

Difficulty ●●○
Current ●●○
Depth ●●○
Reef ★★☆
Fauna ★★☆

Access about 22 mins from Willemstad

**Level** Open Water

## Location

Jan Thiel, Curaçao
GPS 12°04.447'N, 68°52.190'W

## Getting there

Lost Anchor is a boat-accessible dive and snorkel site located just inside Caracasbaai. The best way to reach this site is through one of the local dive operators located along Curaçao's southeast coast.

## Access

Currents are often mild to moderate at Lost Anchor, and the visibility is usually good. This site is suitable for divers and snorkelers of all experience levels.

## Description

Lost Anchor is located along the cliff edge to the northeast of Beacon Point. It is the first site fully located within the Curaçao National Marine Park. This steeply sloping reef, which begins at about 20 feet (6 meters) and drops sharply into the depths, has lots of healthy coral and sponge cover. Divers often report seeing moray eels here, as well as barracuda, Nassau grouper and tiger grouper.

The currents at this site are somewhat unpredictable and can even change both strength and direction over the course of a single dive or snorkel. A large anchor chain runs down the reef slope into the depths, which gives the site its name. This chain is hidden within the structure of the reef and can be hard to find.

Greens and Blues/Shutterstock©

## DID YOU KNOW?

At the onset of the Second World War, the Dutch government installed an anti-submarine fence near Beacon Point to protect the vital refueling station that existed in Caracasbaai. The underwater fence ran from east to west, across the entrance to the entire bay. The anchor chain that runs along the seabed at anchor Point is part of what remains of this feature. Other elements can still be found on the seabed on the opposite side of the bay at *Tugboat* (page 228).

# LA PALAPA

Difficulty ●●○
Current ●●○
Depth ●●○
Reef ★☆☆
Fauna ★★★

Access (boat) about 23 mins from Willemstad
Access (car) about 15 mins from Willemstad
Access (swim) about 15 mins from shore

**Level** Open Water

## Location

Caracasbaai, Curaçao
GPS 12°04.572′N, 68°51.970′W (reef)
12°04.643′N, 68°51.879′W (shore access)

## Getting there

Head south on Schottegatweg Zuid from Willemstad. Take the exit onto Kaya C. Winkel and the second exit at the roundabout onto Caracasbaaiweg. Follow this road for 4.5 miles (7.2 kilometers) until you reach another roundabout. Take the second exit, and continue on Caracasbaaiweg for 0.3 miles (0.5 kilometers) and then turn left into the large, free parking lot adjacent to the shore. Park as close to the western end of the parking lot as possible – adjacent to the Palapa Beach Resort & Marina. While the parking lot is large, this beach is popular with locals and spaces fill up fast, particularly on the weekend. The total distance from Willemstad is approximately 6 miles (9.6 kilometers)

## Access

Divers should gear up at their car and walk down onto the beach as close as possible to the western end of the parking lot. Some divers prefer to walk along the beach and enter the water by the boat channel at the western end of the bay. This distance is significantly greater than simply entering the water adjacent to the parking lot, swimming out to the reef line, which is approximately 300 feet (91 meters) from the beach, and then following the reef line around the edge of the bay to the same point.

The sandy back reef slopes gradually down from the beach to a small fringing reef wall, which bottoms out at about 45 feet (14 meters). It is easy to follow this wall underwater or from the surface, which is the best way for divers to conserve air and bottom time. The reef breaks at the entrance to the channel but it continues on the other side toward the west. Just west of the channel, the La Palapa reef extends out from shore at an angle. In total the distance to reach the reef when circumnavigating the bay is approximately 0.25 miles (0.4 kilometers).

Some divers chose to cross the open water from the beach directly to La Palapa reef in a southwesterly direction, rather than follow the shoreline. This is the more direct route, but it requires advanced compass skills and buoyancy control, as divers need to stay well above the bottom to conserve their bottom time. La Palapa is usually calm and free of strong currents, and the visibility is often good. This site is suitable for divers and snorkelers of all experience levels.

## Description

La Palapa is believed to be named after the Palapa Beach Resort & Marina located along the shore adjacent to this site. It could be a reference to the palm-shaped reef here, which juts out from the shore just south of the boat channel. The site is also sometimes called Turtle Rock.

The reef here consists of a long, curved berm that extends just over 0.1 miles (200 meters) from the shoreline along the northern edge of Caracasbaai. This berm has a noticeable saddle in

### SAFETY TIP

Walking or swimming long distances with heavy scuba gear in warm conditions can cause divers to lose water through body sweat. Dehydration can significantly increase the risk of decompression sickness, or the bends, in divers. La Palapa requires divers to travel a long distance to reach the dive site and this is before any potential current is taken into consideration. Divers should consider this carefully before shore diving this site. Many local operators will visit La Palapa by boat, which can be a much safer option, especially for divers who are not in top physical shape.

## DID YOU KNOW?

Palapa is a Spanish word that originates from the Tagalog language, which is a dialect of Filipino – the national language of the Philippines. The word is widely used in Mexico, Honduras and other Central American countries to describe an open-sided dwelling with a thatched roof made of dried palm leaves. This traditional Filipino construction was believed to have been carried to Nueva España (New Spain), along with coconuts, via Spanish trading galleons that operated between the Mexico and the Far East between the mid-1500s and the mid-1800s.

its middle that drops from 60 feet (18 meters) to about 75 feet (23 meters) at its lowest point. The reef branches into two major lobes at the end, which rise up from the seabed, from over 120 feet deep (36.5 meters). There are several peaks – some rising to as shallow as 40 feet (12 meters) in depth.

La Palapa is not the most pristine reef, but the site is famous for hosting a high density of sea turtles, particularly green and hawksbill turtles. These creatures can often be found resting on the reef and receiving a good cleaning from some of the other reef residents. Divers may also

Sea turtles are often found resting on the reef and sponges at La Palapa.

Richard Whitcombe©

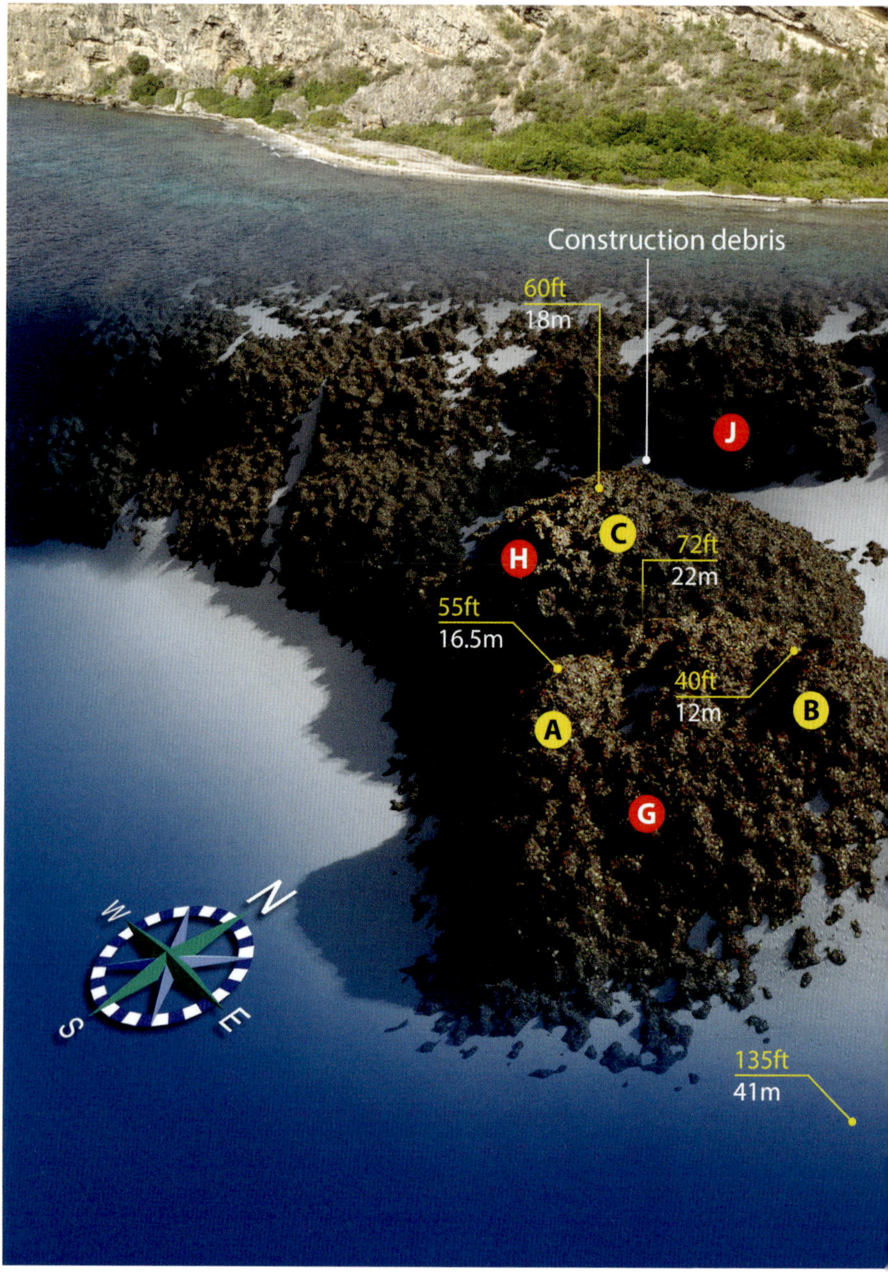


find angelfish, moray eels, jacks, and barracuda at this reef.

A small pile of wreckage and debris can be found in the angle formed by the main reef wall and La Palapa reef. This structure can be interesting to explore, but the main features of this site are undoubtedly the sea turtles, which can only be found on the reef.

## Route

Divers will need to conserve as much air and bottom time as possible to fully explore this relatively deep reef. Most divers choose to swim along the reef slope toward the channel, and then cross over toward the large spur that makes up this site. Once at the site, most divers focus their time and exploration on the end of the reef, which is the shallowest part of the dive

at approximately 40 feet (12 meters). This is also where the greatest number of sea turtles can be found. Divers will need to monitor their air and bottom time closely to ensure they have enough left to make the return trip along the top of the reef slope and all the way back to their original point of entry.

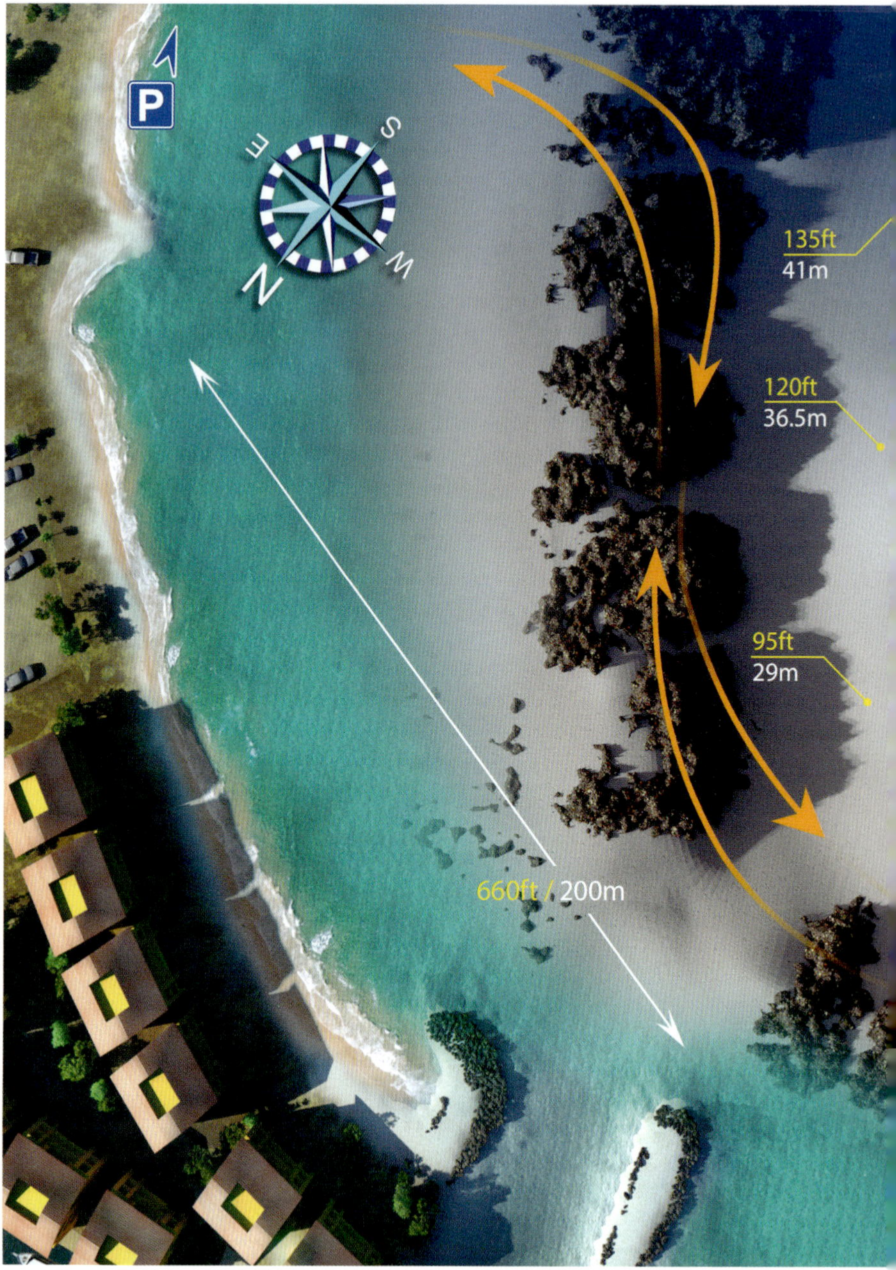


## ECO TIP

When exploring any natural ecosystem, it is always important to view and not interact with any wild animals that may be encountered. Research has shown that virtually any human interaction can affect individual animals, populations, and even entire communities of wildlife, and that direct harassment can affect behavior, reproductive success, and the overall fitness of animals. This has been well-documented in both marine and terrestrial environments, and across a wide range of species. For example, boat traffic has been

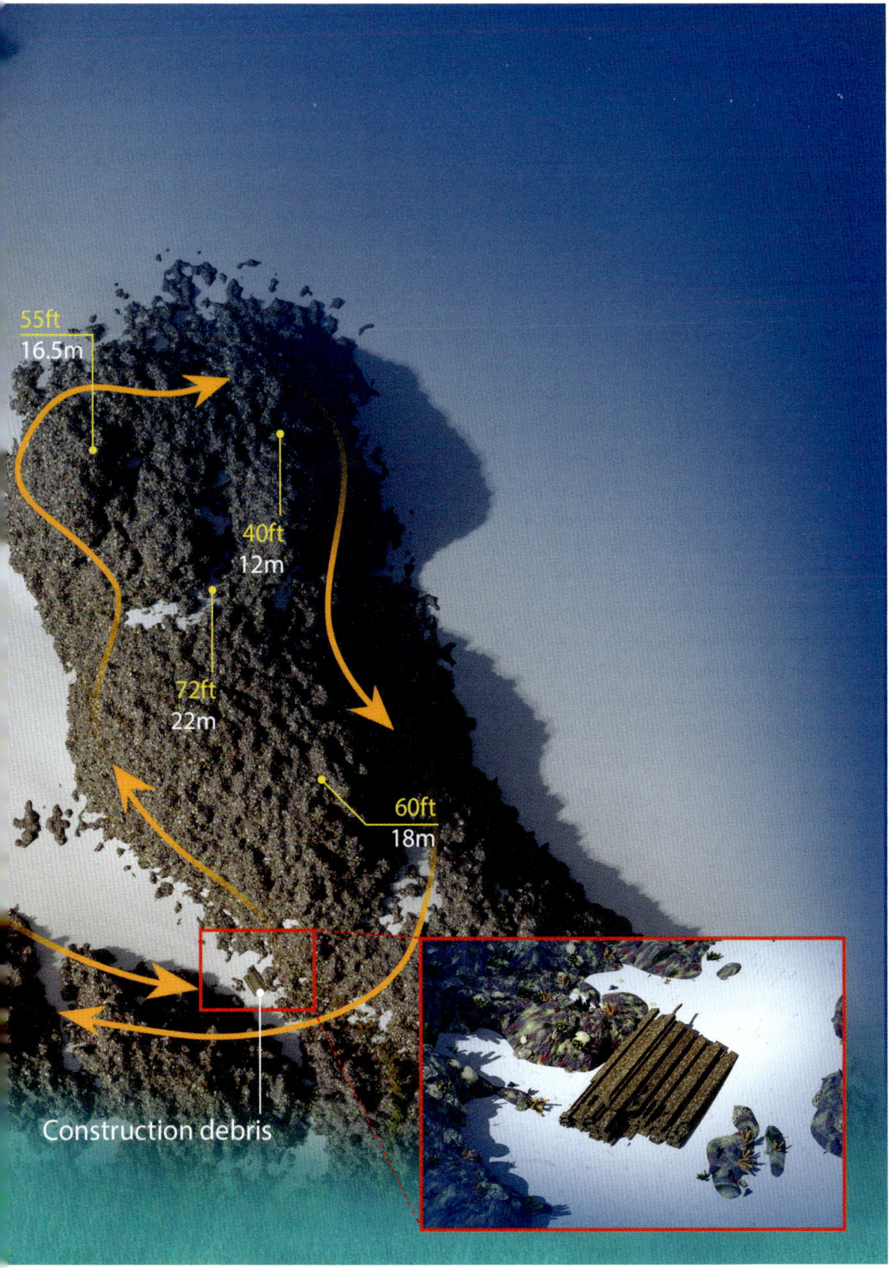


documented to cause female humpback whales and their calves to abandon certain areas of ocean in Hawaii. While in the Florida panhandle, interactions with bottlenose dolphins have habituated many of them to the presence of humans. One study showed that dolphins spent 77 percent of their time interacting with humans, which substantially decreased their time spent foraging. From the other side of the equation, there have also been several cases of severe injuries to humans in swim-with-dolphin experiences in both captive and wild settings.

# CARACASBAAI

Difficulty ●○○
Current ●○○
Depth ●●○
Reef ★☆☆
Fauna ★★☆

Access (boat) about 24 mins from Willemstad
Access (car) about 15 mins from Willemstad
Access (swim) about 4 mins from shore

**Level** Open Water

## Location

Caracasbaai, Curaçao
GPS 12°04.562'N, 68°51.780'W

## Getting there

Head south on Schottegatweg Zuid from Willemstad. Take the exit onto Kaya C. Winkel and the second exit at the roundabout onto Caracasbaaiweg. Follow this road for 4.5 miles (7.2 kilometers) until you reach another roundabout. Take the second exit, and continue on Caracasbaaiweg for 0.3 miles (0.5 kilometers) and then turn left into the large, free parking lot adjacent to the shore. Park near the building located at the center of the beach. It once hosted a restaurant called the Golden Seahorse, which is now closed. While the parking lot is large, this beach is popular with locals and spaces fill up fast, particularly on the weekend. The total distance from Willemstad is approximately 6 miles (9.7 kilometers).

## Access

Divers and snorkelers should gear up at the car and aim to enter the water near the building at the center of the beach. Playa Caracasbaai is mostly sandy, but the bottom soon transitions to rocks, so divers and snorkelers will need boots when visiting this site. The back reef extends from shore about 300 feet (91 meters) but is usually calm and current-free. Visibility is usually good, and this site is suitable for divers and snorkelers of all experience levels.

## Description

Caracasbaai, which is known as Caracas Bay in English, has a central back reef area that slopes gradually from the beach to the drop-off, which begins at about 20 feet (6 meters). There are several features worth exploring here, including a large concrete block and a structure made of metal wreckage, both of which host a wide range of coral reef species, including grunts, goatfish, snapper and trumpetfish. These are particularly good spots for snorkelers to explore.

## RELAX & RECHARGE

**Brisa Do Mar,** also known as Pop's Place, is located at the southeastern end of Playa Caracasbaai. The restaurant is open from 8am to 11pm. The breakfast menu includes salmon rolls, sweet or savory pancakes, and a wide selection of egg dishes, ranging from Huevos Rancheros to breakfast tacos. There's literally something for everyone here. Lunch and dinner options include wraps, paninis, burgers, salad, pasta, stews and steaks. The prego sandwich, made with tenderloin, arugula and pesto mayo, and served on a type of traditional Portuguese flatbread called bolo do caco, is one of the more unique items worth trying. Many people simply chill out with an ice-cold beer, cocktail or soft drink and enjoy many of the à-la-carte snacks, which include shrimp tempura, mussels, calamari, conch fritters, bitter balls and a range of other options. If you happen to be here on a Friday night, then you're in luck because that means it is Espetada Night, which is when seasoned meats are barbecued on skewers.
Visit: **Brisadomarpopsplace.everyorder.io**

The main reef slope contains a decent mix of corals and sponges and continues to a depth of about 110 feet (33.5 meters) before transitioning to sand and rubble. The coral cover is not particularly high at this site, but the reef still hosts a wide range of fish species, including scorpionfish, trunkfish, parrotfish, hamlets and moray eels. Divers and snorkelers may find sea turtles and anemones at this site.

In the southwest corner of the beach, in front of the restaurant Brisa Do Mar, the reef extends out from shore in a long, narrow, finger, which starts at 30 feet (9 meters) and drops gently to a depth of about 50 feet (15 meters). There is a sand channel here and the reef becomes noticeably steeper. This site is also popular as a night dive, due to its ease of access and its suitability for divers of all experience levels.

## DID YOU KNOW?

Fort Beekenburg was built in 1703 to defend the large bay known as Spaanse Water (Spanish Water), located in land from Playa Caracasbaai. At the time, this bay was the only suitable place to load and unload ships in Curaçao. Many of the rocks used to build the fort where formerly used as ship ballast and can be traced back to the Netherlands and Belgium. While active, the fort was armed with numerous cannons, including eight-pounders and twelve-pounders, but was officially abandoned in the mid-19th century. It remains one of the best-preserved forts on the island, and visitors can still walk around the complex today.

# 72 TUGBOAT CURAÇAO

Difficulty ● ○ ○
Current ● ○ ○
Depth ● ● ○
Reef ★★★
Fauna ★★★

Access about 24 mins from Willemstad
Access about 22 mins from Willemstad
Access about 2 mins from shore

**Level** Open Water

## Location

Caracasbaai Peninsula, Curaçao
GPS 12°04.120'N, 68°51.723'W

## Getting there

Head south from Willemstad on Presidente Rómulo Betancourt Boulevard, which becomes Schottegatweg Zuid. After 5.3 miles (8.5 kilometers), turn right onto Kaya C. Winkel and take the second exit at the roundabout onto Nieuwe Caracasbaaiweg. Continue along this road for 4.5 miles (7.2 kilometers) until the roundabout at Caracasbaai and turn left. The road runs along the beach before bending inland slightly and passing Fort Beekenberg. At the intersection after the fort, turn right to reach Tugboat Beach. The total distance from Willemstad is approximately 7 miles (11.4 kilometers).

## Access

This shore-accessible dive and snorkel site can be reached directly from the beach, which is free to enter. There is a decent-sized parking lot and a bar adjacent to the beach, as well as an art and souvenir shop where you can paint your own signs on driftwood. This small, west-facing bay is well protected from currents and waves, which makes it ideal for the whole family. The beach, which is located at the northern end of the small bay, is adjacent to a large pier for commercial ships. The bottom consists of a mix of sand and rocks, so divers and snorkelers are advised to wear booties when entering the water. The *Tugboat* wreck is located at the southern end of the bay – a distance of approximately 570 feet (174 meters) from the beach entry point.

## Description

*Tugboat Curaçao*, and its adjacent reef and wall, is one of the most popular sites in the whole of Curaçao. This picturesque wreck, sometimes simply called *Tugboat*, is the central feature of the site. It is located at the southern end of a shallow sandy plateau that ranges in depth from about 15 to 20 feet (4.5 to 6 meters). The wreck itself is only 6 feet (3 meters) beneath the surface in some places, which makes it ideal for exploration by both divers and snorkelers. *Tugboat* is also a great night-diving spot.

*Tugboat*, which is only 30 feet (9 meters) in length, was sunk by accident in the 1990s when a large ship anchor crashed onto its deck. The wreck has since become overgrown with numerous corals and sponges, and it plays host to a wide variety of reef creatures including blue parrotfish, sea turtles, schooling snapper and grunts, moray eels, lobsters, octopuses and even seahorses. Small schools of squid are often found above the wreck.

Seaward of the wreck, the reef drops away sharply to depths of over 100 feet (30 meters). Divers and snorkelers may encounter numerous anemones along the top of the slope. The wall itself supports sponges and soft corals, which often host flamingo tongues. At the northern end of the plateau, closer to the commercial shipping pier, the reef slope has a pronounced sandy ledge where stingrays and tarpon are often found. The pier, with its tall columns, is also a fascinating place for divers to explore provided there is no ship at anchor there.

## RELAX & RECHARGE

**Tugboat Beach Bar** has a friendly and relaxed vibe that even extends to the cats, dogs and iguanas that are often found chilling around the bar. Cold beer, wine, spirits and soft drinks are all served here, along with coffee and tea for those who require a little caffeine, and hot dogs and fries for those with an appetite. Sun loungers, snorkeling gear and even barbeques are available for rent. But most people just come here to chill, watch the world go by, and enjoy the décor, which consists of decorations that are about as varied as the marine life that lies off the beach. Visit: **Tugboat-beach.com**

## DID YOU KNOW?

The ruins of Curaçao's historic Quarantine House are located on the cliff above Tugboat Beach. Constructed in 1882, this building functioned as a quarantine station for sailors who were suspected of carrying contagious diseases, particularly yellow fever, which was a significant cause of death for those in the West Indies during colonial times. At the time, it was believed that yellow fever was spread by person-to-person contact, but by the turn of the century, scientists had determined that the disease was spread by mosquitoes. Extensive eradication efforts were implemented across the region in the early 20th century, and by 1925, Quarantine House had closed. The building began to fall into disrepair soon after.

The area around *Tugboat* also features many elements that make this site enjoyable to explore. Three large mooring towers are located off the stern of the wreck. Each of these structures features a thick chain that runs down the reef slope. A large anchor can be found closer to the beach at a depth of about 16 feet (5 meters). There are also several artificial reefs constructed of various metal debris and car tires located nearby. Divers and snorkelers may also see numerous coral frames from the active coral restoration project located directly out from the beach, anchored in the sandy ledge.

## ECO TIP

Fish feeding has become a popularly activity at *Tugboat*. While feeding allows divers and snorkelers to get up close and personal with the fish life, it significantly changes their natural behavior and can even make the fish sick, depending on what they are fed. The sergeant majors and yellowtail snapper at tugboat have become very aggressive, approaching divers and snorkelers very closely in anticipation of being fed, which can worry some people, particularly less proficient swimmers. There are even cases of these fish accidentally biting some people. Try to avoid feeding wild animals whenever possible and instead focus on observing their natural behavior. It's better for you and better for the environment.

*Tugboat* is a wonderful depth for both divers and snorkelers to explore.

NaturePicsFilms/Shutterstock©

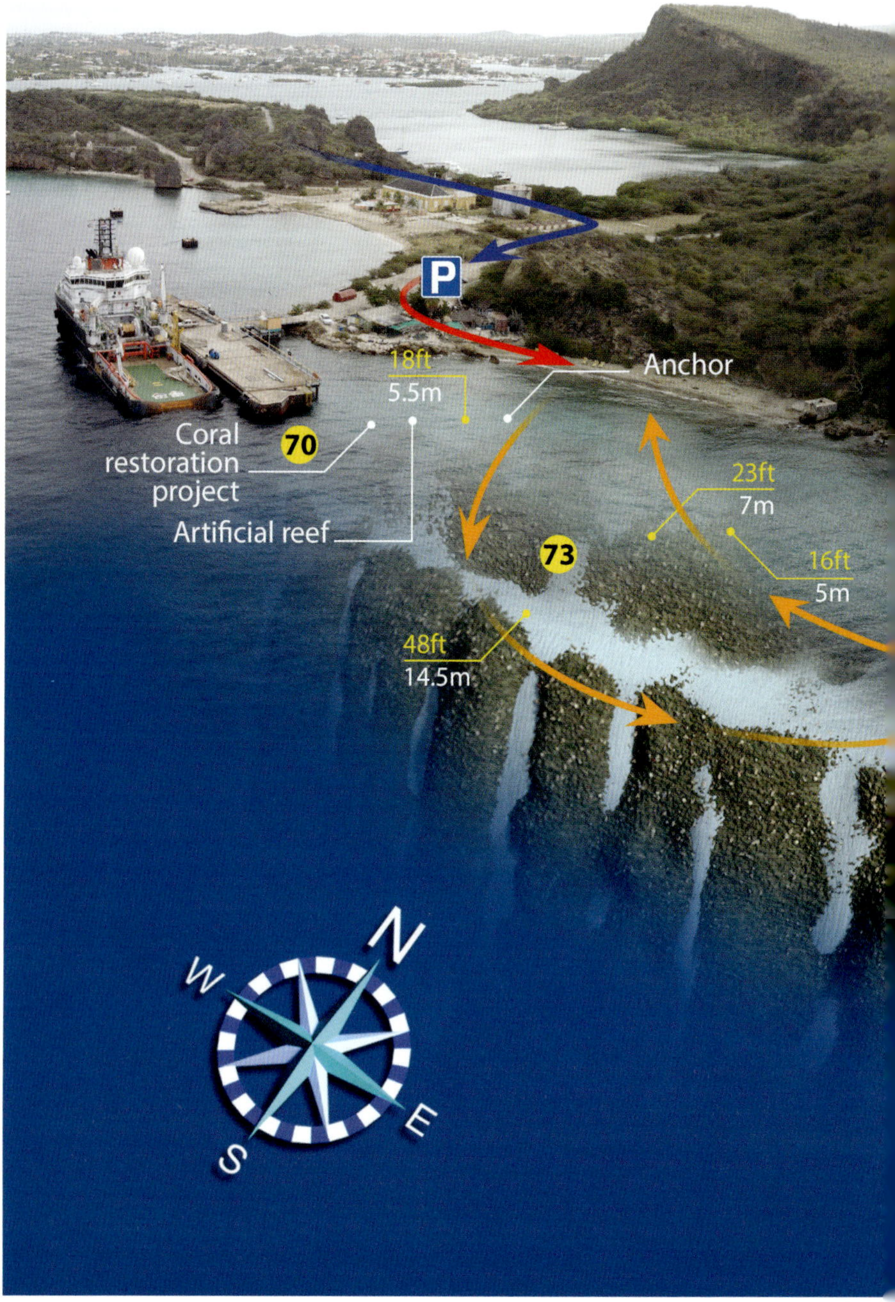


**Route**

Divers and snorkelers usually enter the water from the beach at the northern end of the site and begin by exploring the artificial reef structures, anchor and coral restoration project located on the sandy plateau. From there, snorkelers usually head directly to the *Tugboat* wreck – swimming toward the mooring pillars in the south of the site can assist with navigation. Meanwhile, divers often descend the reef slope adjacent to the pier and gradually move shallower while heading south along the wall before exploring the mooring towers and the *Tugboat* wreck as part of their safety stop.

Tugboat
18ft
5.5m

23ft
7m
S
W
E
N
6ft
2m
B

| | | | |
|---|---|---|---|
| **Name:** | *Tugboat Curaçao* | **Last owner:** | n/a |
| **Type:** | tugboat | **Sunk:** | 1990s |
| **Previous names:** | n/a | | |
| **Length:** | 30ft (9m) | | |
| **Tonnage:** | n/a | | |
| **Construction:** | n/a | | |

# DIRECTOR'S BAY

Difficulty ●○○
Current ●○○
Depth ●●○
Reef ★★☆
Fauna ★★☆

Access (boat) about 25 mins from Willemstad
Access (car) about 24 mins from Willemstad
Access (swim) about 1 mins from shore

**Level** Open Water

**Location**
Caracasbaai Peninsula, Curaçao
GPS 12°03.963'N, 68°51.602'W

## Getting there

Follow the directions to *Tugboat* (page 228), but instead of turning right at the intersection after Fort Beekenberg, which leads to Tugboat Beach, turn left. The road twists and turns for about 0.45 miles (0.65 kilometers) until a road exits on the left-hand side. Take this left turn and stay on this road for an additional 0.45 miles (0.65 kilometers). The road ends at a small parking lot that faces the ocean, adjacent to Director's Bay Beach. The total distance from Willemstad is approximately 7.6 miles (12.2 kilometers).

## Access

This shore-accessible dive and snorkel site can be reached directly from the beach, which is free to enter. Divers and snorkelers should gear up at their vehicle and walk down the short path and staircase that leads to the beach. There are several palapas on the beach that provide shade, as well as some vegetation, but there are no other amenities at this site. The beach consists mainly of coral rubble, so boots are advised. The water here is relatively well protected from currents and waves, which makes entering and exiting the water easy. The reef is less than 70 feet (21 meters) from the beach. Visitors should avoid leaving valuables in their car in this remote location.

## Description

Director's Bay is a stunning shore-accessible dive and snorkel site located on the Caracasbaai Peninsula, between the *Tugboat* and Small Wall sites. The site is also sometimes known as Kabaye. In the past, Director's Bay was considered a private swimming area for company directors of the Royal Dutch Shell Group, which is how the site got its name. The site has the remains of numerous large posts, some of which are embedded in the sand, as well as other debris that was once used to hold protective nets in place around the beach. It is believed that these were installed to ensure a safe, shark-free bathing experience prior to the first royal visit of Queen Juliana to the island in 1955. These posts extend from the middle of the beach out toward the drop-off for about 100 feet (30 meters), before running along the edge of the drop-off and then returning to shore about 200 feet (61 meters) farther south. Many of the pipes have fallen down the slope and those that remain are encrusted with corals and sponges.

The reef at Director's Bay features a spectacular wall that forms two large, scalloped indentations beginning at the beach access point and heading south. Narrow, broken spurs extend the length of the drop-off, separated by wide channels of sand and coral rubble that vary in width. The plateau at this site is particularly narrow adjacent to the beach and has a depth of only about 15 feet (4.5 meters). However, it extends out over 500 feet (150 meters) from shore farther to the south, where it forms a large, triangular plateau that shelters the bay from the open ocean. The adjacent site of Small Wall forms the ocean-side of the plateau.

There are dense areas of pencil coral at the top of the reef slope, which is a great area for snorkelers to explore. Large sponges and domed corals are scattered all along the wall, which features a series of undercuts and overhangs along the edges of the broken spurs. This complex reef habitat hosts a variety of reef fish, including blue parrotfish, scorpionfish, frogfish and octopuses. Divers and snorkelers also commonly report seeing barracuda and sea turtles at this site. To the north, the bay has a very steep, near-vertical, wall that curls around the headland and joins the adjacent *Tugboat* site.

## Route

Divers and snorkelers usually enter the water at the beach. The most common route involves swimming south into what is usually the prevailing current and exploring the steep reef in the direction of Small Wall. Most divers will only have enough air to explore the first scalloped indentations of the wall. For those divers who do explore all the way out beyond the second indentation, they should be aware the currents can pick up near the southern plateau where the prevailing currents can be strong outside of the bay.

The posts in the water at Director's Bay can be interesting to explore.

Turtle & Ray©

Divers may also choose to explore the northern part of this site as well, along the wall toward *Tugboat*. Divers and snorkelers can actually swim along the wall to the Tugboat site, which is a distance of approximately 0.2 miles (0.32 kilometers). Although this would likely require a second dive as there is generally not enough air to explore in both directions here. Snorkelers usually swim parallel with the shoreline along the edge of the drop-off, where there is plenty of marine life to see. Snorkelers should restrict their exploration to the first scalloped indentation of the bay, as surface currents can get strong out on the large plateau that marks the southern edge of the bay.

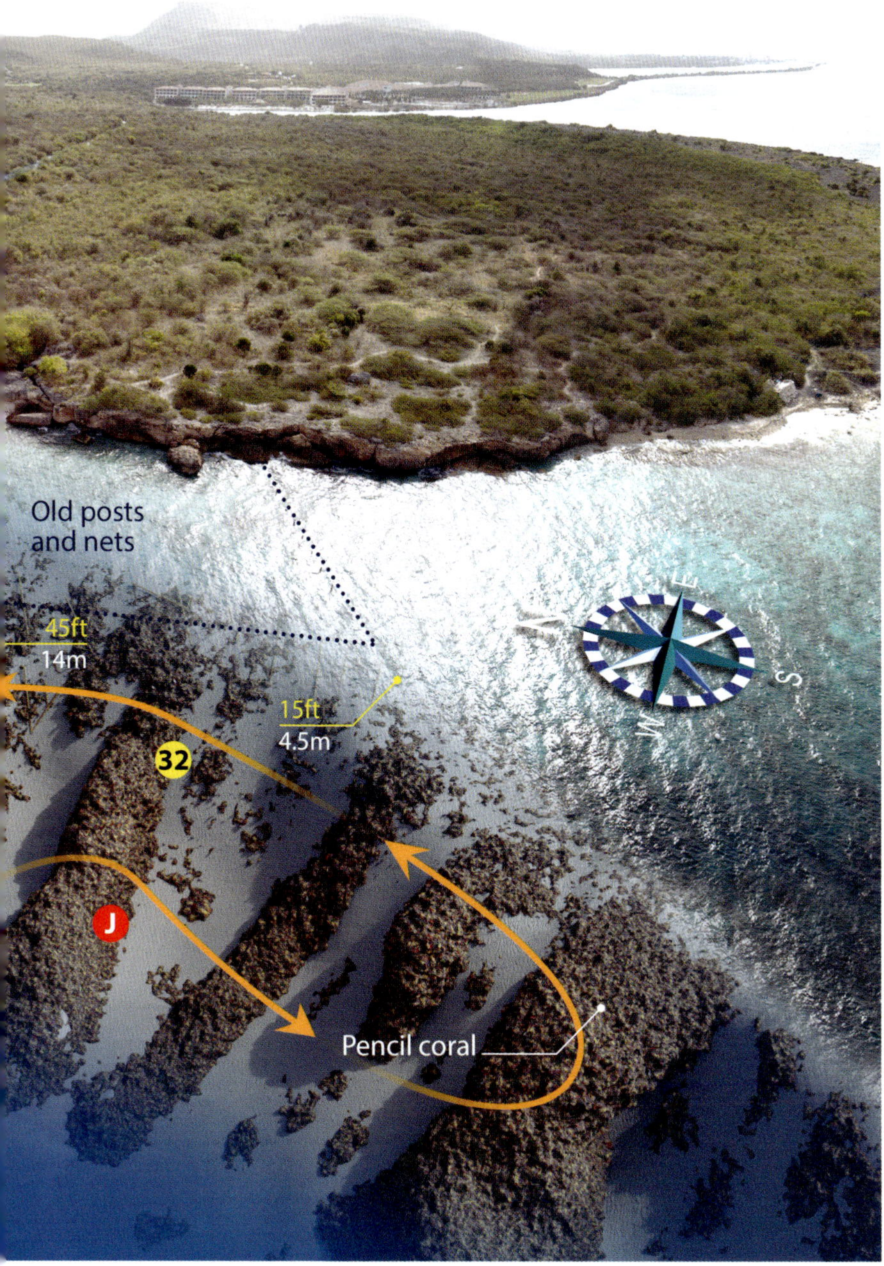
Old posts
and nets
45ft
14m
15ft
4.5m
32
J
Pencil coral
N
E
S
W

74

WILLEMSTAD

# SMALL WALL

Difficulty ●●○
Current ●●○
Depth ●●○
Reef ★★★
Fauna ★★☆

Access about 25 mins from Willemstad

**Level** Open Water

**Location**
Caracasbaai, Curaçao
GPS 12°03.800'N, 68°51.593'W

## Getting there

When conditions allow, experienced divers are able to access Small Wall from the adjacent sites of Director's Bay (page 234) and Barracuda Point (page 240). The site itself does not have direct shore access, however. The best way to reach this site is through one of the local dive operators located along Curaçao's southeast coast.

## Access

Small Wall is generally accessed by boat only. Currents are often moderate here, but they can be strong at times. Seas can also be choppy given the exposed nature of the site. Small Wall is suitable for divers and snorkelers of all experience levels, although experience with wall diving and drift diving is useful to fully explore the site.

## Description

Small Wall features a coral-filled plateau next to a nearly sheer drop-off that begins at between 35 and 40 feet (10.5 and 12 meters) and

## SAFETY TIP

Some divers explore Barracuda Point, Small Wall and Director's Bay as a multi-site drift dive. It is only possible to do this under ideal conditions. A strong current from the southeast is usually required to push divers through all three sites. The total bottom time is approximately 90 minutes, so exceptional air consumption is required, unless divers use a double-tank set up or bring a larger tank, such as a 100-cubic-foot (12-liter) tank. Additionally, the only exit point is at Director's Bay, which is a 0.45-mile (0.72-kilometer) walk back to the Barracuda Point entry. Divers will need to plan for this by arranging a pickup or hiking back to the start while leaving someone to watch their gear.

continues to depths well beyond recreational scuba limits. Only the first 15 feet (4.5 meter) of this drop-off is actually a wall, hence the name Small Wall. The rest of the wall is more like a steep slope, consisting of sand and coral rubble. Caves and undercuts can be found along this transition, where divers often find moray eels, lobsters, soldierfish and glasseye snapper.

Sand channels periodically cut through the wall, bounded by large coral mounds. Near the northwestern end of the site, adjacent to Director's Bay, the wall disappears entirely and the reef forms more of a slope, descending into the depths, which is dominated by soft corals, gorgonians and sponges, including plenty of orange elephant ear sponges and tube sponges. Sea whips are present along deeper sections. Divers are also likely to see French angelfish, Spanish hogfish and grouper, while above the reef, creole wrasses are present in high numbers along with the occasional barracuda.

# BARRACUDA POINT

Difficulty ●●○
Current ●●●
Depth ●●○
Reef ★★★
Fauna ★★★

Access about 27 mins from Willemstad
Access about 26 mins from Willemstad
Access about 15 mins from shore

**Level** Open Water

## Location

Caracasbaai, Curaçao
GPS 12°03.973′N, 68°51.232′W (shore access)

## Getting there

Follow the directions to *Tugboat* (page 228), but instead of turning right at the interaction after Fort Beekenberg, which leads to Tugboat Beach, turn left. The road twists and turns for about 0.45 miles (0.65 kilometers) until a road exits on the left-hand side. Take this left turn and then take the next left turn after another 500 feet (150 meters) onto a dirt road. The road ends at a parking lot adjacent to the water after an additional 850 feet (260 meters). The total distance from Willemstad is approximately 8 miles (13 kilometers). Barracuda Point can be challenging to access from shore, so the best way to access this site is often through one of the local dive operators on Curaçao's southeast coast.

## Access

Diver and snorkelers should gear up at their vehicle and walk down the short path to the water's edge. Entering the water involves

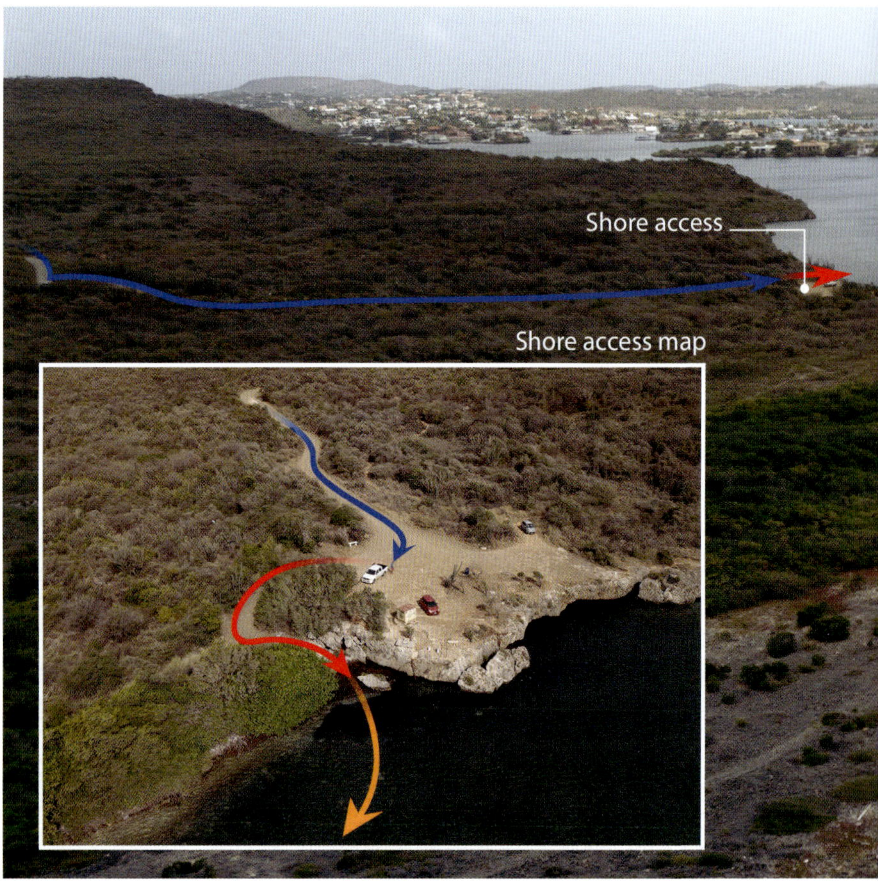

wading out approximately 140 feet (43 meters) across a submerged mudflat, which contains seagrass. Boots are recommended. Divers and snorkelers must then swim along the western edge of the channel for 630 feet (190 meters) to reach the site. In the process divers will need to traverse a sand berm that crosses the channel. Barracuda Point is located to the west of the inlet. Divers are advised to bring a surface marker buoy (SMB) when exploring this site as the channel provides boat access to Spanish Water and can get busy. Visitors should avoid leaving valuables in their car in this remote location.

## Description

Barracuda Point reportedly gets its name from the many barracuda that can be found along this healthy stretch of coral reef. This site, which is also known as Punt'i Piku, is marked by complex reef habitat along the shallow plateau. Large stands of elkhorn and staghorn coral, pillar coral, yellow pencil coral and large dome-shaped brain coral abound in the shallows, which supports one of the healthiest coral reef habitats on the island.

The reef forms a point as it exits the inlet, and then curves around to the west, where it develops into a distinct wall that tops out at 25 feet (7.5 meters) and bottoms out between 50 and 60 feet (15 and 18.5 meters). At its base, the wall disappears into a steep rubble and sand slope that descends into the depths, and undercuts and overhangs often mark its base as it continues to the west.

Near the western edge of the site, the base of the wall shallows and turns into a smaller wall as it transitions into the adjacent site, aptly named Small Wall, even as the slope below the wall remains steep. The wall is dominated by soft corals and gorgonians, along with large sponges. Barracuda are plentiful in the water column near the point, while creole wrasses, foureye butterflyfish, stoplight parrotfish and sea turtles abound in the complex reef habitat of the plateau and upper reef slope.

# EEL VALLEY

Difficulty ●○○
Current ●○○
Depth ●●○
Reef ★★☆
Fauna ★★☆

Access about 8 mins from Spanish Water

**Level** Open Water

## Location

Santa Barbara, Curaçao
GPS 12°03.515′N, 68°50.621′W

## Getting there

Eel Valley is a boat-accessible dive site located in the Santa Barbara area of Curaçao. The best way to reach this site is through one of the local dive operators located along Curaçao's southeast coast.

## Access

Currents can be easy to moderate, and the visibility is often good. There is typically a mooring buoy anchored at the top of the reef slope at this site, which helps make it accessible to divers of all experience levels.

## Description

Eel Valley is located just seaward of the 3rd hole of the famous Old Quarry Golf Course, and it extends along the breakwater that marks the edge of nearby Fuikbaai. The site gets its name from the brown garden eels that are found in high concentrations along the shallow sandy plateau toward the eastern end of the site. This plateau extends approximately 330 feet (100 meters) from shore along the western end of the site but gets wider toward the eastern side of the site as the drop-off curves slightly southward and away from shore. This plateau is also known to host other unique species, including stingrays, hogfish, slender filefish and a wide diversity of butterflyfish.

The transition from sand to reef happens relatively quickly along the top of the drop-off, which sits at a depth of around 25 feet (7.5 meters). The reef slope is very steep at Eel Valley, almost wall-like in some places, and features large, distinct spurs that descend into the depths. To the west of the mooring buoy, the steep slope consists of sand and rubble with small patches of hard and soft corals and large tube sponges scattered along the slope. The main focus of Eel Valley is generally to the east of the buoy, where the habitat is marked by a series of spurs.

Hard coral mounds occur at varying depths, while the slope itself curves inward gently between the spurs. Dominated by sand, these wide channels are peppered with small coral patches, particularly along the top near the back reef plateau. Large barrel sponges mark the edge of the spurs with orange elephant ear sponges more common in the deeper areas. Observant divers will notice a few of the coral mounds form distinct shapes, such as one with a hole through the middle like a donut standing on its side, which sits at a depth of 36 feet (10.5 meters). These coral shapes can help divers keep track of where they are on the reef as they head out and then again on their return leg.

Nearly two-thirds of the way along the slope toward the turnaround point, the reef slope is marked by two coral ridges that border a deep V-shaped channel of sand that is set back into the reef slope. The western edge of this channel is a very broad spur that cuts back against the general angle of the slope, pointing almost due west. The sandy slope beyond this broad

### SCIENTIFIC INSIGHT

Most reef fish swallow their prey by creating a negative pressure space in their throats, which pulls the prey down toward their stomach. The unique physiology of moray eels means they are unable to do this. Instead, they have an interesting adaptation known as pharyngeal jaws that helps them swallow their prey. This highly maneuverable set of jaws is located just behind their first, main set of jaws, and it launches forward to bite down on the prey. The pharyngeal jaws pull the prey down the eel's throat. The moray's pharyngeal jaws were only discovered in 2007 by scientists at the University of California, Davis.

spur does not cut back toward shore as it does in earlier sections of the dive. Instead, the sand beyond the spur is flush with the leading edge of the spur, creating a new slope that projects farther out from the plateau.

This section of reef slope has its own set of spurs as well as a series of ledges and a small wall that sits at a depth of around 70 feet (21.5 meters). The turnaround point for the site is just beyond this new transition. A final spur marks a transition back to a reef slope dominated by scattered coral patches and rubble similar to the reef that lies to the west of the buoy.

Back up on the reef plateau, a large ridge of scattered hard corals and gorgonians marks the halfway point of the site. A coral restoration project is located next to this ridge, with small frames located at a depth of 20 feet (6 meters).

Soft corals provide wonderful habitat for reef fish at Eel Valley.

Turtle & Ray©

These frames support dozens of coral fragments. Divers will see plenty of brown garden eels on the plateau, along with anemones and yellow goatfish.

### Route

Most divers focus their time exploring the section of reef slope that features the prominent spur-like ridges. These features produce more complex habitat that supports a variety of reef life. Blue chromis are often seen up in the water column above the spurs forming large schools with creole wrasses. Divers can count the spurs starting with the one immediately adjacent to the buoy or simply make their way to the west until they reach the halfway point in their air

consumption. As with most dive sites in Curaçao, the most interesting habitat is found at a depth of between 40 and 70 feet (12 and 21.5 meters).

Most return routes hug the sand-reef transition along the edge of the plateau, veering shoreward to explore the coral nursery and the shallow ridge of hard and soft corals that mark the halfway point of the dive. The plateau is shallow enough that it offers a way to recover some bottom time after diving along the wall, as well as to conduct an extended safety stop on the way back to the buoy.

# 77 NEWPORT/BOOBY TRAP

Difficulty ●●●
Current ●●●
Depth ●●○
Reef ★★★
Fauna ★★☆

**Level** Advanced

**Location**
Newport, Curaçao
GPS 12°02.948'N, 68°49.990'W



Newport (spelled Nieuwpoort in Dutch) is located just off shore of the Fuikbaai natural harbor, where the docks for the nearby Table Mountain phosphorus mines are located. The site is also known as Fuikbaai, and the northwestern end of the site is often referred to as Booby Trap. The only safe way to access this site is by boat, usually through one of the dive centers located in the southeast of Curaçao. The site consists of a beautiful steep sloping reef packed with dome-shaped brain and star coral as well as gorgonians. The site also hosts a wide diversity of sponges. This diverse habitat attracts a range of reef creatures, including schoolmaster snapper, butterflyfish and parrotfish, including the relatively rare blue parrotfish. Large schools of bait fish are common at this site, which attract a higher than normal density of barracuda and bar jacks. Divers and snorkelers may also spot nurse sharks, eagle rays and sea turtles here.

# 78 KATHY'S PARADISE

Difficulty ●●●
Current ●●●
Depth ●●●
Reef ★★★
Fauna ★★★

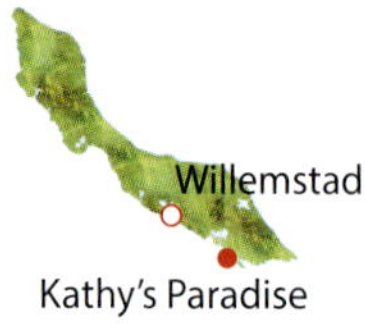


**Level** Advanced

**Location**
Newport, Curaçao
GPS 12°02.573'N, 68°49.115'W

Kathy's Paradise, which is named after an avid diver who loved this site, is also known as Barank'i Karanito. The site is located off shore from the southeastern end of Fuikbaai. The back reef has a dense cover of corals, including lettuce coral, brain coral, finger coral, pencil coral and gorgonians, which makes it a great place for snorkeling when the conditions are right. Unfortunately, this site commonly features strong currents and significant wave action, which makes snorkeling challenging. The high density of hard and soft corals flows down the reef slope and into the depths, which becomes noticeably less steep below a depth of approximately 70 feet (21 meters). The reef slope has numerous undercut areas where divers may find lobsters, moray eels and the occasional nurse shark. The site ends at a distinct ridge line that cuts sharply back toward shore.

Greens and Blues/Shutterstock©

## DID YOU KNOW?

Salt pans, such as those shown in this image, are found across Curaçao. They are often referred to as saliñas, which is the Papiamentu word for salt pan. Salt production played a significant role in shaping Curaçao's early economy and history.

The origins of the industry in Curaçao can be traced back to the island's discovery by Spanish explorers, but it was the Dutch, and more specifically the Dutch West Indies Company, who developed the industry and transformed Curaçao into a major salt exporter. Sadly, much of this development relied heavily on enslaved labor until it was abolished in 1863.

In the latter half of the 20th century, the salt industry in Curaçao experienced a decline from reduced demand and increased competition. Salt mining still occurs in Curaçao today, albeit on a smaller scale than in the past. And smaller in scale relative to neighboring Bonaire. Today, virtually all of the salt produced on the island is exported to Honduras.

# SMOKEY'S

| | |
|---|---|
| Difficulty | ●●● |
| Current | ●●○ |
| Depth | ●●● |
| Reef | ★★★ |
| Fauna | ★★★ |

**Level** Advanced

**Location**
Newport, Curaçao
GPS 12°02.413'N, 68°48.627'W

Smokey's is located to the southeast of Kathy's Paradise. The shallow back reef plateau at this site is slightly more sheltered from the wind and waves than at neighboring sites, which means it may be more suitable for snorkeling. The current is often moderate to strong, however, and can change rapidly. The current also tends to increase toward the southeast point, where the plateau widens noticeably. Large fields of staghorn and elkhorn coral can be found in the back reef, providing habitat for a wide range of reef creatures, including schools of grunts, goatfish and butterflyfish. The reef slope descends steeply to about 100 feet (30 meters) where it transitions to more of a slope with coral rubble and sand. Large sponges can be found here, including barrel, vase and tube sponges, as well as large elephant ear sponges. When these sponges reproduce, they often appear to be "smoking," which is how the site came to be named. Lobsters, moray eels and large grouper are also common in the deeper parts of the site.

# GULIAW

Difficulty ●●○
Current ●●○
Depth ●●○
Reef ★★★
Fauna ★★★

Access about 24 mins from Spanish Water

**Level** Advanced

## Location

Oostpunt, Curaçao
GPS 12°02.196'N, 68°48.122'W

## Getting there

Guliaw is a dive site located near Oostpunt that is only accessible by boat. The best way to reach this site is through one of the local dive operators located along Curaçao's southeast coast. Its remote location means this east point site is not visited as frequently as more centrally located dive sites.

## Access

Access to this site depends on the weather, particularly the strength and direction of the winds. Currents are often strong, and seas can be choppy since this section of coastline is very exposed. Drift diving is almost always the only option for exploring the reefs in this area of Curaçao. This site is better suited to advanced divers. And while sections of the reef plateau are shallow enough to be accessible to snorkelers, the conditions are often too rough at the surface to allow snorkeling.

## Description

Guliaw is located just west of the southernmost tip of the island, and part of the reef extends along the narrow strip of rocky beach that borders Lagun Blanku. Like the adjacent Smokey's, this site is also sometimes known as Punti Sanchi. While the GPS coordinates provided mark an excellent section of explorable reef, the reality is that divers can expect to see a spectacular, near-pristine reef pretty much anywhere along this stretch of coastline. And since there is no permanent mooring ball here, many operators use their own names and have their own preferred drop points in this area.

The east end of the island is almost entirely undeveloped. It is privately owned and thus inaccessible to the public, which is why this site is not shore accessible despite being mere steps from the beach. Fortunately, the relative inaccessibility and the undeveloped nature of this part of the island means the reefs along this stretch of coastline are rarely visited and are largely undisturbed. That means the lucky divers who do venture this far east are in store for an incredible experience.

The reef plateau at Guliaw extends roughly 250 feet (75 meters) from the rocky beach and reaches a depth of around 25 to 35 feet (7.5 to 10.5 meters) at its seaward edge. It is dominated by large mounds of star coral, big boulder brain corals and sea fans. Soft corals and gorgonians are scattered among the hard corals, and the whole area looks like an underwater garden – one with heavy surge in the shallow areas.

Along its seaward edge, the plateau gives way to a steep reef slope that is covered in brain coral, star coral, lettuce coral, pillar coral and small groups of soft corals and gorgonians. Large purple tube sponges stand as much as 7 feet (2 meters) above the reef in some instances, while plate-form corals dominate the deeper areas of the slope. The plateau ends in a sharp drop-off to a wall in some places along its edge, whereas other sections feature a gentler transition to the slope below. Multiple large depressions on the edge of the reef plateau are filled with sand that feed narrow channels that descend the reef slope below. Large, wide spurs dotted with healthy corals frequently extend out from the wall in between these channels, giving the slope an undulating feel in some sections.

The features are dramatic along this stretch of the reef, which often makes divers feel small next to the towering reef slope. The coral cover is dense, and the substrate is very rugose, all of which create incredible habitat for a variety of marine life. Divers will come across everything from large, predatory barracuda to skittish snook. Trumpetfish and filefish are often seen among the gorgonians while yellowtail snapper, bar jacks and eagle rays are often spotted above the reef. Large lionfish are also often spotted here. In short, the health of the reef is on full display at

## SCIENTIFIC INSIGHT

Rugosity is a measurement of the complexity of a surface. It is often used in studies of coral reefs to help quantify the structure of a reef to compare one reef to another. It is expressed as a ratio between the length of a chain or line that is run along the surface of the reef and the linear distance between those same two points. A flat plane has no rugosity (a value of 1.0), but a reef with many coral heads and crevices is said to have high rugosity (values much greater than 1.0). A high-rugosity environment is not only an indication of higher coral coverage, it also means there is more surface area for new corals to colonize. High rugosity habitats also support more coral reef creatures because there are more places for them to hide.

Guliaw and most divers will find it is worth the extra effort to get out to see this part of Curaçao.

## Route

Most divers explore these east point sites as drift dives. The lack of permanent mooring buoys give operators flexibility on dropping divers in favorite spots along the shoreline and letting them explore to the east or the west, depending on the strength and direction of the current. As with many Curaçao dive sites, the reef itself descends to great depth, but the best experience is often in relatively shallow water, typically between 40 and 70 feet (12 and 21.5 meters). The features are most pronounced here and the coral cover is more dense.

As bottom time becomes a limiting factor, divers often shallow up and explore the incredible diversity and density of corals found along the reef plateau. Many divers enjoy drifting along the plateau during an extended safety stop, although they will need to swim away from shore to allow a safe pickup by the boat at the end of the dive.

Some of the large soft corals on the island are present at Guliaw.

Turtle & Ray©

35ft
10.5m
37ft
11.5m
17
J
88ft
27m
85ft
26m
N
W
E
S

1
51
71
G
26ft
8m
90ft
27.5m

# BEST REEF

Difficulty ●●●
Current ●●●
Depth ●●●
Reef ★★★
Fauna ★★★

Access about 29 mins from Spanish Water

**Level** Advanced

## Location

Oostpunt, Curaçao
GPS 12°02.357'N, 68°47.067'W

## Getting there

Best Reef is a dive site located in the Newport area of Curaçao that is only accessible by boat. The best way to reach this site is through one of the local dive operators located along Curaçao's southeast coast.

## Access

Currents are often strong at Best Reef and the visibility is usually good. Seas can be choppy at times. This site is better suited to advanced divers.

## Description

Best Reef is located directly off shore from the Awa Blanku lagoon, which is the alternate name of this site. The strong current here often makes drift diving the only option,

## SCIENTIFIC INSIGHT

Staghorn and elkhorn corals (*Acropora cervicornis* and *A. palmata*, respectively), sometimes referred to collectively as acropora corals, are the fastest growing coral species in the Caribbean. Along with star corals, these species have been the most dominant reef building corals in the region over the past 5,000 years. Stony corals grow by secreting a calcium carbonate skeleton. This process is incredibly slow, with growth rates of less than 0.4 inches (1 centimeter) per year for most coral species. Staghorn and elkhorn corals however, can grow at a much faster rate, sometimes more than 4 inches (10 centimeters) per year under ideal conditions. Their rapid growth and branching form, which creates complex habitat for a wide range of reef creatures, makes acropora corals ideal for reef restoration programs throughout the Caribbean.

which is why this is a dive site for advanced divers with a drift specialty. These conditions make this site particularly pristine, even by Curaçao standards. The back reef, which is not particularly wide at this site, is covered in soft corals and branching staghorn and elkhorn corals. This would be a great site for snorkelers to explore if the seas were calm, but unfortunately conditions are often rough here. The reef slope is mostly vertical, with steep walls that are occasionally split by cascading sand channels. Numerous ledges are cut into the face of the slope with overhanging roofs. Divers often report nurse sharks sheltering in these areas, as well as lobsters and moray eels. Barracuda and eagle rays can often be spotted up in the water column.

Greens and Blues/Shutterstock©

# PIEDRA PRETU (BLACK ROCK)



Difficulty ●●○
Current ●●○
Depth ●●○
Reef ★★★
Fauna ★★★

Access about 34 mins from Spanish Water

**Level** Advanced

## Location

Oostpunt, Curaçao
GPS 12°02.643'N, 68°46.265'W

## Getting there

Black Rock is a dive site located near Oostpunt that is only accessible by boat. The best way to reach this site is through one of the local dive operators located along Curaçao's southeast coast. Its remote location means this east point site is not visited as frequently as more centrally located dive sites.

## Access

Access to this site depends on the weather, particularly the strength and direction of the winds. Currents are often strong, and seas can be choppy since this section of coastline is very exposed. Drift diving is almost always the only option for exploring the reefs in this part of Curaçao. This site is better suited to advanced divers. And while sections of the reef plateau are shallow enough for snorkeling, this site is only accessible for snorkelers when conditions are calm enough to allow it.

## Description

Piedra Pretu, or Black Rock as it is known in English, gets its name from the black rock that once served as a shoreline landmark for dive operators. The site also goes by the name Midway, as it sits midway between the southernmost tip of the island and the easternmost point. While the GPS coordinates provided mark an excellent section of explorable reef, the reality is that divers can expect to see a spectacular, near-pristine reef pretty much anywhere along this stretch of coastline. And since there is no permanent mooring ball here, many operators use their own names and have their own preferred drop points in this area.

The east end of the island is almost entirely undeveloped, giving divers who venture out this far east an idea of what it may have looked like to early settlers centuries ago. In similar fashion, the reef itself hearkens back to a different time. Healthy mounds of star coral dominate the plateau along with smaller mounds of lettuce and mustard hill corals. Scattered among these hard corals stand 10-foot-tall (3-meter) soft corals and gorgonians that have grown to the size of trees. The massive elkhorn corals and wide fields of staghorn corals further testify to the health of this reef and the quality of the water as it arrives from the open ocean.

Eagle rays are often spotted cruising the reef at east point sites such as Black Rock.

The reef plateau at Black Rock extends roughly 250 feet (75 meters) from the rocky beach and reaches a depth of around 25 to 30 feet (7.5 to 9 meters) at its seaward edge. The plateau gives way to a reef slope covered in brain coral, star coral, lettuce coral and pillar coral, along with a dense covering of smaller soft corals and gorgonians. The reef along this stretch alternates between sections of vertical wall and slopes of varying steepness. Wide and narrow spurs mark the slope along its entire length, providing divers with a sense of progress – and a means of navigation, if necessary – as they explore along the reef. Sharp, narrow sand channels cut through the slope as well, often creating notches along the top of the wall that offer divers a peek at the wealth of corals dominating the plateau above.

The features along this stretch of reef are all oversized. Towering coral mounds, massive soft corals, wide spurs and deep grooves all serve to make divers feel small as they drift along with the prevailing currents. So too does the marine life along this stretch of rarely visited reef. Massive barracuda, snapper and jacks patrol the water column above the reef and along the walls, while large grouper hide among the large coral mounts, waiting to ambush prey. Blue and brown chromis, creole wrasses and other pelagic fish flit about in the water column feasting on the plankton brought in by the ocean currents. Sea turtles, nurse sharks and large eagle rays are also often spotted along this length of the reef, attracted by the density of marine life present here.

## Route

Most divers explore these east point sites as drift dives. The lack of permanent mooring buoys give operators flexibility on dropping divers in favorite spots along the shoreline and letting

Turtle & Ray©

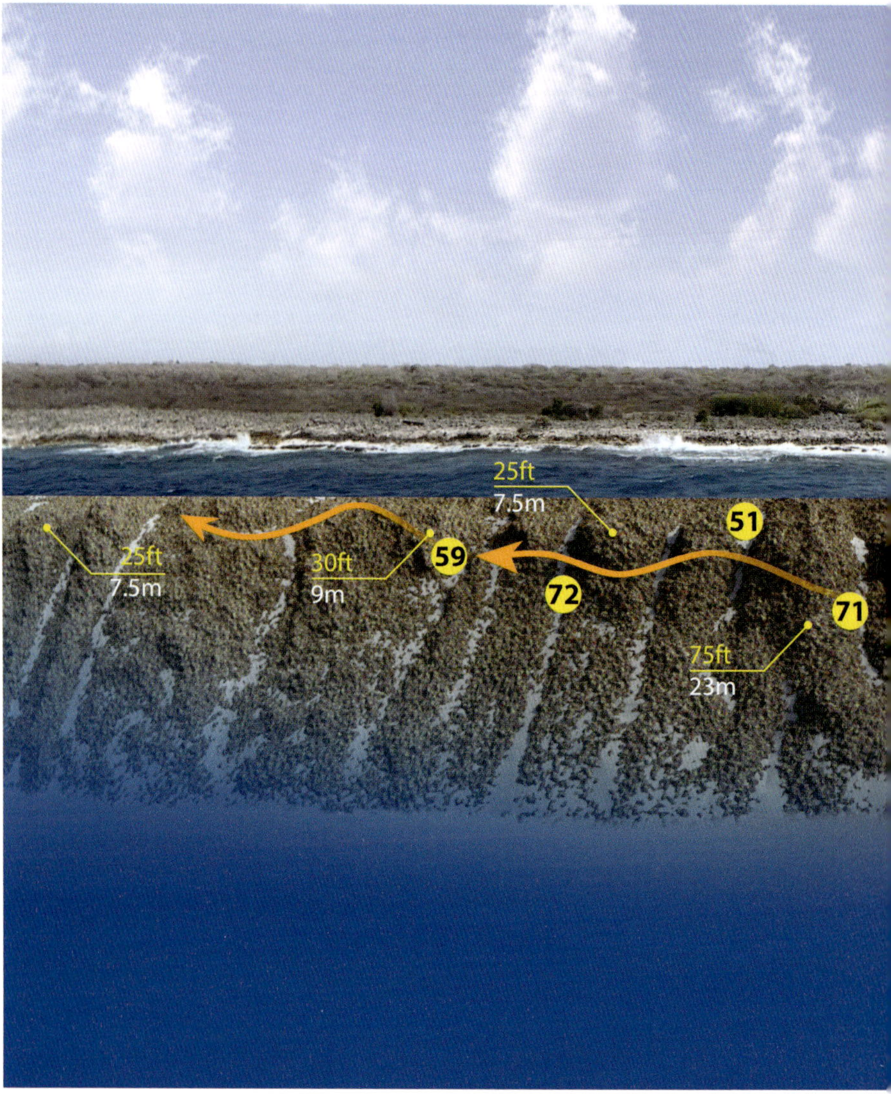


them explore to the east or the west, depending on the strength and direction of the current. As with many Curaçao dive sites, the reef itself descends to great depth, but the best experience is often in relatively shallow water, typically between 50 and 70 feet (15 and 21.5 meters). The features are most pronounced here and the coral cover is densest.

As bottom time becomes a limiting factor, divers often shallow up and explore the incredible diversity and density of corals found along the reef plateau. Many divers enjoy drifting along the plateau during an extended safety stop, although they will need to swim away from shore to allow a safe pickup by the boat at the end of the dive.

## DID YOU KNOW? ?

Orange cup corals (*Tubastraea coccinea*) are originally from the Indo-Pacific region. These non-reef-building corals were first observed in the Caribbean in 1943, specifically in the waters around the island of Curaçao. Scientists believe they arrived attached to the hulls of vessels traveling from the Pacific to the Atlantic. They are hard corals that resemble an anemone, and they feed by using their tentacles to grab small

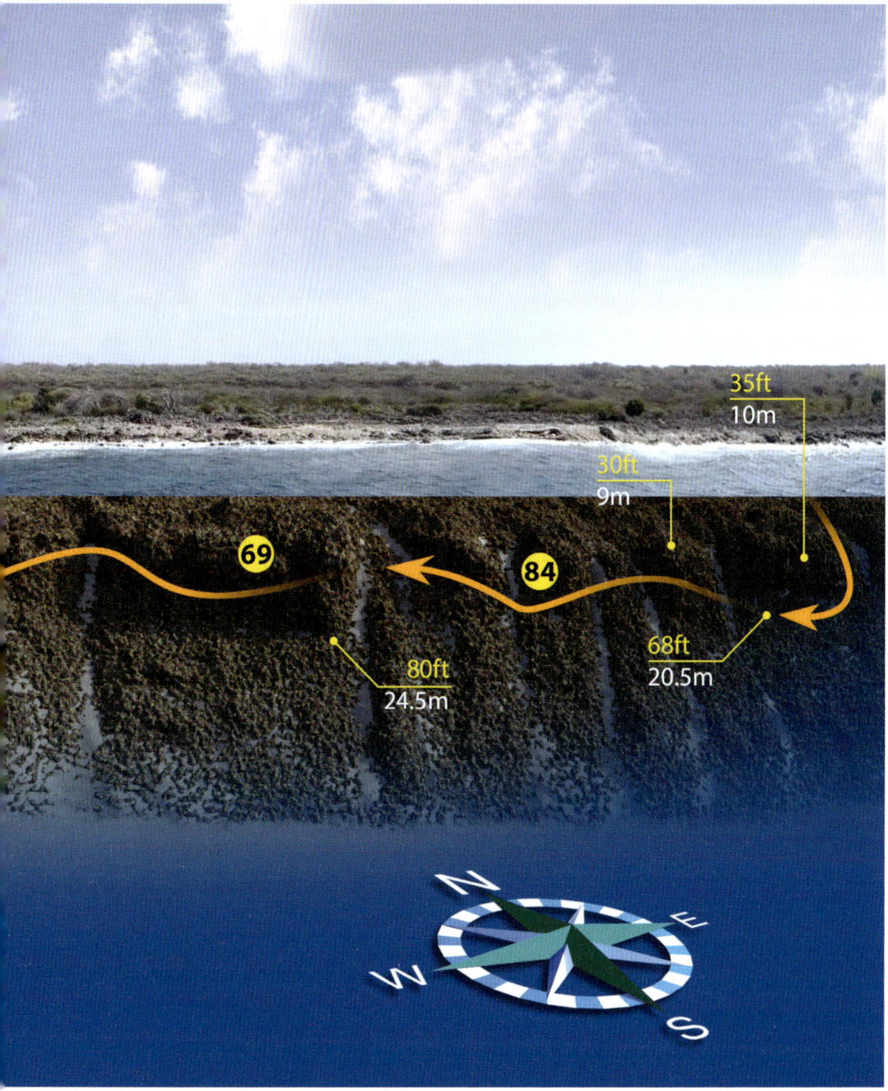


animals and organic particles as they flow by. Unlike native hard corals, they do not rely on photosynthetic algae in their tissues. As a result, they do best in water that is constantly flowing, which is why they have thrived along the island's eastern and western points. They can also be found in darker areas of the reef that other light-dependent corals find harder to survive.

Real estate is a hot commodity on reefs, and these invasive corals are constantly fighting a battle for space against native corals for the best reef locations. Orange cup corals are aided by the fact that they have no natural predators in their adopted home of the Western Atlantic. At this point, it is unlikely that orange cup corals will be eradicated from the reefs around Curaçao as they are simply too well established in the region. They are located throughout the Caribbean Sea and the Gulf of Mexico and have been found as far north as Alaska.

# PUNT KANON

Difficulty ● ● ●
Current ● ● ●
Depth ● ● ●
Reef ★★★
Fauna ★★★

Access about 41mins from Spanish Water

**Level** Advanced

## Location

Oostpunt, Curaçao
GPS 12°02.448'N, 68°44.390'W

## Getting there

Punt Kanon is a dive site located close to Curaçao's East Point. It is only accessible by boat. The best way to reach this site is through one of the local dive operators located along Curaçao's southeast coast.

## Access

Currents are often strong at Punt Kanon and the visibility is usually good. Seas can be choppy. This site is better suited to advanced divers.

## Description

Punt Kanon, sometimes spelled Punt Canon, is a dive site located close to the East Point of Curaçao, which is why this site is sometimes referred to as Oostpunt, or East Point in English. The site is actually off shore from the Awa di Oostpunt lagoon.

The reef at this site slopes steeply into the depths and has a high density of healthy corals and sponges, including pillar corals. Drift diving is the most common way to explore this site, but when currents cooperate, divers can complete a circular route that ends on the shallow back reef plateau, which averages about 20 feet (6 meters) and often contains cushion sea stars. On the reef, eagle rays, tarpon and nurse sharks are often found.

jimcatlinphotography.com/Shutterstock©

Nurse sharks are a common sight on east point sites such as Punt Kanon.

NaturePicsFilms/Shutterstock©

# TARPON BRIDGE

Difficulty ●●●
Current ●●●
Depth ●●○
Reef ★★★
Fauna ★★★

Access about 45 mins from Spanish Water

**Level** Advanced

## Location

Oostpunt, Curaçao
GPS 12°03.018'N, 68°44.377'W

## Getting there

Tarpon Bridge is a dive site located just north of Curaçao's eastern point. It is only accessibly by boat. The best way to reach this site is through one of the local dive operators located along Curaçao's southeast coast.

## Access

Currents are often strong at Tarpon Bridge, and the visibility is usually good. Seas can be choppy. This site is better suited to advanced divers.

## Description

The central feature of Tarpon Bridge is a large underwater archway where tarpon often congregate – it is this feature that gives this site its name. This structure is located at a depth of approximately 60 feet (18 meters) and is large enough for divers to swim through. The width of this arch is significantly wider than its height, so divers will need to have good buoyancy control to swim through the 20 feet (6 meters) of clearance without impacting the structure. If in doubt, it is best to observe this beautiful feature from a distance.

Orange cup corals can be found around the arch, and the seafloor is covered with waving gorgonians and other species of soft coral, as well as small dome-shaped corals and sponges. Beyond the tarpon that always seem to be present at this site, divers may also encounter large barracuda, eagle rays and sea turtles.

Divers often drift to the northwest when exploring this site, gradually shallowing along the gently sloping ledge, which ends abruptly at the shoreline in a small vertical wall. A small, sand-bottomed, underwater cave is located here, which is cut into the cliff face. This feature is referred to by some as Love Cave and may occasionally contain nurse sharks resting on the floor.

Tarpon are often found sheltering beneath the natural arch found at this site.

## SCIENTIFIC INSIGHT

Tarpon (*Megalops atlanticus*) can grow to an incredible 8 feet (2.5 meters) and weigh as much as 350 pounds (160 kilograms). Individuals have also been aged to over 60 years. Tarpon have a long and storied association with humans through history. The species has been fished for centuries and their scales have been used as nail files and jewelry. Their scales have also been crushed for medicinal purposes – a practice that continues in Brazil today. A tarpon is even depicted on the ceiling of the Vatican's Sistine Chapel, which was painted by Michelangelo over 500 years ago, even though this species is not present in the adjacent Mediterranean Sea. Biologically, this species has a unique underslung jaw and distinctive body shape. They are one of the oldest living fish, having evolved approximately 18 million years ago. They are able to live in both saltwater and fresh water, and they are capable of filling their swim bladders with air, like a primitive lung, which enables them to survive in water that has low oxygen levels, such as brackish lagoons.

NaturePicsFilms/Shutterstock©

**SAFETY TIP**

The north coast of Curaçao has some spectacular diving, but most of these sites can only be visited on a few days each year in the late summer, which is when the conditions allow safe access.

All sites on the north coast have very strong currents and large waves. They are also hard to find, extremely challenging to access and far from emergency medical services. All these factors make diving on this coast extremely dangerous.

Shore diving and boat diving are both possible on this coast, with most vessels departing from Playa Kanoa. Shore diving tends to be the most dangerous of the two options, as most sites can only be reached from a single limited location on shore, which is also the only safe point to exit the water. This is because most of the north coast consists of sheer cliffs with sharp rocks and only a few limited bays. As such, excellent navigation skills are essential to successfully return to the point of entry and avoid a dangerous situation.

Diving should only be conducted on the north coast of Curaçao by advanced divers under the direct supervision of suitably experienced and certified local guides.

# JORISBAAI

Difficulty ●●●
Current ●●●
Depth ●●○
Reef ★★☆
Fauna ★★☆

**Level** Advanced

**Location**
North coast, Curaçao
GPS 12°07.735′N, 68°48.330′W

Sint Jorisbaai is a large inland body of water that is connected to the open ocean through a shallow and relatively narrow channel only 650 feet (200 meters) wide. The bay itself is often used for windsurfing and kiteboarding. Surfers can sometimes be seen riding the breakers at the end of the channel, which can provide some indication of how challenging the conditions can be at this advanced dive site. The currents in the channel can change depending on the tide and wind, which makes this site potentially dangerous to explore. Those able to access the outer reef will encounter a gently sloping site that extends farther to the north than to the south. Gorgonians dominate the seabed and sea turtles are commonly spotted here.

Tunnel of Doom and the adjacent Boca Labadera.

## 86 TUNNEL OF DOOM

Difficulty ●●●
Current ●●●
Depth ●●●
Reef ★★☆
Fauna ★★☆

**Level** Advanced

**Location**
North coast, Curaçao
GPS 12°09.495'N, 68°49.778'W

The name of this site alone can strike fear into the hearts of divers. Tunnel of Doom is literally a tunnel that begins on land before passing through the cliff and terminating underwater on the reef beyond at a depth of 17 feet (5 meters). The tunnel is close to 100 feet (30 meters) in length, at least half of which is underwater. The tunnel is dark and the exit point on the reef is not always visible. Divers have reported seeing glassy sweepers in Tunnel of Doom, while tarpon and nurse sharks are often present around the exit of the tunnel. The reef itself starts at about 50 feet (15 meters) and slopes gently down to a depth of 80 feet (24.5 meters). It sits approximately 0.2 miles (0.3 kilometers) beyond the tunnel exit, which can be quite a swim if the currents and swell are strong. Locating the tunnel on the return portion of the dive can be difficult but this is the safest way to exit. Those divers who cannot locate the tunnel exit will need to attempt an exit in nearby Boca Labadera, immediately to the southeast. However, large swells and sharp rocks can make exiting here extremely challenging.

## PLAYA KANOA 87

Difficulty ●●●
Current ●●●
Depth ●●○
Reef ★★☆
Fauna ★★★

**Level** Advanced

**Location**
North coast, Curaçao
GPS 12°10.538'N, 68°51.868'W



Playa Kanoa, sometimes spelled Playa Canoa, is one of the few locations on the north coast of Curaçao where boats can be safely put into the water to access nearby dive sites. Surfers are often found on the break to the west of the boat dock, where the gently sloping seabed produces a clean right-hander – when the wind and swell cooperate. Divers can enter the water on the eastern side of the bay when the conditions allow and loop around the headland to explore the seaward side of the cliff in either direction. The reef begins relatively close to shore and consists mainly of plate-form star corals, mixed with sponges and orange cup corals. Divers often report seeing lobsters, moray eels and barracuda at this site.

Greens and Blues/Shutterstock©

# 88 BOCA SAN PEDRO/ HOUTJESBAAI

Difficulty ●●●
Current ●●●
Depth ●●●
Reef ★★☆
Fauna ★★★

**Level** Advanced

**Location**
North coast, Curaçao
GPS 12°15.043'N, 69°01.887'W

Boca San Pedro and the neighboring site of Houtjesbaai both lie in the shadow of the giant wind turbines located just north of the airport. These sites are only accessible on a few rare days each year because of strong currents and waves that are virtually always present at these exposed sites. A sloping reef exists between approximately 50 feet (15 meters) and 115 feet (35 meters), consisting of plate-form star corals, along with sponges and orange cup corals. This is one of the few sites in Curaçao that divers have consistently reported seeing reef sharks. Other species encountered here include nurse sharks, stingrays, eagle rays and large tarpon.

# 89 BOCA ASCENSION

Difficulty ●●●
Current ●●●
Depth ●●●
Reef ★★☆
Fauna ★★★

**Level** Advanced

**Location**
North coast, Curaçao
GPS 12°16.532'N, 69°02.843'W

Boca Ascension lies just 1.5 miles (2.4 kilometers) northwest of Boca San Pedro/Houtjesbaai. The long, thin channel that leads to the dive site extends inland for nearly 0.5 miles (0.8 kilometers), which means divers have a long walk out and must then swim against the swell to reach the dive site, which is itself quite a way from shore. As such, this site is only for those in peak physical condition. A massive sand patch lies approximately 0.2 miles (0.3 kilometers) due east from the entrance to the channel. This sand patch is located at a depth of approximately 90 feet (27.5 meters) and measures several football fields across. Stingrays are often found in this area and green and hawksbill sea turtles come to feed in the seagrass beds located at this site.

# 90 BOCA PATRICK



| | |
|---|---|
| Difficulty | ●●● |
| Current | ●●● |
| Depth | ●●○ |
| Reef | ★★★ |
| Fauna | ★★★ |

**Level** Advanced

**Location**
North coast, Curaçao
GPS 12°17.265'N, 69°03.032'W

Boca Patrick lies 0.85 miles (1.35 kilometers) north of Boca Ascension. This is widely regarded as one of the best dive sites on the north coast. Nurse sharks are frequently spotted here, while other species, such as lemon and bull sharks, are present, albeit with less regularity. It is possible to access the site from either of the adjacent, twin bays, although the southern bay tends to be easier and has less fire coral close to shore. Divers can explore the reef in either direction. The reef is gently sloping and has plenty of plate-form star corals, as well as a scattering of sponges and soft corals.

The long thin channel that leads to the sea at Boca Ascension.

## DID YOU KNOW?

There are numerous other locations along the north coast where it is possible to dive but access is restricted for one reason or another. For instance, Bartolbaai is often described as a shore-accessible dive site, however, this site is located on property owned by the Ministry of Defense and can only be accessed with permission.

Another example: Boka Tabla is often described as shore-accessible, but this site is located within the Shete Boka National Park, which is an ecologically sensitive area important for turtle nesting. As such, diving here is discouraged by the park's management. In addition, the constant wave action at Boka Tabla has created numerous caves and blowholes along the shoreline that present an additional safety concern. When conditions here are rough, the pounding waves can sometimes feel like an earthquake underfoot. As water is forced through the various blowholes, it often appears as a fine spray above the shoreline bluff, which is often referred to as the "Breath of Curaçao" by locals.

Divers should also consider the environmental impact of diving in remote and unofficial sites. Not only does diving along the north coast carry potential safety risks for divers, it also carries potential risks to the habitat. Attempting to access a site that may otherwise be inaccessible can contribute to erosion of the shoreline, damage to shallow reefs and disturbance of sensitive habitats. Divers should use discretion when selecting a dive site to explore.

# KLEIN CURAÇAO

Klein Curaçao is a popular trip for divers and snorkelers looking for a completely unique experience, both above and below the water. According to many divers and snorkelers who have visited this pristine region, everything is larger in Klein Curaçao, and sea turtle sightings are almost guaranteed. It is even possible to see dolphins at some sites as well as during the boat crossing to and from the remote island.

Diving and snorkeling can occur at numerous locations in the crystal-clear water around the island of Klein Curaçao, but there are five well established sites that are most frequently visited by operators. Some of these sites are suitable to divers and snorkelers of all experience levels, although they often require the ability and experience to explore the site via a drift dive.

This uninhabited island measures 1.5 miles (3.9 kilometers) in length and 0.5 miles (1.3 kilometers) across at its widest point. It is located just over 6.5 miles (10.5 kilometers) off the southeast point of Curaçao and represents less than 0.3% of Curaçao's total area – the island is small.

It can take between one and two hours to travel to the island by boat, depending on the departure location and sea conditions. The island has a wonderful white sandy beach on the southeast coast, as well as an abandoned lighthouse in the middle. Several graves and shipwrecks lie along the shoreline, and should not be disturbed.

# THE CAVE (NORTH POINT)

Difficulty ●●●
Current ●●●
Depth ●●●
Reef ★★★
Fauna ★★★

**Level** Advanced

**Location**
Klein Curaçao
GPS 12°00.057'N, 68°38.873'W

Klein Curaçao's North Point dive site, or The Cave as it is often called, is located at the northern end of the island where strong currents, predominantly from the east, curl around the point and slide down the west coast. This dive site is only accessible under certain conditions – rough seas from the northeast will often require dive operators to focus their activities on the southern side of the island. Drift diving is usually required for this site, which is one of the reasons it ranks as an advanced dive site. The reef has a wide back reef plateau at an average depth of only 15 feet (5 meters), which is covered in branching elkhorn and staghorn corals. The reef drops sharply about 600 feet (183 meters) from shore and is covered with large corals and sponges and particularly large sea fans. The large open cave that gives this site its name is located at a depth of approximately 100 feet (30 meters). Nurse sharks can often be found in the cave. Divers may also encounter barracuda, green morays and numerous species of parrotfish.

Gail Johnson/Shutterstock©

## 92 THE EDGE (NORTHWEST KLEIN CURAÇAO)

Difficulty ●●○
Current ●●●
Depth ●●○
Reef ★★☆
Fauna ★★☆

**Level** Open Water

**Location**
Klein Curaçao
GPS 11°59.802'N, 68°38.958'W

This site is located on the northwest coast of Klein Curaçao. The current at this site is usually moderate to strong and runs in a southerly direction. The reef starts out as a fairly steep incline in the north, but it transitions to more of a slope as divers drift to the south. This transition is also marked by an increasing number of sand patches across the face of the reef. Moray eels and grouper are common here. The farther south divers swim, the more likely they are to spot sea turtles, which tend to congregate off the beach closer to the southwest. The reef plateau becomes narrower and more densely covered in sand to the south, which allows divers to spot slightly different species throughout their dive. Stingrays are more common in the southern parts of the site.

## 93 EASY GOING (SOUTHWEST KLEIN CURAÇAO)

Difficulty ●○○
Current ●●○
Depth ●●○
Reef ★★☆
Fauna ★★★

**Level** Open Water

**Location**
Klein Curaçao
GPS 11°59.025'N, 68°38.730'W

Southwestern Klein Curaçao is one of the best places on the island to snorkel. The water stays shallow for a long way out and numerous sea turtles are usually present in the seagrass beds that thrive just off the beautiful sandy beach – which is how most snorkelers access the site. The dive and snorkel site known as Easy Going runs all the way from the island's southern point up to the boat dock in the north – a distance of 0.7 miles (1.1 kilometers) along the western edge of the island. Divers are usually dropped close to the southern point, and with a favorable current, they can sometimes follow the reef all the way up the west coast. The reef here curves gently as it hugs the shoreline in a wide crescent, and it is punctuated with numerous sandy channels that cascade down the face of the reef slope. Snorkelers that wish to explore coral reefs must do so on the plateau toward the southern end of the site, as the north and mid-sections of the site consist largely of sandy areas and seagrass beds. Snorkelers venturing south must take care, however, as currents increase significantly toward South Point.

## 94 SOUTH POINT (CANNON PILE)

Difficulty ●●●
Current ●●●
Depth ●●○
Reef ★★★
Fauna ★★★

**Level** Advanced

**Location**
Klein Curaçao
GPS 11°58.645'N, 68°38.500'W

As the name suggests, South Point is located just around the corner from the island's tapering southernmost point. The dive actually starts on Klein Curaçao's east coast and takes experienced divers on a drift dive that curls around the point and into the adjacent dive site known as Easy Going. The current is often very strong at this site and divers will need to follow the curve of the reef, which slopes steeply from a depth of approximately 25 feet (7.5 meters) down to over 100 feet (30 meters) before transitioning to sand and coral rubble. The reef, which is also known as Cannon Pile because of the supposed presence of cannons at this, is densely covered in hard and soft corals and sponges. Green morays, grouper, barracuda and large dog and cubera snapper can be found here – along with the occasional pod of dolphins.

# KLEIN CURAÇAO EAST



Difficulty ●●●
Current ●●●
Depth ●●●
Reef ★★☆
Fauna ★★★

**Level** Advanced

**Location**
Klein Curaçao
GPS 11°59.335'N, 68°38.335'W

It is only possible to dive the east coast of Klein Curaçao under calm conditions, which is relatively rare here. The reef at this site drops sharply into the depths and often has a strong current that pushes divers along its face. While the health of this reef is unquestioned, the diversity of corals, particularly in the shallower areas of the reef, is slightly higher closer to the north and south points of the island. Large marine organisms are often present at this site, including large grouper, barracuda, parrotfish and sea turtles. Divers have even reported seeing ocean sunfish at this site, also known as mola mola.



The abandoned lighthouse at Klein Curaçao is one of several unique features on the small island.

# Species

Identifying coral reef organisms is an enjoyable part of any underwater adventure. Not only can you appreciate the diversity and wonder that surrounds you on a reef, but you will be better able to understand the story that is unfolding right before your eyes.

For example, you will know where and when to look for certain species, as well as what they eat, who eats them, how big they get and how long they will live. But more specifically, you will understand certain behaviors that can be observed on coral reefs, such as why damselfish attack larger creatures, or which creatures form symbiotic relationships and why?

Many times, behavior is an integral part of the identification process. In some cases, understanding how a particular fish behaves,

**SAFETY TIP**

The section on dangerous species that follows is intended to provide the information you need to recognize the handful of species that can cause injury. These species should not be considered "active threats," but rather organisms that have the potential to cause harm. Most injuries occur because the organism in question has felt threatened and because a diver or snorkeler has not recognized the warning signs. By engaging in safe and conscientious diving and snorkeling practices, and by keeping in mind a few key safety tips, you can avoid having your experience ruined by an unpleasant sting or bite.

Schools of blue tangs are frequent visitors to back reef plateaus.

Nassau grouper are on the of many species of grouper found on Curaçao. nicolasvoisin44/Shutterstock ©

Turtle & Ray©

such as whether it is active during the night or day, or whether it is an ambush predator or active forager, can be more useful in determining its identity than its color or shape.

Many reef organisms may appear very similar at first glance, and the wide diversity of species on coral reefs can appear to be a chaotic jumble. But by combining an understanding of animal behavior with some basic identification information, you can start to tease apart that puzzle and experience the wonder of the coral reef.

The information provided in this guidebook represents the most up-to-date scientific knowledge available at the time of publication. It covers some of the most common reef species you will find during your time in the waters of Curaçao. However, it should be noted that coral reef ecologists continue to discover new information about species, their behaviors and their interactions. Later editions of this book may contain modifications that reflect new knowledge.

The following pages are divided into three sections, featuring information about sea turtles, which have a rather unique life history; dangerous species, including details on the kind of threat they pose and how to treat injuries caused by them; and finally, a general species section that helps you identify and learn about the most common species found at the Curaçao sites featured in this guide.

# Sea turtle identification

A

## GREEN TURTLE
### CHELONIA MYDAS

Maximum size: 4ft (1.4m)
Longevity: Up to 75 years
Habitat: Seagrass beds, reefs
Diet: Jellyfish and crustaceans when young; algae and seagrass as adults
Sightings: Common
Behavior: Green turtles can be found grazing on vegetation in shallow water or cruising the reef. Most green turtles migrate short distances along the coast to reach nesting beaches, but some may migrate up to 1,300 miles (2,100 kilometers) to reach nesting beaches.
Predators (adults): Tiger sharks, orcas (killer whales)

B

## HAWKSBILL SEA TURTLE
### ERETMOCHELYS IMBRICATA

Maximum size: 3ft (0.9m)
Longevity: Up to 50 years
Habitat: Reefs
Diet: Sponges, tunicates, squid, shrimp
Sightings: Common
Behavior: Hawksbills can be found feeding throughout the day or resting with their bodies wedged into reef cracks and crevices. Some hawksbills do not migrate at all, while others migrate over thousands of miles.
Predators (adults): Tiger sharks, orcas (killer whales)

## SEA TURTLE CONSERVATION STATUS: ENDANGERED

All species of sea turtles are endangered (Kemp's ridleys are critically endangered) and many human activities contribute to their decline.

- Turtles are hunted in many parts of the world, targeting their meat and eggs for food, and their shells to make jewelry, eyeglass frames and curios. Many others drown in fishing nets intended for shrimp or fish, or are struck and killed by passing boats.
- Turtles eat and choke on plastic and other trash, while pollution increases the frequency of turtle disease.
- Coastal development is rapidly reducing the number of active nesting beaches.

### ECO TIP

Sea turtles need our help to survive and thrive alongside our coastal communities. Consider the following tips:

**LIGHTS OUT**
Turn out lights visible from the beach to avoid disorienting nesting turtles and hatchlings.

**DON'T LITTER**
Plastic cups, bags and other trash can kill turtles when they mistake them for food.

**DON'T DISTURB**
Turtles you see on the beach or in the water, whether nesting, feeding or hatching, should be left alone and observed from a distance – without flashlights.

**PLEASE DON'T FEED**
Human food can make sea turtles sick and can leave them vulnerable to capture.

**VOLUNTEER**
Support your local turtle conservation programs, including participating in beach cleanups.

C

## LOGGERHEAD SEA TURTLE
### CARETTA CARETTA

Maximum size: 3.5ft (1.1m)
Longevity: Up to 60 years
Habitat: Reefs and open ocean
Diet: Crabs, shrimp, jellyfish, vegetation
Sightings: Common
Behavior: Loggerheads are occasionally found in the open ocean, but regularly move inshore to feed on reef invertebrates. Loggerhead sea turtles can migrate for thousands of miles to reach new feeding grounds before returning to the same nesting beaches.
Predators (adults): Tiger sharks, orcas (killer whales)

D

## LEATHERBACK TURTLE
### DERMOCHELYS CORIACEA

Maximum size: Up to 10ft (3m)
Longevity: Up to 80 years
Habitat: Open ocean
Diet: Jellyfish and tunicates
Sightings: Rare
Behavior: Leatherbacks feed in deep water during the day and at the surface at night, following the daily migratory patterns of their favorite food: jellyfish. During the mating season, leatherbacks may migrate up to 3,000 miles (4,800 kilometers) from their feeding grounds to their nesting beaches.
Predators (adults): Tiger sharks, orcas (killer whales)

A loggerhead turtle swims slowly past as it explore the top of a reef drop-off. NaturePicsFilms/Shutterstock ©

# Sea turtle ecology

## Nesting

Females crawl onto the beach at night (or during the day in the case of Kemp's ridleys) and dig a shallow nest. They lay up to 200 small white eggs before covering the nest and returning to the sea. The eggs incubate for 45 to 70 days, depending on the species.

## Mating

Most sea turtles reproduce in the warm summer months except for the leatherback, whose mating season spans fall and winter. Many species migrate great distances to return to the their customary nesting beach. Courtship and mating occur in the shallow waters off shore.

Stephan Kerkhofs /Shutterstock ©

Arnunthorn R /Shutterstock ©

## Adulthood

In adulthood, some sea turtle species return to coastal waters where coral reefs and nearshore waters provide plenty of food and protection from predators.

UWPhotog /Shutterstock ©

David Evison/Shutterstock ©

David Evison/Shutterstock ©

Omaly Darcia/Shutterstock ©

**Hatching**
When they hatch, hundreds of tiny turtles dig their way out of the nest and head away from the darkness of land, and toward the light reflecting off the sea. As many as 90 percent are eaten by predators as eggs or as hatchlings within the first few hours of their lives.

Laura Dinraths /Shutterstock ©

**Juvenile stage**
Young turtles drift through the open ocean for years, often associating with floating sargassum (seaweed) mats. They feed on plankton and small jellyfish. Little is known about this stage of their lives.

# Dangerous species

## MEDICAL DISCLAIMER

The treatment advice contained in this book is meant for informational purposes only and is not intended to be a substitute for professional medical advice, either in terms of diagnosis or treatment. Always seek the advice of your physician or other qualified health provider if you are injured by a marine organism. Never disregard professional medical advice or delay seeking it because of something you have read in this book.

### CARIBBEAN REEF SHARK

**CARCHARHINUS PEREZII**

E

Maximum size: 10ft (3m) (10ft)
Longevity: Unknown, but possibly 20 years or more
Typical depth: 3–213ft (1–65m)
Behavior: The Caribbean reef shark is the most common shark species encountered on Caribbean coral reefs. They tend to inhabit drop-offs and the seaward edges of reefs, where they feed on most reef fish species, as well as stingrays and eagle rays.
Predators: Larger shark species, such as bull and tiger sharks

**WARNING:** Caribbean reef sharks rarely attack humans, but they have been known to cause injury if threatened or cornered. Warning signs of an attack include head swings, exaggerated swimming, back arching and lowered pectoral fins. Attacks usually result in biting or raking with the teeth, which can cause deep lacerations. There have been numerous documented attacks on humans by Caribbean reef sharks but no known fatalities.

**TREATMENT:** Exit the water as soon as possible. Rinse the bite with soap and water, and apply pressure to control bleeding. Shark attacks often result in shock, so keep the patient warm, calm and shaded. Elevate the feet unless that may cause additional injury. Do not provide anything to eat or drink. Seek medical attention as soon as possible, since even minor bites require cleaning and suturing.

### SOUTHERN STINGRAY

**DASYATIS AMERICANA**

F

Maximum size: 7ft (2m) disk diameter, 300lbs (136kg)
Longevity: Unknown, but probably over 10 years
Typical depth: 0–170ft (0–53m)
Behavior: Stingrays are most active at night when they hunt for hard-shelled prey such as snails, crabs, lobsters and occasionally fish. During the day, they are often found buried up to their eyes in sand.
Predators: Sharks and large grouper

**WARNING:** Stingrays have a serrated venomous spine at the base of their tail that they use for defense. The area around a puncture wound from this spine may become red and swollen, and you may experience muscle cramps, nausea, fever and chills.

**TREATMENT:** If you are stung, exit the water immediately. Apply pressure above the wound to reduce bleeding, clean the wound and soak the area with hot water, ideally around 113°F (45°C), to reduce the pain. Apply a dressing and seek medical attention. Antibiotics may be needed to reduce the risk of infection. Stingray injuries can be very painful, often reaching a peak around one hour after the injury and lasting up to two days. But they are rarely fatal unless the injury is to the head, neck or abdomen.

## GREAT BARRACUDA

### SPHYRAENA BARRACUDA

G

Maximum size: 6ft (2m), 110lbs (50kg)
Longevity: Around 20 years
Typical depth: 1–100m (3–330ft)
Behavior: Barracuda are most active during the day, feeding on jacks, grunts, grouper, snapper, squid and even other barracuda. They are often solitary in nature, but occasionally school in large numbers. They have even been documented "herding" fish they plan on consuming. Barracuda use their keen eyesight to hunt for food. They are one of the fastest fish in the ocean, capable of bursts of speed up to 30mph (48kph). Along with their two sets of razor sharp teeth, there are few prey capable of escaping a barracuda once it decides to attack.
Predators: Sharks, tuna and large grouper

**WARNING:** Barracuda do not usually attack divers or snorkelers unless provoked. However, evidence suggests they are attracted to objects that glint or shine, such as necklaces, watches or regulators, which they may mistake for prey. The bite of the barracuda is not toxic, but their teeth can produce a severe laceration or deep puncture wound.

**TREATMENT:** Exit the water as soon as possible and apply pressure to reduce bleeding. The wound should be cleaned and dressed. Medical attention may be necessary for severe bites, including sutures to close the wound and antibiotics to reduce the risk of infection.

## SPOTTED SCORPIONFISH

### SCORPAENA PLUMIERI

H

Maximum size: 18in (45cm)
Longevity: Around 15 years
Typical depth: 3–197ft (1–60m)
Behavior: Spotted scorpionfish spend much of their time lying motionless on the seabed, using camouflage to ambush fish and crustaceans. They have a large, expandable mouth capable of creating a vacuum to suck in prey, which they swallow whole.
Predators: Large snapper, sharks, rays and moray eels

**WARNING:** Scorpionfish have a dozen venomous dorsal spines for self-defense. The spines can penetrate skin (most commonly when stepped on), injecting a toxin that causes severe pain that can last from several hours to several days. The area around the injury may also swell and become red.

**TREATMENT:** Exit the water quickly and rinse the affected area with seawater. Remove any spines and use pressure to control any bleeding. Apply the hottest water you can stand to reduce pain, ideally around 113°F (45°C). Let the wound heal uncovered, but antibiotics may be required to avoid infection. The toxin can be painful, but it is not usually fatal. However, seek medical attention if concerned or if symptoms are worse than described.

## RED LIONFISH
### PTEROIS VOLITANS

I

Maximum size: 15in (38cm)
Longevity: Around 10 years
Typical depth: 7–180ft (2–55m)
Behavior: Red lionfish are originally from the Indo-West Pacific, and are considered an invasive species in the Western Atlantic. They are most active at dusk and during the night when they hunt for fish, shrimp, crabs and other reef creatures. Lionfish can live without food for up to three months.
Predators: Occasional predation by certain sharks and grouper

**WARNING:** Lionfish have up to 16 venomous dorsal and anal spines that can deliver a powerful neurotoxin when they puncture skin. Lionfish do not generally attack divers and snorkelers, but may sting in self-defense if you get too close. Divers and snorkelers may feel intense pain after being stung, followed by swelling and redness around the wound.

**TREATMENT:** Exit the water as soon as possible and remove any pieces of the spines that may remain in the wound. Use pressure to control the bleeding and apply the hottest water you can stand, ideally around 113°F (45°C), to reduce the pain. Some people experience shortness of breath, dizziness and nausea. There have been no known fatalities from a lionfish sting, but there is always a risk of complications for vulnerable individuals, including congestive heart failure. Seeking medical attention is advised. The pain may last anywhere from several hours to several days.

## GREEN MORAY EEL
### GYMNOTHORAX FUNEBRIS

J

Maximum size: 8ft (2.5m), 65lbs (30kg)
Longevity: Unknown
Typical depth: 3–164ft (1–50m)
Behavior: Green morays are solitary animals that hide in reef cracks and crevices during the day. At night, they prey on fish, octopuses, crustaceans and even other eels, primarily using smell to hunt as their eyesight is poor.
Predators: Unknown

**WARNING:** Moray eels have sharp teeth that can produce a painful wound, but thankfully they rarely attack unless provoked. There is evidence that the bite of some morays may contain toxins that increase pain and bleeding, but more research is needed. Although all morays can bite, larger species such as the green moray eel can cause more severe injuries than smaller species.

**TREATMENT:** Exit the water as soon as possible. Treat the wound by immediately cleaning the affected area with soap and water. Apply pressure to reduce the bleeding, then apply a topical antibiotic before dressing the wound to reduce the risk of infection. Sutures may be required in some cases. If in doubt or if the wound becomes infected, seek medical attention.

## JELLYFISH & SIPHONOPHORES

**K**

### HYDROIDOMEDUSAE & SIPHONOPHORAE

Maximum size: 7ft (2m) with tentacles extending much farther
Longevity: From a few hours to several years
Typical depth: 0–66ft (0–20m)
Behavior: Jellyfish and siphonophores are both types of cnidaria. Jellyfish are individual animals, while siphonophores are colonies of specialized cells called zooids, such as the Portuguese man o' war. They both drift in the water and use stinging cells called nematocysts to capture and paralyze prey, including plankton and small fish.
Predators: Salmon, tuna and some sharks and sea turtle species

**WARNING:** Jellyfish and siphonophores have stinging cells called nematocysts located on their tentacles that can inject a toxin when brushed against bare skin. Depending on the species, jellyfish toxin can cause mild tingling to intense pain, and can be fatal in some rare cases. The contact site may also become red and blistered. Even dead jellyfish on the beach can sting, so avoid touching them.

**TREATMENT:** Exit the water as quickly as possible, watching out for other jellyfish. Rinse the affected area with seawater to remove any pieces of tentacle on the skin. Do not rinse with fresh water, which can trigger any remaining nematocysts to sting. The best treatment for jellyfish stings may depend on the species, but most can be treated by rinsing the affected area with vinegar or creating a paste using baking soda and seawater. The papain enzyme found in meat tenderizer and papaya can also help. Consider seeking medical attention.

## FIRE CORAL

**L**

### MILLEPORIDAE

Maximum size: 3ft (1m)
Longevity: Unknown, but likely decades
Typical depth: 3–130ft (1–40m)
Behavior: Several fire coral species occur in the Caribbean, attaching to the reef substrate and growing in branching, blade and encrusting forms. Fire corals are hydroids with a hard skeleton, and are more closely related to jellyfish than corals. They get their energy from photosynthetic zooxanthellae in their tissues, but also from feeding on plankton.
Predators: Fireworms, certain nudibranchs and filefish

**WARNING:** Microscopic fire coral polyps are located throughout the surface of the hard skeleton. Each polyp has hair-like tentacles that are covered in stinging cells called nematocysts, which they use to paralyze their tiny prey. Fire corals cause a lingering, burning sensation when they contact bare skin. A rash or blistering may occur in some individuals and may last several days, but is not usually dangerous.

**TREATMENT:** Exit the water as soon as possible and rinse the affected area with vinegar or alcohol to inactivate the fire coral toxin. Do not rinse with fresh water, which can increase the pain by causing untriggered nematocysts to discharge into the skin. Apply hydrocortisone cream to the area once dry. The papain enzyme found in meat tenderizer and papaya can also reduce swelling, pain and itching.

## FRENCH ANGELFISH 1
### POMACANTHUS PARU

Maximum size: 24in (60cm)
Longevity: Up to 15 years
Typical depth: 10–330ft (3–100m)
Behavior: French angelfish dine primarily on sponges, but may also feed on gorgonians and algae. Juveniles often act as cleaners, eating the parasites from other reef fish. At dusk, French angelfish find shelter from nocturnal predators in reef cracks and crevices.
Predators: Large grouper and sharks

## QUEEN ANGELFISH 2
### HOLACANTHUS CILIARIS

Maximum size: 18in (45cm)
Longevity: Up to 15 years
Typical depth: 3–230ft (1–70m)
Behavior: Queen angelfish are often found swimming gracefully between sea fans, sea whips and corals, alone or in pairs. They feed almost exclusively on sponges, but have been known to snack on algae and tunicates as well. Young Queen angelfish also clean parasites off larger fish.
Predators: Large grouper and sharks

## ROCK BEAUTY 3
### HOLACANTHUS TRICOLOR

Maximum size: 14in (35cm)
Longevity: Up to 20 years (in captivity)
Typical depth: 10–115ft (3–35m)
Behavior: Adult rock beauties are often found on rock jetties, rocky reefs and rich coral areas, while juveniles tend to be found near fire corals. These angelfish are not picky eaters and will feed on tunicates, sponges, zoantharians and algae.
Predators: Grouper, snapper and sharks

## BLUE TANG 4
### ACANTHURUS COERULEUS

Maximum size: 16in (40cm)
Longevity: Around 20 years
Typical depth: 3–130ft (1–40m)
Behavior: Blue tangs are often found grazing on algae during the day, either individually or as part of large schools that may also contain surgeonfish, doctorfish, goatfish and parrotfish. At dusk, they settle into a reef crack or crevice to hide for the night.
Predators: Grouper, snapper, jacks and barracuda

## DOCTORFISH 5
### ACANTHURUS CHIRUGUS

Maximum size: 15.5in (39cm)
Longevity: Up to 30 years
Typical depth: 6–213ft (2–65m)
Behavior: Doctorfish can be found in shallow, inshore reef habitats and rocky areas. They forage on benthic algae, including the thin algal mat covering sandy bottoms. They generally swim together in loose schools, often with ocean surgeonfish and blue tangs. They have sharp spines near their tail fin that they can use in defense against predators.
Predators: Large carnivorous fish, including tuna

## OCEAN SURGEONFISH 6
### ACANTHURUS BAHIANUS

Maximum size: 15in (38cm)
Longevity: Up to 32 years
Typical depth: 6–130ft (2–40m)
Behavior: Adult surgeonfish often form large schools to graze on benthic algae and seagrasses in shallow coral reefs and inshore rocky areas. Juveniles rarely school, sheltering instead in the back reef. Researchers have observed spawning aggregations of up to 20,000 individuals in the winter months off of Puerto Rico.
Predators: Sharks, grouper, barracuda and snapper

## BANDED BUTTERFLYFISH 7
### CHAETODON STRIATUS

Maximum size: 6in (16cm)
Longevity: Unknown, but probably around 10 years
Typical depth: 10–60ft (3–20m)
Behavior: Banded butterflyfish are most active during the day when they search the reef for food, which includes polychaete worms, zoanthids, anemones and fish eggs. Banded butterflyfish are often found in monogamous pairs and they defend a joint territory together with their mate.
Predators: Moray eels and large carnivorous fish

## FOUREYE BUTTERFLYFISH 8
### CHAETODON CAPISTRATUS

Maximum size: 6in (15cm)
Longevity: Around 8 years
Typical depth: 6–65ft (2–20m)
Behavior: Foureye butterflyfish are active during the day when they feed on small invertebrates. Their pointed mouth allows them to pull prey from small crevices. They are often found in pairs, and males and females bond early in life and form long-lasting monogamous pairs.
Predators: Barracuda, grouper, snapper and moray eels

## BLUE CHROMIS 9

### CHROMIS CYANEA

Maximum size: 5in (12cm)
Longevity: Unknown, possibly 5 years
Typical depth: 10–70ft (3–20m)
Behavior: Blue chromis gather in schools above the reef to feed on small plankton and jellyfish during the day. They hide in reef crevices at night. Territorial males defend egg nests in the spring and summer.
Predators: Trumpetfish, grouper and snapper

## BROWN CHROMIS 10

### CHROMIS MULTILINEATA

Maximum size: 8in (20cm)
Longevity: Unknown, possibly 5 years
Typical depth: 3–300ft (1–91m)
Behavior: Brown chromis forage in medium-sized schools above the coral reef, feasting on plankton, mainly copepods. They are frequently seen schooling with blue chromis during the day, although their more territorial congeneric tends to chase them out from hiding places in the reef at night.
Predators: Trumpetfish, grouper and snapper

## SERGEANT MAJOR 11

### ABUDEFDUF SAXATILIS

Maximum size: 9in (23cm)
Longevity: Unknown, possibly 5 years
Typical depth: 3–33ft (1–10m)
Behavior: Sergeant majors get their name from their telltale black bars that resemble military stripes. They are usually found in shallow water, typically along the tops of reefs, and often form large feeding schools of up to a few hundred individuals.
Predators: Grouper and jacks

## YELLOWHEAD JAWFISH 12

### OPISTOGNATHUS AURIFRONS

Maximum size: 4in (10cm)
Longevity: Unknown, possibly up to 5 years
Typical depth: 10–131ft (3–40m)
Behavior: Jawfish live in burrows in the sediment that they line with stones and bits of crushed shell and coral. Active during the day, they often hover over their burrow and feed on zooplankton. They rarely move far from their burrow and often retreat tail-first when threatened.
Predators: Snapper, grouper and lionfish

## ROSY RAZORFISH
### XYRICHTYS MARTINICENSIS
13

Maximum size: 6in (15cm)
Longevity: Around 3 years
Typical depth: 7–69ft (2–21m)
Behavior: Rosy razorfish are commonly found in open sandy areas near coral reefs. They are active during the day as they feed on small sand-dwelling invertebrates such as crabs, shrimp and worms. Large males often defend a harem of females within their territory.
Predators: Grouper, snapper, barracuda and dolphins

## BLUEHEAD WRASSE
### THALASSOMA BIFASCIATUM
14

Maximum size: 10in (25cm)
Longevity: 3 years
Typical depth: 0–131ft (0–40m)
Behavior: Bluehead wrasses can be found on reefs, near inshore bays and over seagrass beds feeding on zooplankton, small benthic animals and even parasites on other fish. They start life as female but eventually become males, gaining an unmistakable bright blue head in their terminal phase.
Predators: Grouper, trumpetfish and soapfish

## YELLOWHEAD WRASSE
### HALICHOERES GARNOTI
15

Maximum size: 7in (19cm)
Longevity: Unknown, possibly between 3 and 5 years
Typical depth: 3–100ft (1–30m)
Behavior: Yellowhead wrasses are mainly found near coral reefs and rocky ledges. Adults feed on invertebrates while juveniles sometimes clean parasites off larger fish. Yellowhead wrasses are protogynous hermaphrodites, meaning they start life as female but become males at around 3in (7cm) in size.
Predators: Mackerel, grouper and snapper

## PUDDINGWIFE
### HALICHOERES RADIATUS
16

Maximum size: 20in (51cm)
Longevity: 10 years or more
Typical depth: 6–180ft (2–55m)
Behavior: Puddingwives are commonly found on reefs, feeding on molluscs, sea urchins, crustaceans and brittle stars. Juveniles typically inhabit shallow coral reefs while adults also frequent deeper reefs. As with other wrasses, adults change color dramatically as they grow and reach terminal phase.
Predators: : Reef sharks, greater amberjacks and snapper

## CREOLE WRASSE 17

### CLEPTICUS PARRAE

Maximum size: 12in (30cm)
Longevity: Unknown, but probably around 10 years
Typical depth: 26–328ft (8–100m)
Behavior: Creole wrasses are often found schooling in large numbers above bank reefs, wrecks and on the seaward slopes of reefs. They are most active during the day, when feeding on plankton and small jellyfish. At night, they retreat into reef crevices to sleep.
Predators: Moray eels, grouper and barracuda

## SPANISH HOGFISH 18

### BODIANUS RUFUS

Maximum size: 16in (40cm)
Longevity: Unknown
Typical depth: 10–230ft (3–70m)
Behavior: Adult Spanish hogfish feed on bottom-dwelling invertebrates, such as brittlestars, crustaceans and sea urchins. Juveniles set up cleaning stations to pick parasites off larger fish. Male hogfish (who start out life as a female) typically manage a harem of three to 12 smaller females.
Predators: Sharks, mackerel and snapper

## PRINCESS PARROTFISH 19

### SCARUS TAENIOPTERUS

Max size: 14in (35cm)
Longevity: Unknown, but probably less than 5 years
Typical depth: 3–82ft (1–25m)
Behavior: Princess parrotfish form large schools during the day to feed on plants, algae, sponges and seagrass. Juveniles are more closely associated with seagrass beds. They start out life as female, but can transition to male if no other large breeding males are around.
Predators: Sharks, grouper, jacks and moray eels

## QUEEN PARROTFISH 20

### SCARUS VETULA

Maximum size: 24 in (61 cm)
Longevity: Up to 20 years
Typical depth: 10–80 ft (3–25 m)
Behavior: During the day, Queen parrotfish feed by scraping algae off rocks and dead coral using their tough, parrot-like beak. At night, Queen parrotfish secrete a membrane of mucus from a gland at the base of the gills which surrounds them like a bubble and masks their scent from nocturnal predators.
Predators: Grouper, eels and sharks

## STOPLIGHT PARROTFISH
### SPARISOMA VIRIDE

**21**

Maximum size: 25in (64cm)
Longevity: Around 9 years
Typical depth: 3–164ft (1–50m)
Behavior: Stoplight parrotfish are only active during the day. Their strong beak-like jaws scrape soft algae off the hard coral. They ingest some coral in the process, grinding it up with the help of specialized teeth in their throats and excreting it as coral sand.
Predators: Sharks, barracuda, grouper, snapper, jacks and moray eels

## BLUE PARROTFISH
### SCARUS COERULEUS

**22**

Maximum size: 4ft (1.2m)
Longevity: About 10 years
Typical depth: 10–82ft (3–25m)
Behavior: The blue parrotfish is easily identified by its prominent bulging snout and color, as it is the only blue parrotfish. It feeds during the day by biting off pieces of the reef in order to consume plants, algae and small organisms. This species can form large schools, particularly during spawning.
Predators: Large grouper, snapper, moray eels and barracuda

## MIDNIGHT PARROTFISH
### SCARUS COELESTINUS

**23**

Maximum size: 30in (77cm)
Longevity: Unknown, but possibly up to 10 years
Typical depth: 16–264ft (5–75m)
Behavior: Midnight parrotfish are among the larger parrotfish species in the Caribbean, and are recognizable for their dark blue-black coloration. They can often be spotted schooling with surgeonfish as they munch on algae-encrusted coral. They are typically associated with coral reefs and sport the telltale beak of all parrotfish.
Predators: Sharks, mackerel and jacks

## RAINBOW PARROTFISH
### SCARUS GUACAMAIA

**24**

Maximum size: 4ft (1.2m)
Longevity: Around 10 years
Typical depth: 10–82ft (3–25m)
Behavior: The rainbow parrotfish is the largest herbivorous reef fish in the Caribbean. During the day, it feeds by biting off pieces of the reef in order to consume the plants, algae and small organisms contained within. Schooling may occur in areas where density is high.
Predators: Large grouper, snapper, moray eels, sharks and barracuda

SPECIES

GRUNTS, SNAPPER

## BLACK MARGATE 25

### ANISOTREMUS SURINAMENSIS

Maximum size: 30in (76cm), 13lb (6kg)
Longevity: Unknown
Typical depth: 0–66ft (0–20m)
Behavior: Black margates can be found alone or in small groups. They are nocturnal, feeding on benthic crustaceans, molluscs, smaller fish and long-spined sea urchins at night. During the day, they can often be found under ledges and sheltering in caves or wrecks.
Predators: Sharks

## CAESAR GRUNT 26

### HAEMULON CARBONARIUM

Max size: 16in (40cm)
Longevity: Unknown, but possibly up to 10 years
Typical depth: 10–82ft (3–25m)
Behavior: Caesar grunts are often found in schools near artificial reefs and over rocky reefs. Like most grunts, they are nocturnal feeders, munching on polychaetes, gastropods and small crustaceans. During the day, they form loose schools under overhangs. Unlike other grunts, however, juveniles settle on shallow reefs and not near mangroves or seagrass beds.
Predators: Sharks, grouper, jacks and moray eels

## FRENCH GRUNT 27

### HAEMULON FLAVOLINEATUM

Maximum size: 12in (30cm)
Longevity: Unknown, could be up to 12 years
Typical depth: 3–400ft (1–60m)
Behavior: French grunts form large schools on rocky and coral reefs. During the day, adults can often be found resting under ledges and near elkhorn coral. Juveniles spend the day hiding near the shore. French grunts are nocturnal and typically feed on small crustaceans, polychaetes and molluscs.
Predators: Grouper, snapper and trumpetfish

## GREY SNAPPER 28

### LUTJANUS GRISEUS

Maximum size: 35in (90cm), 44lb (20kg)
Longevity: Around 20 years
Typical depth: 16–590ft (5–180m)
Behavior: Grey snapper are often found schooling, sometimes in large numbers. They feed mainly at night on a range of organisms, including shrimp, crabs, worms and small fishes, rarely moving far to feed.
Predators: Moray eels, sharks, large grouper and barracuda

## MAHOGANY SNAPPER 29
### LUTJANUS MAHOGONI

Maximum size: 19in (48cm)
Longevity: Around 20 years
Typical depth: 3–330ft (1–100m)
Behavior: This smaller snapper forms large schools during the day, typically in shallower waters over coral reefs. At night, mahogany snapper feed on small fish, shrimp, crabs and cephalopods. They frequent warmer waters and only stray into temperate climates during the heat of summer.
Predators: Sharks, mackerel and other snapper

## SCHOOLMASTER SNAPPER 30
### LUTJANUS APODUS

Maximum size: 26in (67cm)
Longevity: Up to 42 years
Typical depth: 6–207ft (2–63m)
Behavior: Schoolmaster snapper are found in shallow coastal waters in coral reefs and mangrove habitats – adults are often associated with elkhorn corals while younger individuals sometimes enter brackish waters. They feed on crustaceans and cephalopods, although adults also show a preference for fish once their mouth can open wide enough to catch them.
Predators: Sharks, barracuda and grouper

## CUBERA SNAPPER 31
### LUTJANUS CYANOPTERUS

Maximum size: 5ft (1.6m); 126lbs (57kg)
Longevity: 20 years, but possibly up to 50 years
Typical depth: 3–280ft (1–85m)
Behavior: Cubera snapper are the biggest of the Atlantic snapper species. Adults are often seen alone on deeper reefs and wrecks, while juveniles are generally in shallower water near vegetation, including estuaries. Cubera snapper feed on fish as well as crustaceans, such as shrimp, crabs and lobsters. Large individuals are rarely removed from the water when caught on fishing lines, due to concerns about ciguatera poisoning.
Predators: Sharks, large grouper, barracuda and mackerel

## YELLOWTAIL SNAPPER 32
### OCYURUS CHRYSURUS

Maximum size: 34in (86cm), 9lb (4kg)
Longevity: Around 13 to 17 years
Typical depth: 3–541ft (1–165m)
Behavior: Yellowtail snapper are typically associated with coral reefs in coastal waters from the U.S. state of Massachusetts, down to the coast of Brazil. They often form schools above reefs and are less commonly seen along the seafloor. They eat plankton and small benthic organisms.
Predators: Sharks, barracuda, mackerel, snapper and grouper

## GLASSEYE SNAPPER

### HETEROPRIACANTHUS CRUENTATUS

33

Maximum size: 20in (51cm)
Longevity: Unknown
Typical depth: 10–115ft (3–35m)
Behavior: Glasseye snapper are secretive fish, hiding alone or in small groups in holes and crevices during the day. At night, they exit their shelters to feed on octopuses, pelagic shrimp, crabs, small fishes and polychaete worms. They sometimes form larger schools at dusk.
Predators: Sharks, tuna, grouper and mahi mahi

## GLASSY SWEEPER

### PEMPHERIS SCHOMBURGKII

34

Maximum size: 6in (15cm)
Longevity: Unknown
Typical depth: 10–98ft (3–30m)
Behavior: The nocturnal glassy sweeper is a small fish that feeds on zooplankton and small crustaceans in the water above the reef. During the day, it shelters in groups, hiding in reef crevices and caves. Juveniles are nearly transparent – likely the origin of their name.
Predators: Rays and grouper

## BLACKBAR SOLDIERFISH

### MYRIPRISTIS JACOBUS

35

Maximum size: 10in (25cm)
Longevity: Unknown
Typical depth: 7–115ft (2–35m)
Behavior: Blackbar soldierfish are nocturnal, often hiding in caves and crevices during the day. They congregate around coral and rocky reefs at night to feed on plankton and invertebrates. They most commonly occur on shallow inshore reefs, but can be found at depths of 330ft (100m).
Predators: Snapper, grouper, jacks and trumpetfish

## CLEANING GOBY

### ELACATINUS GENIE

36

Maximum size: 2in (4cm)
Longevity: 3 to 5 years
Typical depth: 3–98ft (1–30m)
Behavior: As their name suggests, cleaning gobies clean other reef creatures by removing their parasites. This behavior is a form of symbiosis known as mutualism, where both parties benefit. The client fish get rid of their ectoparasites, while the cleaners get an easy meal.
Predators: Grouper, snapper and moray eels

## REDLIP BLENNY 37

### OPHIOBLENNIUS ATLANTICUS

Maximum size: 7in (19cm)
Longevity: Around 2 years
Typical depth: 0–27ft (0–8m)
Behavior: Redlip blennies are common in shallow reef areas with relatively high wave action. Their body shape and modified fins let them "hold on" to the reef. They are herbivorous and territorial, defending a patch of algae during the day and hiding in the reef at night.
Predators: Grouper, snapper and trumpetfish

## FLYING GURNARD 38

### DACTYLOPTERUS VOLITANS

Maximum size: 21in (50cm)
Longevity: Unknown, but likely more than 5 years
Typical depth: 3–262ft (1–80m)
Behavior: Flying gurnards are often found along sand-bottomed areas near the reef, foraging for benthic crustaceans, crabs, clams and small fishes. They get their name from their fan-like pectoral fins that make it look like they are flying when they swim.
Predators: Sharks, tuna, mahi mahi, grouper and bigeye

## SPOTTED GOATFISH 39

### PSEUDUPENEUS MACULATUS

Maximum size: 12in (30cm)
Longevity: At least 7 years
Typical depth: 0–115ft (0–35m)
Behavior: Spotted goatfish are most often encountered in shallow water over rocky or sandy habitat near reefs. They feed on bottom-dwelling crabs, shrimp and small fish. Spotted goatfish are easily recognizable by the three dark blotches along their back and the telltale barbels they use to stir up the sand when they hunt.
Predators: Sharks, snapper and jacks

## YELLOW GOATFISH 40

### MULLOIDICHTHYS MARTINICUS

Maximum size: 15in (39cm)
Longevity: Unknown
Typical depth: 0–115ft (0–35m)
Behavior: Yellow goatfish are commonly found swimming in large schools over sandy bottoms. They use their long, sensitive barbels to locate polychaete worms, clams, isopods, amphipods and other crustaceans in the sand. When not feeding, they are often found in groups, sheltering in the reef.
Predators: Sharks, tuna, mahi mahi, grouper and jacks

## LONGLURE FROGFISH
### ANTENNARIUS MULTIOCELLATUS

41

Maximum size: 8in (20cm)
Longevity: Unknown, but probably around 10 years
Typical depth: 0–215ft (0–66m)
Behavior: The longlure frogfish is a bottom-dwelling fish that can change color and texture to blend in with its surroundings. It is an ambush predator, feeding mainly on other fish and crustaceans. Frogfish have one of the fastest attacks in the animal kingdom.
Predators: Moray eels and other frogfish

## SAND TILEFISH
### MALACANTHUS PLUMIERI

42

Maximum size: 28in (70cm)
Longevity: Unknown, but potentially as much as 40 years
Typical depth: 33–164ft (10–50m)
Behavior: Sand tilefish build tunnels and mounds in the sand- and rubble-bottomed areas near reefs and seagrass beds. Tunnel entrances can reach 10ft (3m) in diameter and the mounds are built out of the sand, coral rubble and shell fragments found during excavation.
Predators: Sharks and snapper

## PEACOCK FLOUNDER
### BOTHUS LUNATUS

43

Maximum size: 18in (46cm)
Longevity: Up to 10 years
Typical depth: 0–66ft (0–20m)
Behavior: Peacock flounders are usually found partially buried in loose sand near coral reefs, mangroves and seagrass beds. They are the most common flounders around coral reefs, and mainly feed on small fishes, but also crustaceans and small octopuses.
Predators: Sharks and snapper

## BROWN GARDEN EEL
### HETEROCONGER LONGISSIMUS

44

Maximum size: 20in (50cm)
Longevity: Unknown
Typical depth: 33–197ft (10–60m)
Behavior: Brown garden eels live in burrows in sandy areas near coral reefs, feeding mainly on plankton that drift by in the current. Individuals rarely leave the safety of their burrows, remaining partially buried with their heads poking out from the sand. They retreat backwards into their burrow when threatened.
Predators: Snake eels and triggerfish

## GOLDENTAIL MORAY EEL 45

### GYMNOTHORAX MILIARIS

Maximum size: 28in (70cm)
Longevity: Unknown
Typical depth: 0–115ft (0–35m)
Behavior: Goldentail moray eels are common in the Caribbean, living alone in holes and crevices in coral reefs. Unlike other types of morays, goldentails are most active during the day. They feed on fish, molluscs and crustaceans.
Predators: Grouper

## SPOTTED MORAY EEL 46

### GYMNOTHORAX MORINGA

Maximum size: 3.3ft (1m), 6lbs (2.5kg)
Longevity: Around 10 years, but possibly up to 30 years
Typical depth: 0–656ft (0–200m)
Behavior: Spotted moray eels are most active at night, when they hunt for a wide variety of prey, including parrotfish, grunts, trumpetfish, crustaceans and molluscs. During the day, they are often seen with their head sticking out of a reef hole or crevice.
Predators: Dog snapper and Nassau grouper

## SPOTTED DRUM 47

### EQUETUS PUNCTATUS

Maximum size: 11in (27cm)
Longevity: Unknown, but probably around 10 years
Typical depth: 10–98ft (3–30m)
Behavior: Spotted drums are found under ledges, jetties and near small caves during the day. They are solitary and mostly active at night, when they hunt for crabs, shrimp and worms. Drums can emit a drumming sound when they feel threatened, which is the origin of their name.
Predators: Moray eels, grouper and barracuda

## SCRAWLED FILEFISH 48

### ALUTERUS SCRIPTUS

Maximum size: 43in (110cm), 5.5lbs (2.5kg)
Longevity: Unknown
Typical depth: 10–394ft (3–120m)
Behavior: Scrawled filefish are commonly found on offshore reefs. They are active during the day, feeding on algae, seagrass, hydrozoans, soft corals and anemones. Juveniles sometimes drift with sargassum mats, explaining how this species is found throughout the tropics, and on many non-tropical reefs.
Predators: Barracuda, mahi mahi and large tuna

## SLENDER FILEFISH
### MONACANTHUS TUCKERI

49

Maximum size: 4in (10cm)
Longevity: Unknown
Typical depth: 7–165ft (2–50m)
Behavior: Slender filefish are almost always found hiding among the branches of gorgonians. During the day, they feed on worms, crabs and zooplankton. At night, they wedge themselves into soft coral with their dorsal spine and stomach appendage, sometimes biting down on a coral polyp while sleeping.
Predators: Grouper and barracuda

## BLACK DURGON
### MELICHTHYS NIGER

50

Maximum size: 20in (50cm)
Longevity: Around 5 years
Typical depth: 0–246ft (0–75m)
Behavior: The black durgon is most common on outer bank reef crests, particularly near drop-offs, where they form loose aggregations of as many as 200 individuals. They feed on plant and animal plankton that drift in the water, as well as on reef algae.
Predators: Large grouper, snapper, moray eels and barracuda

## ATLANTIC TRUMPETFISH
### AULOSTOMUS MACULATUS

51

Maximum size: 3ft (1m)
Longevity: Unknown, but likely around 10 years
Typical depth: 6–82ft (2–25m)
Behavior: Trumpetfish are often found camouflaged within the branches of gorgonian corals. They are generally ambush predators that consume small or juvenile reef fish and crustaceans. As known shadow-feeders, they sometimes stalk their prey while swimming alongside other reef fish, using them as cover.
Predators: Grouper, snapper and moray eels

## HONEYCOMB COWFISH
### ACANTHOSTRACION POLYGONIUS

52

Maximum size: 20in (50cm)
Longevity: Unknown
Typical depth: 7–262ft (2–80m)
Behavior: Honeycomb cowfish are protected by hexagon scales that form a rigid carapace over much of their bodies. They are relatively slow and wary, which makes their external armor an essential defense against potential predators. They usually forage alone, feeding on sponges, tunicates and shrimp.
Predators: Sharks

## SMOOTH TRUNKFISH 53
### LACTOPHRYS TRIQUETER

Maximum size: 18.5in (47cm)
Longevity: Unknown
Typical depth: 0–164ft (0–50m)
Behavior: Smooth trunkfish are easily recognized by their black mouth and white-spotted, triangular, shape. They are slow, relying on their armor and toxins for protection. They are easily approached and are often seen hunting bottom invertebrates by jetting water from their mouths to shift sand and locate their prey.
Predators: Mahi mahi, cobia and large carnivorous fish

## PORCUPINEFISH 54
### DIODON HYSTRIX

Maximum size: 35in (90cm)
Longevity: Up to 10 years
Typical depth: 7–164ft (2–50m)
Behavior: Porcupinefish are solitary nocturnal predators that feed on snails, crabs and sea urchins. During the day, they are often found sheltering in reef caves or crevices. They can inflate their bodies up to twice their normal size by drawing in water or air.
Predators: Dolphins, and large pelagic fish such as sharks and tuna

## CARIBBEAN SHARPNOSE PUFFER 55
### CANTHIGASTER ROSTRATA

Maximum size: 5in (12cm)
Longevity: Unknown, but possibly up to 10 years
Typical depth: 3–130ft (1–40m)
Behavior: Sharpnose puffers prefer reefs where gorgonian corals are common. They are most active during the day as they search for small reef invertebrates such as crabs, shrimp, worms and snails. They are territorial, so if you happen to see two individuals near one another, they may be engaged in defensive displays.
Predators: Grouper, snapper, barracuda and moray eels

## CONEY 56
### CEPHALOPHOLIS FULVA

Maximum size: 17in (43cm)
Longevity: 11 years, possibly as much as 19 years
Typical depth: 3–148ft (1–45m)
Behavior: Coneys hide in caves and crevices in the reef during the day, venturing out at night to forage for small reef fish and crustaceans. They are approachable but wary, and the males are territorial. They start out as female, becoming male at around 8in (20cm).
Predators: Sharks, grouper and snapper

## GRAYSBY
### CEPHALOPHOLIS CRUENTATA
57

Maximum size: 16in (40 cm)
Longevity: Approximately 12 years
Typical depth: 7–561ft (2–170m)
Behavior: Graysbies are found in reef areas that contain caves, crevices or hollow sponges where they hide during the day. At night, they hunt for reef fish, such as chromis, squirrelfish, gobies and crustaceans. Some individuals hunt alongside moray eels at night.
Predators: Barracuda, sharks and larger grouper

## TIGER GROUPER
### MYCTEROPERCA TIGRIS
58

Maximum size: 3ft (1m)
Longevity: Up to 40 years
Typical depth: 33–130ft (10–40m)
Behavior: A solitary ambush predator, tiger grouper are easily identified by the tiger stripes that run from the dorsal fin down either side of the fish. They vary in color from black, red, tan and yellow. They feed on a variety of fish, including grunts, parrotfish, croakers, angelfish and damselfish. A hermaphroditic species, smaller individuals are females while larger fish are males.
Predators: Sharks, large grouper and mackerel

## BLACK GROUPER
### MYCTEROPERCA BONACI
59

Maximum size: 5ft (1.5m), 220lbs (100kg)
Longevity: More than 30 years
Typical depth: 19–246ft (6–75m)
Behavior: Black grouper are abundant in Curaçao waters but rarely seen. They tend to shy away from swimmers. Commercially fished in many places, their populations are generally declining as a result. They are solitary except when they congregate to spawn. Adults feed on smaller reef fish such as grunts and snapper.
Predators: Sharks

## GOLIATH GROUPER
### EPINEPHELUS ITAJARA
60

Maximum size: 8ft (2.5m), 1,000lbs (455kg)
Longevity: Nearly 40 years
Typical depth: 0–330ft (0–100m)
Behavior: Goliath grouper are the largest grouper species in Curaçao. This massive, solitary fish does not have a large home range, but will defend its territory aggressively against intruders by making loud "barking" noises with its swim bladder. They have even been known to charge divers, so beware. Goliath grouper feed on lobsters, fish and even turtles and stingrays.
Predators: Sharks

## GREATER SOAPFISH 61

### RYPTICUS SAPONACEUS

Maximum size: 14in (35cm)
Longevity: Up to 6 years
Typical depth: 6–115ft (2–35m)
Behavior: Soapfish are solitary, nocturnal fish that feed on crustaceans and small fish. They are often seen hiding at the base of corals and in crevices in the reef. They secrete a toxic mucus as a deterrent to predators. The mucus covers their bodies and lathers up to a soapy foam when the fish is disturbed, hence the name soapfish.
Predators: Sharks and eagle rays

## BARRED HAMLET 62

### HYPOPLECTRUS PUELLA

Maximum size: 6in (15cm)
Longevity: Unknown
Typical depth: 10–75ft (3–23m)
Behavior: Hamlets are often found on the seaward side of reefs. They feed during the day on crustaceans, particularly shrimp and crabs, and occasionally small fish. Hamlets are fiercely territorial, and are often observed fighting with members of their own species.
Predators: Grouper, snapper, jacks and barracuda

## FAIRY BASSLET 63

### GRAMMA LORETO

Maximum size: 3in (8cm)
Longevity: Around 6 years, but up to 12 years
Typical depth: 3–180ft (1–60m)
Behavior: Fairy basslets are often found on reef walls that are full of caves and ledges. They are most active during the day, feeding mainly on crustaceans – although they occasionally act as a cleaner fish. At night, they retreat into the safety of a familiar reef shelter.
Predators: Snapper, grouper and moray eels

## BERMUDA CHUB 64

### KYPHOSUS SECTATRIX

Maximum size: 30in (76cm), 13lbs (6kg)
Longevity: Unknown
Typical depth: 3–330ft (1–10m)
Behavior: Bermuda chub are a schooling fish found in shallow waters above sandy areas, seagrass beds and near coral reefs. They feed on benthic algae, but also on small crabs and molluscs. Juveniles often associate with floating sargassum mats, letting them disperse across great distances.
Predators: Sharks, barracuda, snapper, moray eels and scorpionfish

## BAR JACK
### CARANX RUBER

65

Maximum size: 23in (59cm)
Longevity: Unknown, possibly up to 30 years
Typical depth: 3–330ft (1–100m)
Behavior: Bar jacks sometimes swim alone, but are usually found schooling in shallow, clear water near coral reefs. They feed on fish, shrimp and other invertebrates. They are the most abundant species of jack in the Caribbean, and are easily approached by divers.
Predators: Grouper, mackerel, mahi mahi and large jacks

## HORSE-EYE JACK
### CARANX LATUS

66

Maximum size: 3ft (1m), 29lbs (13kg)
Longevity: Unknown
Typical depth: 3–66ft (0–20m)
Behavior: Horse-eye jacks are schooling pelagic fish that frequent the waters above offshore reefs, although juveniles are often seen inshore along sandy beaches. Adults feed on fish, shrimp and other invertebrates. They often approach divers boldly, but without posing much of a threat.
Predators: Sharks, barracuda and mahi mahi

## RAINBOW RUNNER
### ELAGATIS BIPINNULATA

67

Maximum size: 6ft (1.8m), 102lbs (56kg)
Longevity: Up to 6 years
Typical depth: 6–33ft (2–10m)
Behavior: Rainbow runners are one of the larger members of the jack family, and they are found near the surface of the water over reefs . Though they can get quite large, individuals measuring 2–3ft (60–90cm) are more common. Rainbow runners can form large schools, where they feed on invertebrates and small fish.
Predators: Sharks and tuna

## PALOMETA / GREAT POMPANO
### TRACHINOTUS GOODEI

68

Maximum size: 20in (50cm)
Longevity: Unknown
Typical depth: 0–40ft (0–12m)
Behavior: Adult palometa tend to form schools over shallow coral reefs. Juveniles, meanwhile, are more common over sand and rubble habitat. They are most active during the day, feeding on crustaceans, worms, molluscs and fish.
Predators: Sharks and barracuda

## CERO 69
### SCOMBEROMORUS REGALIS

Maximum size: 6ft (1.8m)
Longevity: Unknown
Typical depth: 3–66ft (1–20m)
Behavior: A member of the mackerel family, the cero is typically found swimming in open water near coral reefs, occasionally in schools. Cero eat smaller fish, including herring, anchovies and silversides, along with squid and shrimp. They are considered a good game fish.
Predators: Sharks, tuna, marlin, king mackerel and wahoo

## TARPON 70
### MEGALOPS ATLANTICUS

Maximum size: 8ft (2.5m), 330lb (150kg)
Longevity: Around 50 years
Typical depth: 3–330ft (0–100m)
Behavior: Tarpon frequent both marine and freshwater ecosystems, from Canada in the north to Brazil in the south. They can feed during both the day and the night on a range of fish and crustaceans. Tarpon have relatively small teeth and tend to swallow their prey whole.
Predators: Sharks and dolphins

## SPOTTED EAGLE RAY 71
### AETOBATUS NARINARI

Maximum size: 10ft (3m) disc width, 500lb (230kg)
Longevity: Up to 20 years
Typical depth: 3–260ft (1–80m)
Behavior: Spotted eagle rays are carnivores that specialize in eating hard-shelled prey such as conch, clams, crabs and lobsters. They sometimes eat octopuses and fish as well, and are often found over sand habitat. They have electro-receptors in their snout to help search for buried prey.
Predators: Tiger, bull, lemon and hammerhead sharks

## NURSE SHARK 72
### GINGLYMOSTOMA CIRRATUM

Maximum size: 14ft (4.3m), 242lbs (110kg)
Longevity: Up to 25 years
Typical depth: 0–430ft (0–130 m)
Behavior: Nurse sharks are large nocturnal reef predators. At night, they search for hard-shelled prey, such as lobsters, crabs and conch, which they consume with their specially designed jaws. During the day, they are often found resting in caves or beneath coral overhangs.
Predators: Larger shark species

## LONGSNOUT SEAHORSE 73
### HIPPOCAMPUS REIDI

Maximum size: 7in (18cm) with tail outstretched
Longevity: Unknown, but probably at least 4 to 5 years
Typical depth: 3–55m (10–180ft)
Behavior: Seahorses are rare throughout the Caribbean. They prefer shallow reef areas. They are often seen clinging to seagrass, macroalgae, gorgonians and sponges with their prehensile tails, while they feed on zooplankton, mysid shrimp and small crustaceans.
Predators: Rays, turtles and crabs

## PEDERSON CLEANER SHRIMP 74
### ANCYLOMENES PEDERSONI

Maximum size: 1in (3cm)
Longevity: Unknown
Typical depth: 3–115ft (1–35m)
Behavior: Pederson cleaner shrimp pick parasites off reef fish. They are found in close association with sea anemones, which help advertise the shrimp's cleaning services and provide shelter. The anemone's stinging tentacles ward off predators but do not sting its resident cleaner shrimp, which can number up to a dozen.
Predators: Unknown

## YELLOWLINE ARROW CRAB 75
### STENORHYNCHUS SETICORNIS

Maximum size: 2in (6cm)
Longevity: Around 5 years
Typical depth: 10–130ft (3–40m)
Behavior: Yellowline arrow crabs are small spider-like creatures with triangular bodies and small purple claws. They are often found inside tube sponges, and among the tentacles of anemones and spines of sea urchins. At night, they forage for algae, detritus, tube worms and bristleworms.
Predators: Grouper, puffers, triggerfish, wrasses and grunts

## CARIBBEAN SPINY LOBSTER 76
### PANULIRUS ARGUS

Maximum size: 18in (45cm)
Longevity: Around 20 years
Typical depth: 0–295ft (0–90m)
Behavior: Caribbean spiny lobsters like to hide in reef caves and crevices during the day. At night, they roam the reef searching for snails, clams, crabs and dead and decaying organisms to eat. They undergo seasonal mass migrations in the fall, marching in single-file toward deeper water.
Predators: Sharks, stingrays, grouper, triggerfish and moray eels

## CARIBBEAN REEF OCTOPUS 77

### OCTOPUS BRIAREUS

Maximum size: 39in (1m) with arms spread, 3lbs (1.5kg)
Longevity: Less than 2 years
Typical depth: 13–82ft (4–25m)
Behavior: Caribbean reef octopuses like to hide in reef caves and crevices during the day. They are masters of camouflage and incredibly hard to spot, since they can change their color, texture and shape. They are most active at night, hunting for crustaceans, clams, snails and small fish.
Predators: Grouper, snapper, nurse sharks and moray eels

## CARIBBEAN REEF SQUID 78

### SEPIOTEUTHIS SEPIOIDEA

Maximum size: 8in (20cm)
Longevity: Around 1 year
Typical depth: 0–98ft (0–30m)
Behavior: Caribbean reef squid are often found in small schools. They capture food in their 10 arms, feeding mainly on small fishes, as well as crustaceans and other molluscs. They have the largest eyes relative to body size of any animal, and they track their food by sight.
Predators: Grouper, snapper and barracuda

## FLAMINGO TONGUE 79

### CYPHOMA GIBBOSUM

Maximum size: 2in (4cm)
Longevity: Unknown, but likely 2 years
Typical depth: 6–45ft (2–14m)
Behavior: Flamingo tongues are a reef gastropod (marine snail) almost always found feeding on sea fans, sea whips and other gorgonians. The flesh of the gorgonians they eat contains toxic chemicals that the flamingo tongue converts into its own predator-deterring toxins.
Predators: Hogfish

## QUEEN CONCH 80

### STROMBUS GIGAS

Maximum size: 12in (30cm)
Longevity: Up to 30 years
Typical depth: 3–98ft (1–30m)
Behavior: Queen conch are the world's largest marine snail. They are found mainly on sandy reef areas and seagrass beds, where they graze on algae and detritus. They are most active at night, and when threatened, can retreat into their shells for protection.
Predators: Nurse sharks, spotted eagle rays and stingrays

## GIANT ANEMONE 81
### CONDYLACTIS GIGANTEA

Maximum size: 12in (30cm)
Longevity: Around 75 years
Typical depth: 3–82ft (1–25m)
Behavior: Giant anemones come in a variety of colors, from white to dark brown, sometimes with pink or purple-tipped tentacles. Some individuals have stinging tentacles that they use to paralyze and capture fish, shrimp and worms. Anemones typically attach to the reef, but are also capable of crawling.
Predators: Hermit crabs, snails and sea slugs

## STAGHORN CORAL 82
### ACROPORA CERVICORNIS

Maximum size: 8ft (2.5m)
Longevity: Individual polyps live 2-3 yrs but colonies can live for centuries
Typical depth: 3–164ft (1–50m)
Behavior: Staghorn corals are usually found in calm back reef areas with clear water. They provide important habitat for a range of different coral reef organisms. The coral polyps feed at night while the zooxanthellae in their tissue photosynthesize during the day. Staghorn coral is the fastest growing coral species in the Western Atlantic.
Predators: Some worm and snail species. The biggest threat is from disease.

## ELKHORN CORAL 83
### ACROPORA PALMATA

Maximum size: 12ft (3.5m)
Longevity: Individual polyps live 2-3yrs but colonies can live for centuries
Typical depth: 3–65ft (1–20m)
Behavior: Elkhorn corals are an important reef-building coral species, producing many large branches that coral reef organisms use as habitat. Elkhorn coral is often found in areas of moderate to high current and wave action. The coral polyps feed at night while the zooxanthellae in their tissue photosynthesize during the day.
Predators: Some worm and snail species. The biggest threat is from disease.

## ORANGE ELEPHANT EAR SPONGE 84
### AGELAS CLATHRODES

Maximum size: 6ft (1.8m)
Longevity: 2,000 years or more
Typical depth: 35–130ft (12–40m)
Behavior: Named for their resemblance to the ear of an elephant, these large sponges are easily spotted in deeper waters on the reef thanks to their bright coloration and large size. It can take different forms, including a thick encrusting form, or lobed and/or ridged forms. Like other sponges, they feed by filtering food particles from the surrounding water.
Predators: Sea turtles, crabs, parrotfish, slugs and many other sea creatures

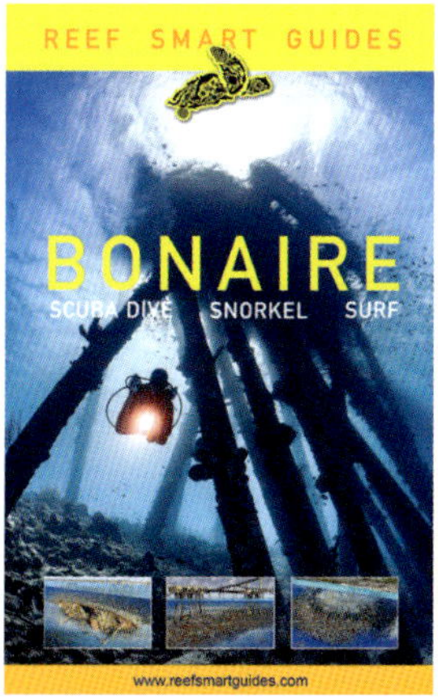

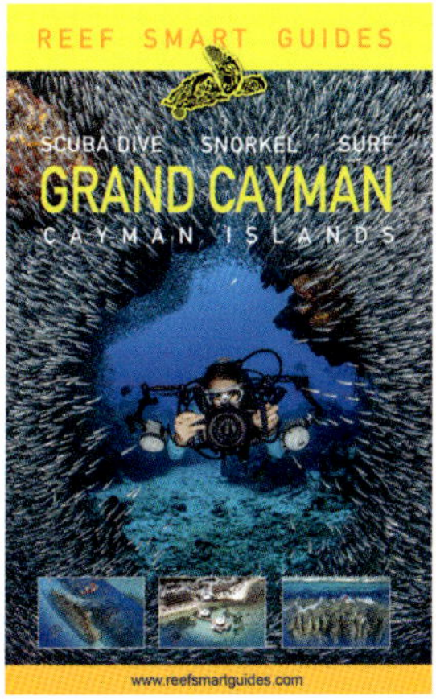

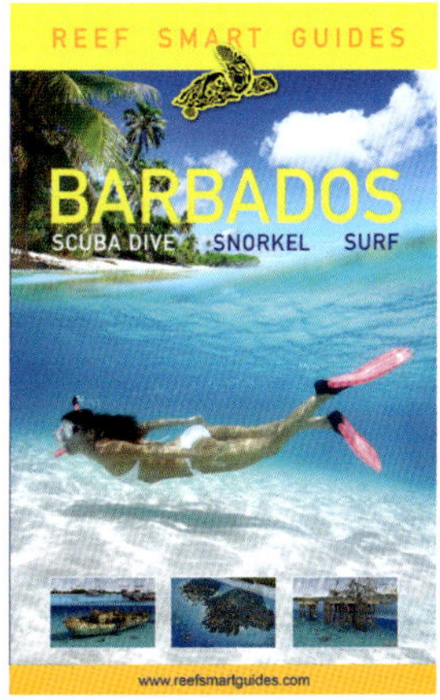

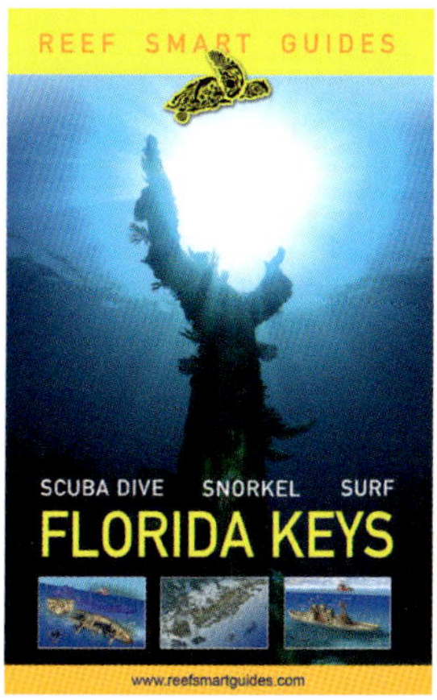

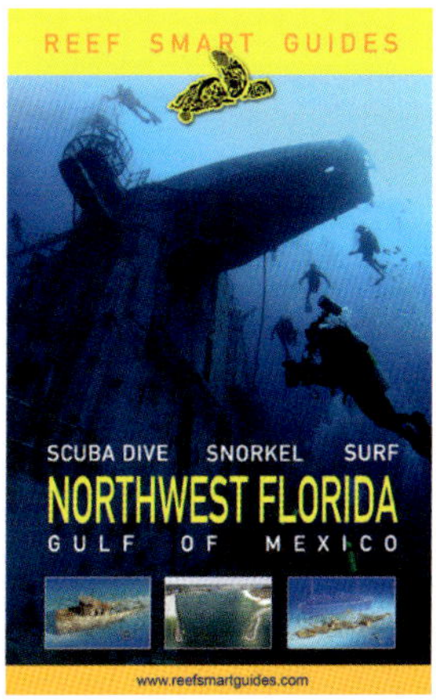

Check out Reef Smart Guides' growing line of regional dive and snorkel guidebooks. For an up-to-date list of locations, visit **Reefsmartguides.com**

# Index of sites

Curaçao is home to some stunning coral diversity, including healthy stands of elkhorn corals like this one.

Turtle & Ray©

# ABOUT THE AUTHORS

**Ian POPPLE**
ian@reefsmartguides.com

Born and raised in the U.K., Ian earned his undergraduate degree in Oceanography from the University of Plymouth in 1994. He worked for five years at Bellairs Research Institute in Barbados, supporting research projects across the region, before completing his Master's in marine biology at McGill University in 2004. He co-founded a marine biology education company, Beautiful Oceans, before founding Reef Smart in 2015, to raise awareness and encourage people to explore the underwater world. Ian has published in both the scientific and mainstream media, including National Geographic, Scuba Diver Magazine and the Globe and Mail. He is a PADI Dive Master with over 3,000 dives in 30 years of diving experience.

**Otto WAGNER**
otto@reefsmartguides.com

Born and raised in Romania, Otto graduated from the University of Art and Design in Cluj, Romania in 1991. He moved to Canada in 1999 where he studied Film Animation at Concordia University in Montreal. In 2006, Otto turned to underwater cartography and pioneered new techniques in 3D visual mapping. He co-founded Art to Media and began mapping underwater habitats around the world. Throughout his 25-year career, Otto has received numerous awards and international recognition for his work, including the Prize of Excellence in Design from the Salon International du Design de Montréal. He has also illustrated seven books. Otto is a PADI Advanced Diver with over 500 dives in 20 years of diving experience.

**Peter McDOUGALL**
peter@reefsmartguides.com

Born and raised in Canada, Peter received his undergraduate and Master's degrees from McGill University. His focus on behavioral ecology and coral reef ecology led him to two field seasons at Bellairs Research Institute in Barbados, in 1999 and again in 2002. After graduating in 2003, Peter moved to the United States and began a career in science communication and writing, publishing in both peer-reviewed academic journals and the popular press. He has written on a variety of coastal ecosystem issues, including extensive work surrounding the science of ocean acidification. He is a PADI Rescue Diver with over 400 dives in 25 years of experience.